SHAKESPEARE FOR TWO

Shakespeare for Two

A Comprehensive Collection of Two-Person Scenes

edited by

Douglas Newell

Heinemann
Portsmouth, NH

Heinemann
A division of Reed Elsevier Inc.
361 Hanover Street
Portsmouth, NH 03801–3912
www.heinemanndrama.com

Offices and agents throughout the world

Library of Congress Cataloging-in-Publication Data
Shakespeare, William, 1564–1616.
[Plays. Selections.]
Shakespeare for two : a comprehensive collection of two-person scenes/ [compiled by] Douglas Newell.
p. cm.
ISBN-13: 978-0-325-00889-9 (acid-free paper)
ISBN-10: 0-325-00889-2 (acid-free paper)
1. Dialogues. I. Newell, Douglas. II. Title.
PR2768.N48 2006
822.3′3–dc22 2006022127

Editor: Lisa A. Barnett
Production service: TechBooks
Production coordinator: Sonja S. Chapman
Cover design: Jenny Jensen Greenleaf
Author photograph: Patricia Conroy
Compositor: TechBooks
Manufacturing: Steve Bernier

Printed in the United States of America on acid-free paper
10 09 08 07 06 VP 1 2 3 4 5

For Donna . . .
who gave me the circus.

CONTENTS

Introduction xi

Scenes for Two Actresses

(1) HELENA AND COUNTESS OF ROSSILLION *All's Well That Ends Well* 1

(2) CELIA AND ROSALIND *As You Like It* 5

(3) CELIA AND ROSALIND *As You Like It* 8

(4) PORTIA AND NERISSA *The Merchant of Venice* 12

(5) MISTRESS FORD AND MISTRESS PAGE *The Merry Wives of Windsor* 15

(6) HERO AND URSULA *Much Ado About Nothing* 18

(7) EMILIA AND DESDEMONA *Othello* 22

(8) JULIET AND NURSE *Romeo and Juliet* 26

(9) LADY CAPULET AND JULIET *Romeo and Juliet* 29

(10) VIOLA AND OLIVIA *Twelfth Night* 32

(11) VIOLA AND OLIVIA *Twelfth Night* 37

(12) JULIA AND LUCETTA *The Two Gentlemen of Verona* 41

(13) JULIA AND SILVIA *The Two Gentlemen of Verona* 47

Scenes for Two Actors

(14) CORIN AND TOUCHSTONE *As You Like It* 51

(15) ANTIPHOLUS OF SYRACUSE AND DROMIO OF EPHESUS *The Comedy of Errors* 54

(16) ANTIPHOLUS OF SYRACUSE AND DROMIO OF SYRACUSE *The Comedy of Errors* 57

(17) COMINIUS AND MENENIUS *Coriolanus* 62

(18) POSTHUMUS AND IACHIMO *Cymbeline* 65

(19) HAMLET AND HORATIO *Hamlet* 71

(20) HAMLET AND FIRST CLOWN *Hamlet* 76

(21) CADE AND IDEN *Henry VI, Part 2* 79

(22) CASSIUS AND BRUTUS *Julius Caesar* 82

(23) HUBERT AND ARTHUR *King John* 87

(24) HUBERT AND KING JOHN *King John* 92

(25) EARL OF GLOUCESTER AND EDGAR *King Lear* 96

(26) LUCIO AND DUKE VINCENTIO *Measure For Measure* 100

(27) FORD AND FALSTAFF *The Merry Wives of Windsor* 104

(28) IAGO AND CASSIO *Othello* 108

(29) IAGO AND OTHELLO *Othello* 111

(30) IAGO AND OTHELLO *Othello* 117

(31) IAGO AND OTHELLO *Othello* 123

(32) IAGO AND RODERIGO *Othello* 125

(33) SECOND MURDERER AND FIRST MURDERER *Richard III* 128

(34) ALCIBIADES AND TIMON *Timon of Athens* 131

(35) SPEED AND PROTEUS *The Two Gentlemen of Verona* 134

(36) SPEED AND LAUNCE *The Two Gentlemen of Verona* 138

(37) CLOWN AND SHEPHERD *The Winter's Tale* 141

(38) CLOWN AND AUTOLYCUS *The Winter's Tale* 144

Scenes for One Actress and One actor

(39) DIANA AND BERTRAM *All's Well That Ends Well* 149

(40) CLEOPATRA AND ANTONY *Antony and Cleopatra* 152

(41) IMOGEN AND IACHIMO *Cymbeline* 157

(42) IMOGEN AND PISANIO *Cymbeline* 163

(43) OPHELIA AND HAMLET *Hamlet* 168

(44) MARGARET AND EARL OF SUFFOLK *Henry VI, Part 1* 171

(45) LADY GREY AND KING EDWARD IV *Henry VI, Part 3* 176

(46) LADY MACBETH AND MACBETH *Macbeth* 180

(47) ISABELLA AND ANGELO *Measure For Measure* 184

(48) ISABELLA AND CLAUDIO *Measure For Measure* 189

(49) HELENA AND DEMETRIUS *A Midsummer Night's Dream* 194

(50) BEATRICE AND BENEDICK *Much Ado About Nothing* 197

(51) DESDEMONA AND OTHELLO *Othello* 201

(52) DESDEMONA AND OTHELLO *Othello* 205

(53) LADY ANNE AND RICHARD, DUKE OF GLOUCESTER *Richard III* 210

(54) QUEEN ELIZABETH AND KING RICHARD III *Richard III* 216

(55) QUEEN ELIZABETH AND KING RICHARD III *Richard III* 220

(56) JULIET AND ROMEO *Romeo and Juliet* 224

(57) KATHARINA AND PETRUCHIO *The Taming of the Shrew* 229

(58) MIRANDA AND FERDINAND *The Tempest* 234

(59) VIOLA AND FESTE *Twelfth Night* 238

(60) HERMIONE AND LEONTES *The Winter's Tale* 241

A Guide to Pronunciation 245

Just the Facts, Ma'am 250

Shakespeare in Brief 265

Outtakes 267

INTRODUCTION

Overview

Entries in *Shakespeare For Two* are collected into three groups. First up are scenes requiring two actresses, followed by those calling for two actors, and finally those written for one actress and one actor.

At the beginning of each entry are the names of the two characters featured in the scene, the title of the play from which the scene is taken, the scene's approximate location in the play, a description of its physical setting, and a brief account of the action or circumstances that have led to the moment at hand.

Line numbers appearing in the margin of each scene refer to the explanatory notes that follow.

At the back of the book are a guide to the pronunciation of names and short overviews of each play's key plot developments, as well as other information that might be useful in finding a particular scene.

The Chosen Ones

Ferreting out two-person scenes from Shakespeare's weighty body of work was for the most part a matter of setting criteria. Issues that demanded to be addressed early on in the process included: How are these scenes going to be used? . . . Who's going to be using them? . . . How short or long must they be? . . . What qualities are essential in an effective scene? . . . What flaws are fatal?

In the case of *Shakespeare For Two,* answering these and other such puzzles eventually led to a collection of more than 400 two-person dialogues that, for better or worse, could legitimately be considered a "scene."

Which is not to say that all 400 of them were prize winners. Some were such fleeting affairs—I.viii of *Coriolanus* runs a mere 16 lines, for example—that little in the way of shape or substance had time to develop. Others were plenty long enough, but were in essence a string of monologues posing as a scene. Check out the Prince Hal/King Henry face-off in IV.v of *Henry IV, Part 2* to see just how little give and take there can be in a scene of some 130 lines.

A number of selections that might have otherwise qualified for membership were rejected because something about the scene required the presence of one or more additional characters. Several pieces met *Shakespeare For Two*'s minimum requirements only to succumb to "narrative disease"—an affliction in which a sequence (like for instance the opening of *The Comedy of Errors*) serves mainly to lay out story particulars and has no discernable pulse of its own. Many more were dispensed with because, once forced to make it by themselves as freestanding pieces, they just weren't very compelling theater.

But without a doubt, the single characteristic that most frequently proved to be the undoing of an otherwise acceptable scene was simply a lack of fair play. Far too often a piece would allot the lion's share of focus to one character, thereby leaving the other role with little more than straight lines. Not so bad, perhaps, if your character is the one doing all the talking. But since the prime directive of *Shakespeare For Two* is to provide an opportunity for *two* actors to explore the wonders of Shakespeare, one-sided scenes were shown the door.

To Edit or Not to Edit

Fortunately, the call to edit an entry in *Shakespeare For Two* was seldom heard. Suitable start and end points were usually self-evident, and the appearance of unnecessary characters or extraneous stage business seldom required more than a quick snip here or there.

There were, however, certain situations where only the gentle and judicious touch of an editor's hand could enable a scene to reach its full potential. For example . . .

- On two or three occasions cuts were made in order to avoid unnecessary distractions. With entry (26), for instance, deleting Lucio's inquiry about Claudio keeps his scene with the Duke from straying at the last minute onto a superfluous matter.
- Now and then, for the good of the scene, a lengthy speech would have to be trimmed a bit. King Richard's 45-line monologue at the beginning of entry (55) is a thing of beauty if you're looking to solo. But for

scene work it proves a cumbersome and ill-advised opening to his otherwise fast-paced confrontation with Queen Elizabeth.

- Sometimes the scene itself was too darn long. Imogen and Pisanio have a wonderful exchange in entry (41), but left to their own devices, they take more than 200 lines to tell their story. Cinching things up a bit results in a more manageable (though still lengthy) selection that loses none of its power.
- And every so often line fragments were linked together in order to keep intact both meter and intended meaning.

With modifications this minor and so few and far between, it was deemed unnecessary to bracket or otherwise draw attention to departures from the original text. The thinking here is that an uncluttered script is easier to work with. And since act, scene and line information is provided for every scene, it's a simple matter to go to the source, should a question arise regarding the entry's integrity.

Finally, there is the question of Shakespeare's glorious linguistic idiosyncrasies. Shakespeare would hardly be Shakespeare, of course, without curious constructions such as *to't* and *i'th'*, or compressed verbs like *wond'red* and *o'erwhelm*. And since a prime function of such contractions is to sustain the meter of verse, it seemed far preferable to keep them as they traditionally appear rather than resort to some sort of misbegotten "modernization."

As to whether or not an extra syllable here or there really matters all that much, well, that's a call for each individual actor to make. Fiddling about with Shakespeare is an endeavor fraught with peril, but theater history is thick with it just the same. Fortunately, most situations calling for Shakespearean scene work are likely to allow for a good deal of flexibility.

It's Greek to Me

An observation originally made in *Shakespeare For One* is just as pertinent here: Acting is tricky . . . and acting Shakespeare is really tricky. As if unraveling the Bard's complex characters and accommodating the imposing demands of blank verse weren't enough, you also have to make sense of that marvelous (and oft times maddening) language of his. Yet even Shakespeare's most inscrutable passages can be successfully navigated if one is properly prepared for the journey. Which is where *Shakespeare For Two* comes in.

Unlike nearly all other editions of Shakespeare, which are designed for those who read and study the plays, *Shakespeare For Two* is a resource aimed squarely at *actors* of Shakespeare. As such, its approach to annotation differs from the norm in two key ways: by erring on the side of caution when deciding whether or not a definition is called for (i.e., when in doubt, define . . .), and by decoding arcane passages with thorough, plain-English explanations instead of terse snippets that assume you have a degree in Elizabethan Studies.

All of the definitions and explanations presented in *Shakespeare For Two* are based on information gleaned from a variety of authoritative sources. Very few stones were left unturned. But in those rare instances when even the collective wisdom of scholars past and present has failed to yield a solution, a consensus best guess, marked with a question mark (?), is offered instead.

Do Your Homework

Hopefully, it goes without saying that the brief plot-related comments leading into each scene are not offered as a substitute for actually reading the play. Instead, they—as well as the "Shakespeare In Brief" synopses at the back of the book—are asked to perform two narrowly-defined roles: one, set the scene a bit for the uninitiated so they don't have to read an entire play just to test-drive its monologues; and two, gently jog the memories of those who might know a given play, but can't quite recall the particulars leading up to the entry at hand.

Should there come a time when more specific plot or character details are required, any of several titles sitting in your local bookstore will do the trick just fine. But be forewarned that even the best of study guides cannot provide the actor with everything he or she will need in the way of background material. The only way an actor can be fully prepared, and can thoroughly appreciate both character and context, is to know the play.

SCENES FOR TWO ACTRESSES

(1) Helena and Countess of Rossillion [I.iii.134]

All's Well That Ends Well

SCENE: The Count of Rossillion's palace.

{Lowly Helena has long been secretly in love with the Countess of Rossillion's son, Bertram. Class considerations being what they are, this is not good. And now that the Countess has learned of Helena's clandestine infatuation, it's no surprise that the poor maid's entrance spurs a spirited interrogation.}

HELENA
What is your pleasure, madam?

COUNTESS
You know, Helen, I am a mother to you.

HELENA
Mine honorable mistress.

COUNTESS
Nay, a mother.
Why not a mother? When I said "a mother,"
Methought you saw a serpent. What's in "mother,"
That you start at it? Does it curd thy blood
To say I am thy mother? What's the matter,
That this distempered messenger of wet,
The many-color'd Iris, rounds thine eye?
Why? That you are my daughter?

HELENA
That I am not.

COUNTESS
I say, I am your mother.

HELENA

Pardon, madam;
The Count Rossillion cannot be my brother.
I am from humble, he from honor'd name;
No note upon my parents, his all noble.
My master, my dear lord he is, and I
His servant live, and will his vassal die.
He must not be my brother.

COUNTESS

Nor I your mother?

HELENA

You are my mother, madam; would you were—
So that my lord your son were not my brother—
Indeed my mother! Or were you both our mothers,
I care no more for than I do for heaven,
So I were not his sister. Can't no other
But, I your daughter, he must be my brother?

COUNTESS

Yes, Helen, you might be my daughter-in-law.
God shield you mean it not! "Daughter" and "mother"
So strive upon your pulse. What, pale again?
My fear hath catch'd your fondness! Now I see
The myst'ry of your loneliness, and find
Your salt tears' head. Now to all sense 'tis gross:
You love my son. Invention is asham'd,
Against the proclamation of thy passion,
To say thou dost not. Speak, is it so?

HELENA

Good madam, pardon me!

COUNTESS

Do you love my son?

HELENA

Your pardon, noble mistress!

COUNTESS

Love you my son?

HELENA

Do not you love him, madam?

COUNTESS
Go not about; my love hath in 't a bond,
Whereof the world takes note. Come, come, disclose
The state of your affection, for your passions
Have to the full appeach'd.

HELENA
Then I confess
Here on my knee, before high heaven and you,
That before you, and next unto high heaven,
I love your son.
My friends were poor, but honest; so 's my love.
Be not offended, for it hurts not him
That he is lov'd of me. I follow him not
By any token of presumptuous suit,
Nor would I have him till I do deserve him,
Yet never know how that desert should be.
I know I love in vain, strive against hope;
Yet in this captious and intenible sieve
I still pour in the waters of my love
And lack not to lose still.

COUNTESS
Had you not lately an intent—speak truly—
To go to Paris?

HELENA
Madam, I had.

COUNTESS
Wherefore? Tell true.

HELENA
I will tell truth, by grace itself I swear.
You know my father left me some prescriptions
Of rare and prov'd effects, such as his reading
And manifest experience had collected
For general sovereignty; and that he will'd me
In heedfull'st reservation to bestow them,
As notes whose faculties inclusive were
More than they were in note. Amongst the rest,
There is a remedy, approv'd, set down,
To cure the desperate languishings whereof
The King is render'd lost.

COUNTESS
This was your motive for Paris, was it? Speak.

HELENA
My lord your son made me to think of this;
Else Paris, and the medicine, and the King
Had from the conversation of my thoughts
Happily been absent then.

COUNTESS
But think you, Helen,
If you should tender your supposed aid,
He would receive it? He and his physicians
Are of a mind: he, that they cannot help him;
They, that they cannot help. How shall they credit
A poor unlearned virgin, when the schools,
Embowel'd of their doctrine, have left off
The danger to itself?

HELENA
There's something in 't,
More than my father's skill, which was the great'st
Of his profession, that his good receipt
Shall for my legacy be sanctified
By th' luckiest stars in heaven; and would your honor
But give me leave to try success, I'd venture
The well-lost life of mine on his Grace's cure
By such a day and hour.

COUNTESS
Dost thou believe 't?

HELENA
Ay, madam, knowingly.

COUNTESS
Why, Helen, thou shalt have my leave and love,
Means and attendants, and my loving greetings
To those of mine in court. I'll stay at home
And pray God's blessing into thy attempt.
Be gone tomorrow, and be sure of this;
What I can help thee to thou shalt not miss.

[Exeunt.]

6 curd curdle **8 distempered** disturbed, upset **messenger of wet** i.e., tear **9 Iris** Roman goddess of the rainbow (The Countess refers to the refracted light—a rainbow of sorts—in Helena's tear.) **rounds** encircles **10 not** i.e., not your daughter-in-law **14 note** mark of distinction **parents** ancestors **16 vassal** menial, servant **19 So that** so long as, provided that **20 both our mothers** mother of us both **21 I . . . heaven** i.e., I would value that as highly as I value heaven **22–23 Can . . . daughter** can it not be other than I, being your daughter **25 shield** forbid **26 strive upon** raise, agitate **27 fear** apprehension, uneasiness **catch'd** ferreted out, caught on to **fondness** (1) love (of Bertram) (2) foolishness **29 head** source **sense** perception **gross** apparent, obvious **30 Invention** ability to devise excuses or plausible answers **31 Against** in the face of **36 Go not about** don't be evasive **37 Whereof . . . note** which society acknowledges **38 affection** feelings **39 appeach'd** informed against you, betrayed you **41 before . . . unto** more than (I love) you and second only to **43 friends** relatives **45–46 I . . . suit** I do not pursue him in an inappropriately forward manner (?) **48 should be** may or will come to be **49 hope** what can reasonably be expected **50 captious** receptive, capacious **intenible** incapable of holding **52 lack . . . still** have enough to continually lose more **54 Wherefore** for what reason **55 grace** God's grace **56 prescriptions** medicines, remedies **58 manifest** practical, tangible **59 general sovereignty** universal effectiveness and application **59–60 will'd . . . them** wished me to dispense them with the utmost care **61–62 As . . . note** i.e., as remedies whose power was greater than generally recognized **62 Amongst the rest** i.e., among them all **63 approv'd** proved, tested **64 languishings** lingering disease **whereof** by means of which **65 King** i.e., King of France **render'd lost** assumed to be dying, considered to be incurable **66 for** i.e., for traveling to **70 Happily** perhaps, haply **71 tender . . . aid** offer the aid you propose **73 of a mind** of like mind, in agreement **help** cure **76 Embowel'd** exhausted, emptied **76–77 have . . . itself** are resigned to letting the disease run its course **79 receipt** prescription, remedy **80 sanctified** blessed **83 well-lost** (i.e., if lost in such a noble cause) **84 such a** a specified **85 knowingly** assuredly **86 leave** permission to depart **89 into** upon **91 miss** lack, go without

(2) CELIA AND ROSALIND [I.III.88]

As You Like It

SCENE: Duke Frederick's palace.

{Just moments ago, Duke Frederick burst into the room, abruptly banished Rosalind from his court, and burst right back out. Understandably taken aback by this sudden turn of events, Rosalind and her faithful cousin, Celia, are nonetheless quick to gather their wits and map out an adventurous strategy.}

CELIA
O my poor Rosalind, whither wilt thou go?
Wilt thou change fathers? I will give thee mine.
I charge thee, be not thou more griev'd than I am.

ROSALIND
I have more cause.

CELIA
Thou hast not, cousin.
Prithee, be cheerful. Know'st thou not, the Duke
Hath banish'd me, his daughter?

ROSALIND
That he hath not.

CELIA
No, hath not? Rosalind lacks then the love
Which teacheth thee that thou and I am one.
Shall we be sund'red? Shall we part, sweet girl?
No, let my father seek another heir.
Therefore devise with me how we may fly,
Whither to go, and what to bear with us.
And do not seek to take your change upon you,
To bear your griefs yourself and leave me out;
For, by this heaven, now at our sorrows pale,
Say what thou canst, I'll go along with thee.

ROSALIND
Why, whither shall we go?

CELIA
To seek my uncle in the forest of Arden.

ROSALIND
Alas, what danger will it be to us,
Maids as we are, to travel forth so far!
Beauty provoketh thieves sooner than gold.

CELIA
I'll put myself in poor and mean attire
And with a kind of umber smirch my face;
The like do you. So shall we pass along
And never stir assailants.

ROSALIND

Were it not better,
Because that I am more than common tall,
That I did suit me all points like a man?
A gallant curtle-axe upon my thigh,
A boar-spear in my hand; and—in my heart
Lie there what hidden woman's fear there will—
We'll have a swashing and a martial outside,
As many other mannish cowards have
That do outface it with their semblances.

CELIA
What shall I call thee when thou art a man?

ROSALIND
I'll have no worse a name than Jove's own page,
And therefore look you call me Ganymede.
But what will you be call'd?

CELIA
Something that hath a reference to my state:
No longer Celia, but Aliena.

ROSALIND
But, cousin, what if we assay'd to steal
The clownish fool out of your father's court?
Would he not be a comfort to our travel?

CELIA
He'll go along o'er the wide world with me;
Leave me alone to woo him. Let's away,
And get our jewels and our wealth together,
Devise the fittest time and safest way
To hide us from pursuit that will be made
After my flight. Now go we in content
To liberty, and not to banishment.

Exeunt

9 sund'red separated **13 change** change of fortune and circumstances **15 pale** cheerless **22 mean** lowly, base **23 umber** brown pigment **27 suit** dress **28 curtle-axe** short, broad-bladed sword **31 swashing** swaggering, swashbuckling **33 outface . . . semblances** bluff their way with mere appearances **36 Ganymede** a boy whom Jupiter ("Jove") chose as his cupbearer **39 Aliena** Latin for "the estranged one" **40 assay'd** tried **44 woo** coax, persuade **48 content** contentment

(3) CELIA AND ROSALIND [III.II.153]

As You Like It

SCENE: The forest of Arden.

{Poor Orlando, completely infatuated with Rosalind, has been running around hanging love poems on the trees of Arden's forest. In fact it's one of Orlando's overwrought odes that Celia, out for a little stroll, has just now finished reciting. Having figured that she was alone, Celia's somewhat taken aback when Rosalind pops out from behind a nearby bush to offer an unsolicited critique.}

ROSALIND
O most gentle Jupiter, what tedious homily of love have you wearied your parishioners withal, and never cried "Have patience, good people!"

CELIA
How now? Didst thou hear these verses?

ROSALIND
O, yes, I heard them all, and more too; for some of them had in them more feet than the verses would bear.

CELIA
That's no matter; the feet might bear the verses.

ROSALIND
Ay, but the feet were lame and could not bear themselves without the verse, and therefore stood lamely in the verse.

CELIA
But didst thou hear without wondering how thy name should be hang'd and carv'd upon these trees?

ROSALIND
I was seven of the nine days out of the wonder before you came; for look here what I found on a palm-tree. I was never so berhym'd since Pythagoras' time, that I was an Irish rat, which I can hardly remember.

CELIA
Trow you who hath done this?

ROSALIND
Is it a man?

CELIA
And a chain, that you once wore, about his neck. Change you color?

ROSALIND
I prithee, who?

CELIA
O Lord, Lord, it is a hard matter for friends to meet; but mountains may be remov'd with earthquakes, and so encounter.

ROSALIND
Nay, but who is it?

CELIA
Is it possible?

ROSALIND
Nay, I prithee now with most petitionary vehemence, tell me who it is.

CELIA
O wonderful, wonderful, and most wonderful wonderful! And yet again wonderful, and after that, out of all hooping!

ROSALIND
Good my complexion! Dost thou think, though I am caparison'd like a man, I have a doublet and hose in my disposition? One inch of delay more is a South-sea of discovery. I prithee, tell me who is it quickly, and speak apace. I would thou couldst stammer, that thou mightst pour this conceal'd man out of thy mouth, as wine comes out of a narrow- mouth'd bottle, either too much at once, or none at all. I prithee, take the cork out of thy mouth that I may drink thy tidings.

CELIA
So you may put a man in your belly.

ROSALIND
Is he of God's making? What manner of man? Is his head worth a hat, or his chin worth a beard?

CELIA
Nay, he hath but a little beard.

ROSALIND
Why, God will send more, if the man will be thankful. Let me stay the growth of his beard, if thou delay me not the knowledge of his chin.

CELIA
It is young Orlando, that tripp'd up the wrestler's heels and your heart both in an instant.

ROSALIND
Nay, but the devil take mocking. Speak sad brow and true maid.

CELIA
I' faith, coz, 'tis he.

ROSALIND
Orlando?

CELIA
Orlando.

ROSALIND
Alas the day, what shall I do with my doublet and hose? What did he when thou saw'st him? What said he? How look'd he? Wherein went he? What makes he here? Did he ask for me? Where remains he? How parted he with thee? And when shalt thou see him again? Answer me in one word.

CELIA
You must borrow me Gargantua's mouth first; 'tis a word too great for any mouth of this age's size. To say ay and no to these particulars is more than to answer in a catechism.

ROSALIND
But doth he know that I am in this forest and in man's apparel? Looks he as freshly as he did the day he wrestled?

CELIA
It is as easy to count atomies as to resolve the propositions of a lover. But take a taste of my finding him, and relish it with good observance. I found him under a tree, like a dropp'd acorn.

ROSALIND
It may well be call'd Jove's tree, when it drops forth such fruit.

CELIA
Give me audience, good madam.

ROSALIND
Proceed.

CELIA
There lay he, stretch'd along, like a wounded knight.

ROSALIND
Though it be pity to see such a sight, it well becomes the ground.

CELIA
Cry "holla" to thy tongue, I prithee; it curvets unseasonably. He was furnish'd like a hunter.

ROSALIND
O, ominous! He comes to kill my heart.

CELIA
I would sing my song without a burden. Thou bring'st me out of tune.

ROSALIND
Do you not know I am a woman? When I think, I must speak. Sweet, say on.

[*Enter Orlando and Jaques.*]

CELIA
You bring me out.—Soft! Comes he not here?

ROSALIND
'Tis he. Slink by, and note him.

[*They stand aside and listen.*]

2 withal with **5 feet** (Rosalind playfully refers to metric feet, the units of stress that maintain the meter of verse.) **7 without** (1) without the help of (2) outside **9 should be** happened to be **9–10 hang'd and carv'd** (see III.ii.1) **11 seven . . . wonder** (Refers to the expression, "a nine day's wonder"; i.e., a short-lived sensation) **12 berhym'd** described in verse **Pythagoras** (An allusion to the Greek philosopher who taught that souls of the dead passed on to other beings.) **13 Irish rat** (Refers to an old belief that Irish enchanters could kill rats and other animals with rhymed spells.) **14 Trow** know **16 And a chain** i.e., yes, it is a man, and with a chain **17 prithee** pray thee, beg you **18 friends . . . mountains** (A play on the proverb, "Friends may meet, but mountains never greet.") **19 remov'd with** moved by **encounter** fight on **22 petitionary vehemence** urgent pleading **24 out of** beyond **hooping** whooping, i.e., power to exclaim **25 Good my complexion!** O, my woman's curiosity! **caparison'd** dressed up **26 doublet and hose** jacket and pants commonly worn by men **26–27 is . . . discovery** will seem the same as a lengthy exploration of the South Seas **27 apace** swiftly **32 of God's making** i.e., a real man, and not merely a poser **35 stay** wait for **37 tripp'd . . . heels** (See I.ii.) **39 sad . . . maid** seriously and truthfully **40 I' faith** in good faith, in truth **47 Gargantua's mouth** (Gargantua is the medieval giant who once swallowed up six men in his salad.) **51 freshly** youthful, filled with vitality **52 atomies** atoms, tiny specks **propositions** questions **53 relish it** enhance its taste **good observance** careful attention **55 Jove's tree** i.e., an oak tree (considered the king of trees) **59 becomes** adorns, adds splendor to **60 "holla"** stop

(Such a cry was used to halt a horse.) **curvets unseasonably** prances about inappropriately **61 furnish'd** equipped **62 heart** (with a play on *hart*, a male deer) **63 burden** accompanying refrain **65 bring me out** put me off, confuse me **Soft!** wait

(4) PORTIA AND NERISSA [I.II.1]

The Merchant of Venice

SCENE: Portia's house.

{Portia is nearly at wits end. Her frustration stems from a provision in her late father's will that dictates she must marry the first suitor who can correctly choose from among three small chests adorned with gold, silver and lead, respectively. Thank goodness faithful servant Nerissa is at hand, ready and willing to help Portia gain a bit of perspective on the situation.}

PORTIA
By my troth, Nerissa, my little body is aweary of this great world.

NERISSA
You would be, sweet madam, if your miseries were in the same abundance as your good fortunes are; and yet, for aught I see, they are as sick that surfeit with too much as they that starve with nothing. It is no mean happiness, therefore, to be seated in the mean; superfluity comes sooner by white hairs, but competency lives longer.

PORTIA
Good sentences and well pronounc'd.

NERISSA
They would be better, if well follow'd.

PORTIA
If to do were as easy as to know what were good to do, chapels had been churches and poor men's cottages princes' palaces. It is a good divine that follows his own instructions; I can easier teach twenty what were good to be done, than to be one of the twenty to follow mine own teaching. But this reasoning is not in the fashion to choose me a husband. O me, the word "choose!" I may neither choose who I would nor refuse who I dislike; so is the will of a living daughter curb'd by the will of a dead father. Is it not hard, Nerissa, that I cannot choose one nor refuse none?

NERISSA
Your father was ever virtuous, and holy men at their death have good inspirations; therefore the lott'ry that he hath devis'd in these three chests of gold, silver and lead, whereof who chooses his meaning chooses you, will no doubt never be chosen by any rightly but one who you shall rightly love. But what warmth is there in your affection towards any of these princely suitors that are already come?

PORTIA
I pray thee, over-name them; and as thou namest them, I will describe them; and, according to my description, level at my affection.

NERISSA
First, there is the Neapolitan prince.

PORTIA
Ay, that's a colt indeed, for he doth nothing but talk of his horse; and he makes it a great appropriation to his own good parts that he can shoe him himself. I am much afeard my lady his mother play'd false with a smith.

NERISSA
Then is there the County Palatine.

PORTIA
He doth nothing but frown, as who should say "An you will not have me, choose." He hears merry tales and smiles not; I fear he will prove the weeping philosopher when he grows old, being so full of unmannerly sadness in his youth.

NERISSA
How say you by the French lord, Monsieur Le Bon?

PORTIA
God made him, and therefore let him pass for a man. In truth, I know it is a sin to be a mocker, but he! Why, he hath a horse better than the Neapolitan's, and a better bad habit of frowning than the Count Palatine. If he would despise me I would forgive him, for if he love me to madness, I shall never requite him.

NERISSA
What say you, then, to Falconbridge, the young baron of England?

PORTIA
You know I say nothing to him, for he understands not me, nor I him. He hath neither Latin, French, nor Italian, and you will come into the court and swear that I have a poor pennyworth in the English. He is a proper man's picture, but, alas, who can converse with a dumb-show?

NERISSA
How like you the young German, the Duke of Saxony's nephew?

PORTIA
Very vilely in the morning, when he is sober, and most vilely in the afternoon, when he is drunk. When he is best, he is a little worse than a man, and when he is worst, he is little better than a beast. An the worst fall that ever fell, I hope I shall make shift to go without him.

NERISSA
If he should offer to choose, and choose the right casket, you should refuse to perform your father's will, if you should refuse to accept him.

PORTIA
Therefore, for fear of the worst, I pray thee, set a deep glass of Rhenish wine on the contrary casket, for if the devil be within and that temptation without, I know he will choose it. I will do any thing, Nerissa, ere I will be married to a sponge.

NERISSA
You need not fear, lady, the having any of these lords. They have acquainted me with their determinations, which is, indeed, to return to their home and to trouble you with no more suit, unless you may be won by some other sort than your father's imposition depending on the caskets.

PORTIA
If I live to be as old as Sibylla, I will die as chaste as Diana, unless I be obtain'd by the manner of my father's will. I am glad this parcel of wooers are so reasonable, for there is not one among them but I dote on his very absence, and I pray God grant them a fair departure.

1 By my troth (a common affirmation of the day on the order of "I'll say this," or "I declare") **3 aught I see** i.e., as far as I can **3–4 surfeit with** indulge in **4 mean** lowly, poor **5 in the mean** between having too much and too little **superfluity . . . by** excess more quickly gets **6 competency** adequate means **7 sentences** maxims **pronounc'd** spoken **10 divine** priest **13 in the fashion** of a kind to help me **15 hard** harsh, severe **19 whereof who** from which (chests) whoever **chooses his meaning** i.e., correctly guesses your father's intentions **23 over-name them** name them again **24 level . . . affection** i.e., you may guess what affection I have for them **27 appropriation** addition **28 false** adulterously **smith** blacksmith **29 County** Count **30 who should** if to **An** if **31 choose** i.e., then do as you like **prove** turn out to be **31–32 weeping philosopher** (refers to Heraclitus of Ephesus, the Greek philosopher known for being particularly downhearted) **32 unmannerly** unbecoming **43 poor pennyworth in** piddling amount of **43–44 proper man's picture** handsome man **44 dumb-show** story played out without words **48 fall** befalls, happens **49 make shift** manage **50 should refuse** would be refusing **52–53 Rhenish wine** German wine from the Rhine valley **53 contrary** wrong **59 sort** manner, way **imposition** conditions **60 Sibylla** prophetess to whom Apollo gave a year of life for every grain of sand she held in her hand **Diana** the goddess of chastity

(5) Mistress Ford and Mistress Page [II.1.31]

The Merry Wives of Windsor

SCENE: In front of Page's house.

{Out of breath and clutching a lascivious love letter she's received from the fat knight Falstaff, Mistress Ford shows up at the Page's doorstep raring to apprise her best mate of this unsavory event.}

[Enter Mistress Ford.]

MISTRESS FORD
Mistress Page! Trust me, I was going to your house.

MISTRESS PAGE
And, trust me, I was coming to you. You look very ill.

MISTRESS FORD
Nay, I'll ne'er believe that; I have to show to the contrary.

MISTRESS PAGE
Faith, but you do, in my mind.

MISTRESS FORD
Well, I do then; yet I say I could show you to the contrary. O Mistress Page, give me some counsel!

MISTRESS PAGE
What's the matter, woman?

MISTRESS FORD
O woman, if it were not for one trifling respect, I could come to such honor!

MISTRESS PAGE
Hang the trifle, woman; take the honor. What is it? Dispense with trifles. What is it?

MISTRESS FORD
If I would but go to hell for an eternal moment or so, I could be knighted.

MISTRESS PAGE
What? Thou liest! Sir Alice Ford! These knights will hack; and so thou shouldst not alter the article of thy gentry.

MISTRESS FORD
We burn daylight. Here, read, read; perceive how I might be knighted. [*Gives her the letter.*] I shall think the worse of fat men, as long as I have an eye to make difference of men's liking. And yet he would not swear; prais'd women's modesty; and gave such orderly and well-behav'd reproof to all uncomeliness, that I would have sworn his disposition would have gone to the truth of his words; but they do no more adhere and keep place together than the Hundredth Psalm to the tune of "Green Sleeves." What tempest, I trow, threw this whale, with so many tuns of oil in his belly, ashore at Windsor? How shall I be reveng'd on him? I think the best way were to entertain him with hope, till the wicked fire of lust have melted him in his own grease. Did you ever hear the like?

MISTRESS PAGE
Letter for letter, but that the name of Page and Ford differs! To thy great comfort in this mystery of ill opinions, here's the twin-brother of thy letter. [*Shows her the letter.*] But let thine inherit first; for, I protest, mine never shall. I warrant he hath a thousand of these letters, writ with blank space for different names—sure, more—and these are of the second edition. He will print them, out of doubt; for he cares not what he puts into the press, when he would put us two. I had rather be a giantess, and lie under Mount Pelion. Well, I will find you twenty lascivious turtles ere one chaste man.

MISTRESS FORD
[*Comparing the two letters.*] Why, this is the very same; the very hand, the very words. What doth he think of us?

MISTRESS PAGE
Nay, I know not. It makes me almost ready to wrangle with mine own honesty. I'll entertain myself like one that I am not acquainted withal; for, sure, unless he know some strain in me that I know not myself, he would never have boarded me in this fury.

MISTRESS FORD
"Boarding," call you it? I'll be sure to keep him above deck.

MISTRESS PAGE
So will I. If he come under my hatches, I'll never to sea again. Let's be reveng'd on him. Let's appoint him a meeting, give him a show of comfort in

his suit, and lead him on with a fine-baited delay, till he hath pawn'd his horses to mine host of the Garter.

MISTRESS FORD
Nay, I will consent to act any villainy against him that may not sully the chariness of our honesty. O, that my husband saw this letter! It would give eternal food to his jealousy.

MISTRESS PAGE
Why, look where he comes; and my good man too. He's as far from jealousy as I am from giving him cause, and that I hope is an unmeasurable distance.

MISTRESS FORD
You are the happier woman.

MISTRESS PAGE
Let's consult together against this greasy knight. Come hither.

[They retire.]

10 Hang never mind **13 hack** (Literally, swing wildly and indiscriminately, together with a likely play on the image of sexual promiscuity.) **14 article of thy gentry** character, nature of your rank **15 burn daylight** waste time **17 make . . . liking** discriminate among different men's appearances **18 orderly** proper, seemly **19 uncomliness** unseemly behavior **19–20 gone . . . of** supported **20–21 adhere . . . together** agree with or suit each other **22 trow** wonder **tuns** large barrels **24 entertain him** engage his thoughts **27 ill** morally corrupt **28 inherit first** (The wordplay here has Page suggesting that Ford's letter should "inherit" Falstaff's knighthood, in that it no doubt arrived first.) **31 out of doubt** no doubt **into the press** into the printing press (with a pun on the image of Falstaff's considerable girth pressing upon the unfortunate woman lying beneath him) **32 Mount Pelion** (Refers to the mountain that the giants of Greek mythology piled on top of Mount Ossa in a futile attempt to scale Mount Olympus.) **33 turtles** turtledoves (which were symbols of faithful love) **36 wrangle with** dispute, quarrel with **37 entertain** treat **withal** with **38 strain** quality **39 boarded** addressed, accosted (with a play on the image of naval warfare) **42 appoint him** arrange with him **comfort in** delight with **43 fine-baited** subtly alluring **pawn'd** forfeited **44 host . . . Garter** (See I.iii.) **46 chariness** scrupulous integrity **47 food** i.e., nourishment, sustenance

(6) HERO AND URSULA [III.1.15]

Much Ado About Nothing

SCENE: Leonato's orchard.

{*Now that Benedick has been duped by Don Pedro and friends into thinking that Beatrice is madly in love with him, the time has come to play the flip side. With Hero and her attendant Ursula running the show, part two of the elaborate ruse begins.*}

HERO
Now, Ursula, when Beatrice doth come,
As we do trace this alley up and down,
Our talk must only be of Benedick.
When I do name him, let it be thy part
To praise him more than ever man did merit:
My talk to thee must be how Benedick
Is sick in love with Beatrice. Of this matter
Is little Cupid's crafty arrow made,
That only wounds by hearsay.

[*Enter Beatrice, behind.*]

Now begin;
For look where Beatrice, like a lapwing, runs
Close by the ground, to hear our conference.

URSULA
The pleasant'st angling is to see the fish
Cut with her golden oars the silver stream,
And greedily devour the treacherous bait.
So angle we for Beatrice; who even now
Is couched in the woodbine coverture.
Fear you not my part of the dialogue.

HERO
Then go we near her, that her ear lose nothing
Of the false sweet bait that we lay for it.

[*They approach the bower.*]

No, truly, Ursula, she is too disdainful;
I know her spirits are as coy and wild
As haggards of the rock.

URSULA

But are you sure
That Benedick loves Beatrice so entirely?

HERO

So says the prince and my new-trothed lord.

URSULA

And did they bid you tell her of it, madam?

HERO

They did entreat me to acquaint her of it;
But I persuaded them, if they lov'd Benedick,
To wish him wrestle with affection,
And never to let Beatrice know of it.

URSULA

Why did you so? Doth not the gentleman
Deserve as full as fortunate a bed
As ever Beatrice shall couch upon?

HERO

O god of love! I know he doth deserve
As much as may be yielded to a man:
But Nature never fram'd a woman's heart
Of prouder stuff than that of Beatrice.
Disdain and scorn ride sparkling in her eyes,
Misprising what they look on, and her wit
Values itself so highly that to her
All matter else seems weak. She cannot love,
Nor take no shape nor project of affection,
She is so self-endeared.

URSULA

Sure, I think so;
And therefore certainly it were not good
She knew his love, lest she'll make sport at it.

HERO

Why, you speak truth. I never yet saw man,
How wise, how noble, young, how rarely featur'd,
But she would spell him backward. If fair-fac'd,
She would swear the gentleman should be her sister;
If black, why, Nature, drawing of an antic,
Made a foul blot; if tall, a lance ill-headed;
If low, an agate very vilely cut;
If speaking, why, a vane blown with all winds;

If silent, why, a block moved with none.
So turns she every man the wrong side out,
And never gives to truth and virtue that
Which simpleness and merit purchaseth.

URSULA
Sure, sure, such carping is not commendable.

HERO
No, not to be so odd and from all fashions,
As Beatrice is, cannot be commendable.
But who dare tell her so? If I should speak,
She would mock me into air; O, she would laugh me
Out of myself, press me to death with wit.
Therefore let Benedick, like cover'd fire,
Consume away in sighs, waste inwardly.
It were a better death than die with mocks,
Which is as bad as die with tickling.

URSULA
Yet tell her of it. Hear what she will say.

HERO
No, rather I will go to Benedick
And counsel him to fight against his passion.
And truly, I'll devise some honest slanders
To stain my cousin with. One doth not know
How much an ill word may empoison liking.

URSULA
O, do not do your cousin such a wrong.
She cannot be so much without true judgment—
Having so swift and excellent a wit
As she is priz'd to have—as to refuse
So rare a gentleman as Signior Benedick.

HERO
He is the only man of Italy,
Always excepted my dear Claudio.

URSULA
I pray you, be not angry with me, madam,
Speaking my fancy: Signior Benedick,
For shape, for bearing, argument and valor,
Goes foremost in report through Italy.

HERO
Indeed, he hath an excellent good name.

URSULA
His excellence did earn it, ere he had it.
When are you married, madam?

HERO
Why, every day tomorrow. Come, go in.
I'll show thee some attires, and have thy counsel
Which is the best to furnish me tomorrow.

[*They begin to walk away.*]

URSULA
She's lim'd, I warrant you. We have caught her, madam.

HERO
If it proves so, then loving goes by haps;
Some Cupid kills with arrows, some with traps.

[*Exeunt Hero and Ursula.*]

2 trace roam, walk **9 only . . . hearsay** wounds by mere rumor **10 lapwing** a type of bird **13 oars** i.e., fins **16 woodbine coverture** shade of honeysuckle **21 coy** haughty, insolent **22 haggards** wild female hawks **rock** i.e., mountain **24 new-trothed** recently betrothed **31 as full as** fully as **35 fram'd** created **38 Misprising** undervaluing **40 All matter else** anyone else's opinion **41 take . . . affection** i.e., come to grips with any conception of what love is **42 self-endeared** full of herself **46 How** no matter how **rarely** unusually fine **47 spell him backward** misconstrue him by seeing his virtues as faults **fair-fac'd** fair of complexion **49 black** dark complexioned **antic** buffoon, grotesque figure **51 agate** (alludes to the tiny figures cut into agate for jewelry) **56 simpleness** sincerity, integrity **purchaseth** deserve **58 from all fashions** contrary to all proper forms of behavior **61 into air** i.e., until I was nothing **62 press . . . death** (Pressing to death with weights was a means of executing one who refused to enter a plea.) **64 Consume . . . sighs** (It was believed by some that each sigh cost the heart a drop of blood.) **70 honest** harmless (Hero intends to invent mild slanders that will not besmirch Beatrice's character.) **77 Signior** (term of address taken from Italian "signore" and equivalent to "Mr.") **79 excepted** excepting **82 shape** appearance **argument** skillful conversation, powers of reasoning **87 every day tomorrow** every day after tomorrow **90 lim'd** ensnared (Putting lime on bushes was a common method of trapping birds.) **91 haps** chance

(7) Emilia and Desdemona [IV.iii.11]

Othello

SCENE: A room in Othello's castle.

{It's all over but the smothering. An agitated Othello, convinced of his wife's infidelity, has just left the room after commanding Desdemona to "get you to bed." But before dutifully—and as things would turn out, fatally—following her husband's instructions, Desdemona pauses for a moment of song and introspection with her attendant and chief confidant, Emilia.}

EMILIA
How goes it now? He looks gentler than he did.

DESDEMONA
He says he will return incontinent,
And hath commanded me to go to bed,
And bade me to dismiss you.

EMILIA
Dismiss me?

DESDEMONA
It was his bidding; therefore, good Emilia,
Give me my nightly wearing, and adieu.
We must not now displease him.

EMILIA
I would you had never seen him!

DESDEMONA
So would not I. My love doth so approve him,
That even his stubbornness, his checks, his frowns—
Prithee, unpin me—have grace and favor in them.

[*Emilia readies Desdemona for bed.*]

EMILIA
I have laid those sheets you bade me on the bed.

DESDEMONA
All's one. Good faith, how foolish are our minds!
If I do die before thee, prithee shroud me
In one of those same sheets.

EMILIA
Come, come you talk.

DESDEMONA
My mother had a maid call'd Barbary.
She was in love, and he she lov'd prov'd mad
And did forsake her. She had a song of "Willow,"
An old thing 'twas, but it express'd her fortune,
And she died singing it. That song tonight
Will not go from my mind; I have much to do
But to go hang my head all at one side
And sing it like poor Barbary. Prithee, dispatch.

EMILIA
Shall I go fetch your nightgown?

DESDEMONA
No, unpin me here.
This Lodovico is a proper man.

EMILIA
A very handsome man.

DESDEMONA
He speaks well.

EMILIA
I know a lady in Venice would have walk'd barefoot to Palestine for a touch of his nether lip.

DESDEMONA
[*Singing.*] "The poor soul sat sighing by a sycamore tree,
Sing all a green willow:
Her hand on her bosom, her head on her knee,
Sing willow, willow, willow:
The fresh streams ran by her, and murmur'd her moans;
Sing willow, willow, willow;
Her salt tears fell from her, and soften'd the stones"—
Lay by these.
[*Singing.*] "Sing willow, willow, willow"—
Prithee, hie thee; he'll come anon.—
[*Singing.*] "Sing all a green willow must be my garland.
Let nobody blame him; his scorn I approve"—
Nay, that's not next—Hark, who is 't that knocks?

EMILIA
It's the wind.

DESDEMONA
[*Singing*.] "I call'd my love false love; but what said he then?
Sing willow, willow, willow;
If I court moe women, you'll couch with moe men"—
So, get thee gone; good night. Mine eyes do itch;
Doth that bode weeping?

EMILIA
'Tis neither here nor there.

DESDEMONA
I have heard it said so. O, these men, these men!
Dost thou in conscience think—tell me, Emilia—
That there be women do abuse their husbands
In such gross kind?

EMILIA
There be some such, no question.

DESDEMONA
Wouldst thou do such a deed for all the world?

EMILIA
Why, would not you?

DESDEMONA
No, by this heavenly light!

EMILIA
Nor I neither by this heavenly light;
I might do 't as well i' th' dark.

DESDEMONA
Wouldst thou do such a deed for all the world?

EMILIA
The world's a huge thing. It is a great price
For a small vice.

DESDEMONA
Good troth, I think thou wouldst not.

EMILIA
By my troth, I think I should; and undo 't when I had done. Marry, I would not do such a thing for a joint-ring, nor for measures of lawn, nor for

gowns, petticoats, nor caps, nor any petty exhibition; but for the whole world—'ud's pity, who would not make her husband a cuckold to make him a monarch? I should venture purgatory for 't.

DESDEMONA
Beshrew me, if I would do such a wrong
For the whole world.

EMILIA
Why, the wrong is but a wrong i' th' world; and having the world for your labor, 'tis a wrong in your own world, and you might quickly make it right.

DESDEMONA
I do not think there is any such woman.

EMILIA
Yes, a dozen; and as many to th' vantage as would store the world they play'd for.
But I do think it is their husbands' faults
If wives do fall. Say that they slack their duties,
And pour our treasures into foreign laps,
Or else break out in peevish jealousies,
Throwing restraint upon us. Or say they strike us,
Or scant our former having in despite.
Why, we have galls, and though we have some grace,
Yet have we some revenge. Let husbands know
Their wives have sense like them; they see and smell
And have their palates both for sweet and sour,
As husbands have. What is it that they do
When they change us for others? Is it sport?
I think it is. And doth affection breed it?
I think it doth. Is 't frailty that thus errs?
It is so too. And have not we affections,
Desires for sport, and frailty, as men have?
Then let them use us well; else let them know,
The ills we do, their ills instruct us so.

DESDEMONA
Good night, good night. God me such uses send,
Not to pick bad from bad, but by bad mend!

[*Exeunt.*]

2 incontinent at once **7 wearing** clothes **11 checks** rebukes, reprimands **12 Prithee** (I) pray thee, beg thee **14 Good faith** in truth **19 mad** wild, i.e., untrue **23–24 I . . . But to** it's all I can do not to **28 Lodovico** (See

IV.iii.1.) **43 hie** hurry **48 moe** more **54 In . . . kind** so flagrantly **57 heavenly light** i.e., moon **63 Good troth** in truth **64 By my troth** (a mild oath affirming one's truthfulness) **undo** reverse, annul **Marry** (a mild oath used to emphasize an assertion) **65 joint-ring** a type of inexpensive finger-ring that can be separated in half **lawn** fine linen **66 exhibition** gift **67 'ud's pity** God's **69 Beshrew me** (a mild oath on the order of "curse me" or "a plague on me") **74 to th' vantage** in addition, to boot **store** populate, fill **77 slack** neglect **duties** marital responsibilities **78 our treasures** (refers to their husband's semen) **foreign laps** i.e., other women **79 peevish** childish **80 restraint** confinement, restrictions **81 scant . . . despite** reduce our allowance just to spite us **82 have galls** possess the sort of spirit that resents wrongdoing or injustice **84 sense like** the same physical senses as **87 change** exchange **sport** a pleasant entertainment, an amusing diversion **88 affection** passion **92 use** treat **93 instruct us so** serve as our example **94 God . . . send** God grant that it be my practice **95 Not . . . mend** i.e., not to model one's behavior on the bad deeds of others (per Emilia's suggestion that "their ills instruct us so"), but rather improve ("mend") ourselves by fully appreciating what badness is.

(8) JULIET AND NURSE [II.v.1]

Romeo and Juliet

SCENE: Capulet's orchard.

{Romance moves quickly here in Verona. Romeo and Juliet have known each other for a mere matter of hours, but even so, Romeo has already concocted a plan by which the two might be secretly married. Nurse, playing the role of the lovers' go-between, now hurries back from Romeo in order to fill Juliet in on the arrangements.}

[*Enter Juliet.*]

JULIET
The clock struck nine when I did send the nurse;
In half an hour she promised to return.
Perchance she cannot meet him—that's not so.
O, she is lame! Love's heralds should be thoughts,
Which ten times faster glide than the sun's beams,
Driving back shadows over louring hills.
Therefore do nimble-pinion'd doves draw Love,
And therefore hath the wind-swift Cupid wings.
Now is the sun upon the highmost hill

Of this day's journey, and from nine till twelve
Is three long hours, yet she is not come.
Had she affections and warm youthful blood,
She would be as swift in motion as a ball;
My words would bandy her to my sweet love,
And his to me.
But old folks, many feign as they were dead—
Unwieldy, slow, heavy and pale as lead.

[*Enter Nurse.*]

O God, she comes! O honey nurse, what news?
Hast thou met with him? —O Lord, why look'st thou sad?
Though news be sad, yet tell them merrily;
If good, thou shamest the music of sweet news
By playing it to me with so sour a face.

NURSE
I am a-weary, give me leave awhile.
Fie, how my bones ache! What a jaunce have I had!

JULIET
I would thou hadst my bones, and I thy news.
Nay, come, I pray thee, speak; good, good nurse, speak.

NURSE
Jesu, what haste! Can you not stay awhile?
Do you not see that I am out of breath?

JULIET
How art thou out of breath, when thou hast breath
To say to me that thou art out of breath?
The excuse that thou dost make in this delay
Is longer than the tale thou dost excuse.
Is thy news good or bad? Answer to that.
Say either, and I'll stay the circumstance.
Let me be satisfied, is 't good or bad?

NURSE
Well, you have made a simple choice; you know not how to choose a man. Romeo? No, not he. Though his face be better than any man's, yet his leg excels all men's; and for a hand, and a foot, and a body, though they be not to be talk'd on, yet they are past compare. He is not the flower of courtesy, but, I'll warrant him, as gentle as a lamb. Go thy ways, wench; serve God. What, have you din'd at home?

JULIET
No, no: but all this did I know before.
What says he of our marriage? What of that?

NURSE
Lord, how my head aches! What a head have I!
It beats as it would fall in twenty pieces.
My back a t' other side—ah, my back, my back!
Beshrew your heart for sending me about
To catch my death with jauncing up and down!

JULIET
I' faith, I am sorry that thou art not well.
Sweet, sweet, sweet nurse, tell me, what says my love?

NURSE
Your love says, like an honest gentleman,
And a courteous, and a kind, and a handsome,
And, I warrant, a virtuous—Where is your mother?

JULIET
Where is my mother? Why, she is within;
Where should she be? How oddly thou repliest!
"Your love says, like an honest gentleman,
Where is your mother?"

NURSE
O God's lady dear!
Are you so hot? Marry, come up, I trow;
Is this the poultice for my aching bones?
Henceforward do your messages yourself.

JULIET
Here's such a coil! Come, what says Romeo?

NURSE
Have you got leave to go to shrift today?

JULIET
I have.

NURSE
Then hie you hence to Friar Laurence' cell;
There stays a husband to make you a wife.
Now comes the wanton blood up in your cheeks;
They'll be in scarlet straight at any news.
Hie you to church; I must another way,

To fetch a ladder, by the which your love
Must climb a bird's nest soon when it is dark.
I am the drudge, and toil in your delight,
But you shall bear the burden soon at night.
Go. I'll to dinner; hie you to the cell.

JULIET
Hie to high fortune! Honest nurse, farewell.

[*Exeunt in separate directions.*]

6 louring gloomy **7 draw Love** pull Venus (whose chariot was drawn by doves) **12 warm** passion-filled **14 bandy** toss **16 feign as** act as if **24 Fie** (an expression of disgust) **jaunce** jolting, i.e., exhausting journey **27 Jesu** Jesus (a mild oath) **stay** wait **34 stay the circumstance** wait for the details **36 simple** foolish **38–39 be . . . on** are nothing to talk about **39 past** beyond **45 as** as if **46 a t' other** on the other **47 Beshrew** (a mild oath on the order of "a curse on") **49 I' faith** truthfully (a mild oath) **59 hot** impatient **Marry, come up** (An expression conveying a strong reprimand.) **62 coil** fuss **63 shrift** confession **65 hie** hurry **67 wanton** excited, impetuous **68 straight** straightaway, promptly **71 a bird's nest** i.e., to Juliet's bedroom (with a bawdy reference to pubic hair) **73 bear the burden** (Nurse extends the off-color imagery she began with "bird's nest.")

(9) LADY CAPULET AND JULIET [III.v.64]

Romeo and Juliet

SCENE: Juliet's bedchamber.

{Romeo has no sooner slipped away from his bridal (i.e., Juliet's) bed than in pops Lady Capulet, blissfully ignorant of her daughter's recent wedding and brimming over with nuptial news of her own.}

LADY CAPULET
[*Within.*] Ho, daughter, are you up?

JULIET
Who is 't that calls? It is my lady mother.
Is she not down so late, or up so early?
What unaccustom'd cause procures her hither?

[*Enter Lady Capulet.*]

LADY CAPULET
Why, how now, Juliet!

JULIET
Madam, I am not well.

LADY CAPULET
Evermore weeping for your cousin's death?
What, wilt thou wash him from his grave with tears?
An if thou couldst, thou couldst not make him live;
Therefore, have done. Some grief shows much of love,
But much of grief shows still some want of wit.

JULIET
Yet let me weep for such a feeling loss.

LADY CAPULET
So shall you feel the loss, but not the friend
Which you weep for.

JULIET
Feeling so the loss,
I cannot choose but ever weep the friend.

LADY CAPULET
Well, girl, thou weep'st not so much for his death,
As that the villain lives which slaughter'd him.

JULIET
What villain madam?

LADY CAPULET
That same villain, Romeo.

JULIET
[*Aside.*] Villain and he be many miles asunder.—
God Pardon him! I do, with all my heart;
And yet no man like he doth grieve my heart.

LADY CAPULET
That is because the traitor murderer lives.

JULIET
Ay, madam, from the reach of these my hands.
Would none but I might venge my cousin's death!

LADY CAPULET
We will have vengeance for it, fear thou not.
Then weep no more. I'll send to one in Mantua,
Where that same banish'd runagate doth live,
Shall give him such an unaccustom'd dram,
That he shall soon keep Tybalt company.
And then, I hope, thou wilt be satisfied.

JULIET
Indeed, I never shall be satisfied
With Romeo, till I behold him—dead—
Is my poor heart so for a kinsman vex'd.
Madam, if you could find out but a man
To bear a poison, I would temper it,
That Romeo should, upon receipt thereof,
Soon sleep in quiet. O, how my heart abhors
To hear him nam'd, and cannot come to him
To wreak the love I bore my cousin
Upon his body that hath slaughter'd him!

LADY CAPULET
Find thou the means, and I'll find such a man.
But now I'll tell thee joyful tidings, girl.

JULIET
And joy comes well in such a needy time.
What are they, beseech your ladyship?

LADY CAPULET
Well, well, thou hast a careful father, child;
One who, to put thee from thy heaviness,
Hath sorted out a sudden day of joy,
That thou expects not, nor I look'd not for.

JULIET
Madam, in happy time, what day is that?

LADY CAPULET
Marry, my child, early next Thursday morn,
The gallant, young and noble gentleman,
The County Paris, at Saint Peter's Church,
Shall happily make thee there a joyful bride.

JULIET
Now, by Saint Peter's Church and Peter too,
He shall not make me there a joyful bride!
I wonder at this haste, that I must wed
Ere he that should be husband comes to woo.

I pray you, tell my lord and father, madam,
I will not marry yet; and, when I do, I swear
It shall be Romeo, whom you know I hate,
Rather than Paris. These are news indeed!

LADY CAPULET
Here comes your father; tell him so yourself,
And see how he will take it at your hands.

[*Enter Capulet and Nurse.*]

3 not down not yet gone to bed **4 unaccustom'd** unusual **procures** brings **hither** here **6 cousin's death** (See III.i.) **8 An if** if **10 still** ever, always **11 feeling** heartfelt **20 like** so much as **26 runagate** renegade **33 find out** locate **34 temper** mix **44 careful** full of concern (for your welfare) **46 sorted out** chosen **sudden** imminent **49 Marry** (a mild oath used to emphasize an assertion) **51 County** (a variation of Count)

(10) VIOLA AND OLIVIA [I.v.164]

Twelfth Night

SCENE: Olivia's house.

{Viola, currently operating in disguise as a boy named "Cesario," comes before Olivia hoping to further the amorous intentions of her employer, Duke Orsino. Unfortunately, Viola's masquerade appears to be undermining her mission, as Olivia seems considerably more impressed by the messenger than she does by his message.}

[*Enter Viola.*]

VIOLA
The honorable lady of the house, which is she?

OLIVIA
Speak to me; I shall answer for her. Your will?

VIOLA
Most radiant, exquisite and unmatchable beauty—I pray you tell me if this be the lady of the house, for I never saw her. I would be loath to cast away my speech; for besides that it is excellently well penn'd, I have taken great pains to con it. Good beauties, let me sustain no scorn; I am very comptible, even to the least sinister usage.

OLIVIA
Whence came you, sir?

VIOLA
I can say little more than I have studied, and that question's out of my part. Good gentle one, give me modest assurance if you be the lady of the house, that I may proceed in my speech.

OLIVIA
Are you a comedian?

VIOLA
No, my profound heart; and yet, by the very fangs of malice I swear, I am not that I play. Are you the lady of the house?

OLIVIA
If I do not usurp myself, I am.

VIOLA
Most certain, if you are she, you do usurp yourself; for what is yours to bestow is not yours to reserve. But this is from my commission. I will on with my speech in your praise, and then show you the heart of my message.

OLIVIA
Come to what is important in 't. I forgive you the praise.

VIOLA
Alas, I took great pains to study it, and 'tis poetical.

OLIVIA
It is the more like to be feign'd. I pray you, keep it in. I heard you were saucy at my gates, and allow'd your approach rather to wonder at you than to hear you. If you be not mad, be gone; if you have reason, be brief. 'Tis not that time of moon with me to make one in so skipping a dialogue. Speak your office.

VIOLA
I bring no overture of war, no taxation of homage. I hold the olive in my hand; my words are as full of peace as matter.

OLIVIA
Yet you began rudely. What are you? What would you? What is your text?

VIOLA
Most sweet lady—

OLIVIA
A comfortable doctrine, and much may be said of it. Where lies your text?

VIOLA
In Orsino's bosom.

OLIVIA
In his bosom? In what chapter of his bosom?

VIOLA
To answer by the method, in the first of his heart.

OLIVIA
O, I have read it; it is heresy. Have you no more to say?

VIOLA
Good madam, let me see your face.

OLIVIA
Have you any commission from your lord to negotiate with my face? You are now out of your text; but we will draw the curtain and show you the picture. Look you, sir, such a one I was this present. [*She unveils herself.*] Is 't not well done?

VIOLA
Excellently done, if God did all.

OLIVIA
'Tis in grain, sir; 'twill endure wind and weather.

VIOLA
'Tis beauty truly blent, whose red and white
Nature's own sweet and cunning hand laid on.
Lady, you are the cruell'st she alive
If you will lead these graces to the grave
And leave the world no copy.

OLIVIA
O, sir, I will not be so hard-hearted; I will give out divers schedules of my beauty. It shall be inventoried, and every particle and utensil label'd to my will: as, item, two lips, indifferent red; item, two grey eyes, with lids to them; item, one neck, one chin, and so forth. Were you sent hither to praise me?

VIOLA
I see you what you are, you are too proud;
But if you were the devil, you are fair.
My lord and master loves you. O, such love
Could be but recompens'd, though you were crown'd
The nonpareil of beauty.

OLIVIA

How does he love me?

VIOLA

With adorations, fertile tears,
With groans that thunder love, with sighs of fire.

OLIVIA

Your lord does know my mind; I cannot love him.
Yet I suppose him virtuous, know him noble,
Of great estate, of fresh and stainless youth;
In voices well divulg'd, free, learn'd and valiant;
And in dimension and the shape of nature
A gracious person. But yet I cannot love him.
He might have took his answer long ago.

VIOLA

If I did love you in my master's flame,
With such a suff'ring, such a deadly life,
In your denial I would find no sense;
I would not understand it.

OLIVIA

Why, what would you?

VIOLA

Make me a willow cabin at your gate,
And call upon my soul within the house;
Write loyal cantons of contemned love
And sing them loud even in the dead of night;
Halloo your name to the reverberate hills,
And make the babbling gossip of the air
Cry out "Olivia!" O, you should not rest
Between the elements of air and earth
But you should pity me!

OLIVIA

You might do much.
What is your parentage?

VIOLA

Above my fortunes, yet my state is well:
I am a gentleman.

OLIVIA

Get you to your lord.
I cannot love him; let him send no more—

Unless, perchance, you come to me again
To tell me how he takes it. Fare you well.
I thank you for your pains. Spend this for me.

[*She offers a purse.*]

VIOLA
I am no fee'd post, lady; keep your purse.
My master, not myself, lacks recompense.
Love make his heart of flint that you shall love,
And let your fervor, like my master's, be
Plac'd in contempt! Farewell, fair cruelty.

[*Exit.*]

OLIVIA
"What is your parentage?"
"Above my fortunes, yet my state is well:
I am a gentleman." I'll be sworn thou art!

4 cast away waste **6 con** memorize **comptible** sensitive, susceptible **7 least sinister usage** slightest discourteous treatment **8 Whence** from where **9 out . . . part** not part of my speech **10 modest** reasonable **12 comedian** actor **13 profound heart** very wise lady **15 do . . . myself** am not an imposter **16 usurp yourself** wrongfully withhold yourself (from Orsino) **17 from** outside of, beyond **18 your praise** praise of you **19 forgive you** excuse you from **22 at my gates** i.e., from my gatekeepers **23 be not mad** do not have madness to account for your "saucy" behavior **reason** sanity, your wits **24 time of moon** (Certain phases of the moon were thought to profoundly influence the insane.) **make one** take part **skipping** frivolous **25 office** business **26 taxation** demand **olive** olive branch of peace **27 matter** substance **28 rudely** unskillfully **30 comfortable** comforting **33 by the method** in the same metaphor (i.e., of delivering a sermon, with imagery such as "doctrine," "chapter" and "heresy") **38 this present** at the present time (Olivia is unveiling herself as if she were unmasking a contemporary portrait of herself.) **41 in grain** ingrained, permanent **42 blent** blended **44 she** woman **46 copy** i.e., child inheriting your beauty (though Olivia subsequently plays on the word's "transcript" or "record" sense) **47 divers** several **schedules** itemized lists **48 utensil** article **label'd** attached **53 if** even if **55 Could . . . though** could be no more than evenly repaid even though **57 fertile** abundant **62 In . . . divulg'd** well regarded by public opinion **63 dimension . . . nature** form and physique **66 in . . . flame** with my master's passion **67 deadly** death-like **70 willow cabin** (Willow was the symbol of unrequited love.) **71 my soul** i.e., Olivia **72 cantons** songs **contemned** rejected, scorned **74 Halloo** shout **reverberate** reverberating **75 babbling . . . air** echo

77 Between . . . earth i.e., anywhere on the face of the Earth **80 state** situation in life **85 pains** efforts **86 fee'd post** messenger to be tipped **88 Love . . . love** may Love furnish a heart of flint to the man you fall in love with **90 cruelty** cruel person

(11) VIOLA AND OLIVIA [III.1.84]

Twelfth Night

SCENE: Olivia's garden.

{Still presenting herself as "Cesario" (see previous scene), Viola returns to take another stab at advancing Duke Orsino's suit for Olivia's affections. This time, though, Olivia drops the coy act and lays at least some of her cards on the table.}

[*Enter Olivia.*]

VIOLA
Most excellent accomplish'd lady, the heavens rain odors on you!

OLIVIA
Give me your hand, sir.

VIOLA
My duty, madam, and most humble service.

OLIVIA
What is your name?

VIOLA
Cesario is your servant's name, fair princess.

OLIVIA
My servant, sir! 'Twas never merry world
Since lowly feigning was call'd compliment.
Y' are servant to the Count Orsino, youth.

VIOLA
And he is yours, and his must needs be yours;
Your servant's servant is your servant, madam.

OLIVIA
For him, I think not on him. For his thoughts,
Would they were blanks, rather than fill'd with me.

VIOLA
Madam, I come to whet your gentle thoughts
On his behalf.

OLIVIA
O, by your leave, I pray you,
I bade you never speak again of him.
But, would you undertake another suit,
I had rather hear you to solicit that
Than music from the spheres.

VIOLA
Dear lady—

OLIVIA
Give me leave, beseech you. I did send,
After the last enchantment you did here,
A ring in chase of you; so did I abuse
Myself, my servant, and I fear me, you.
Under your hard construction must I sit,
To force that on you, in a shameful cunning
Which you knew none of yours. What might you think?
Have you not set mine honor at the stake
And baited it with all th' unmuzzled thoughts
That tyrannous heart can think? To one of your receiving
Enough is shown; a cypress, not a bosom,
Hides my heart. So, let me hear you speak.

VIOLA
I pity you.

OLIVIA
That's a degree to love.

VIOLA
No, not a grize; for 'tis a vulgar proof,
That very oft we pity enemies.

OLIVIA
Why, then, methinks 'tis time to smile again.
O world, how apt the poor are to be proud!
If one should be a prey, how much the better
To fall before the lion than the wolf! [*A clock strikes.*]
The clock upbraids me with the waste of time.
Be not afraid, good youth, I will not have you;
And yet, when wit and youth is come to harvest,

Your wife is like to reap a proper man.
There lies your way, due west.

VIOLA

Then westward ho!
Grace and good disposition attend your ladyship.
You'll nothing, madam, to my lord by me?

OLIVIA

Stay.
I prithee tell me what thou think'st of me.

VIOLA

That you do think you are not what you are.

OLIVIA

If I think so, I think the same of you.

VIOLA

Then think you right. I am not what I am.

OLIVIA

I would you were as I would have you be.

VIOLA

Would it be better, madam, than I am?
I wish it might, for now I am your fool.

OLIVIA

[*Aside.*] O, what a deal of scorn looks beautiful
In the contempt and anger of his lip!
A murd'rous guilt shows not itself more soon
Than love that would seem hid; love's night is noon.—
Cesario, by the roses of the spring,
By maidhood, honor, truth, and every thing,
I love thee so, that maugre all thy pride,
Nor wit nor reason can my passion hide.
Do not extort thy reasons from this clause,
For that I woo, thou therefore hast no cause,
But rather reason thus with reason fetter:
Love sought is good, but given unsought better.

VIOLA

By innocence I swear, and by my youth,
I have one heart, one bosom and one truth,
And that no woman has; nor never none
Shall mistress be of it, save I alone.

And so adieu, good madam. Never more
Will I my master's tears to you deplore.

OLIVIA
Yet come again; for thou perhaps mayst move
That heart, which now abhors, to like his love.

[*Exeunt.*]

1 odors perfumes **6 'Twas . . . world** life has never been as pleasant **7 lowly feigning** exaggerated humility, sycophancy **was call'd** was first called **9 must needs** necessarily must **11 For** as for **14 by your leave** (a gentle interjection on the order of "please say no more") **18 music . . . spheres** (Refers to the notion that exquisite but inaudible music was produced by the movement of transparent spheres that surrounded planets and other celestial objects.) **20 enchantment you did** spell you cast (i.e., on Olivia) **21 ring in chase** (See I.v, II.ii.) **abuse** dishonor, wrong **23 hard** harsh **construction** appraisal, interpretation **24 To force** for forcing **26–27 Have . . . thoughts** (The imagery here comes from the "sport" of bear-baiting; Olivia fears her honor is being assailed by Viola/Cesario's thoughts in the same way a defenseless bear, chained to a stake, was tormented ("baited") by unmuzzled dogs.) **28 tyrannous** cruel **receiving** intelligence, perception **29 cypress** an almost transparent black fabric **31 degree** step **32 grize** step **a vulgar proof** commonly known **34 smile** i.e., dispense with the melancholy of love **35 apt** ready, prepared **36 should be** is to be, must be **37 lion . . . wolf** i.e., noble adversary (Orsino) than a lowly one (Cesario) **40 wit** cleverness, intelligence **41 like** likely **proper** worthy **42 westward ho!** call of boatmen on the Thames river as they headed from central London to the city's western region **43 good disposition** a peaceful state of mind **44 You'll nothing** you've nothing to convey **45 prithee** pray thee, beg you **46 not . . . are** i.e., in love with a man (while "what you *are*" is in love with a woman posing as a man) **47 If . . . you** (Olivia seems to think that Viola, with her curious reply, has just accused her of being so mad with passion that she is "not herself." By suggesting in return that she thinks "the same of" Viola, Olivia may be hinting at a suspicion that this young "man" is not what he appears to be.) **52 fool** plaything, sport **53 deal** certain amount **56 would seem hid** would like to remain hidden **love's . . . noon** i.e., love's idea of secrecy is actually love plain as day **58 maidhood** maidenhood, virginity **59 maugre** in spite of **60 Nor** neither **61–62 Do . . . cause** do not derive your reasons (for not pursuing me) from this premise; because I am the wooer, you have no reason (to woo me in return) **63 reason . . . fetter** bind together these two reasons (to accept my love) **64 Love sought** i.e., the love Olivia seeks (and hopes to receive) from "Cesario" **given unsought** i.e., the love "Cesario" does not seek (but Olivia would gladly give) **70 deplore** lament, express grief **72 That heart** i.e., my heart

(12) JULIA AND LUCETTA [I.II.1]

The Two Gentlemen of Verona

SCENE: The garden of Julia's house.

{Julia is one popular gal, no doubt about it. So much so, in fact, that she must solicit the help of her maid, Lucetta, to sort through a string of would-be suitors. Funny thing is, it's only when the name of "Proteus" comes up that the exercise turns acrimonious.}

JULIA
But say, Lucetta, now we are alone,
Wouldst thou then counsel me to fall in love?

LUCETTA
Ay, madam, so you stumble not unheedfully.

JULIA
Of all the fair resort of gentlemen
That every day with parle encounter me,
In thy opinion which is worthiest love?

LUCETTA
Please you repeat their names, I'll show my mind
According to my shallow simple skill.

JULIA
What think'st thou of the fair Sir Eglamour?

LUCETTA
As of a knight well-spoken, neat and fine;
But, were I you, he never should be mine.

JULIA
What think'st thou of the rich Mercatio?

LUCETTA
Well of his wealth; but of himself, so so.

JULIA
What think'st thou of the gentle Proteus?

LUCETTA
Lord, Lord! To see what folly reigns in us!

JULIA
How now? What means this passion at his name?

LUCETTA
Pardon, dear madam; 'tis a passing shame
That I, unworthy body as I am,
Should censure thus on lovely gentlemen.

JULIA
Why not on Proteus, as of all the rest?

LUCETTA
Then thus: of many good I think him best.

JULIA
Your reason?

LUCETTA
I have no other but a woman's reason;
I think him so because I think him so.

JULIA
And wouldst thou have me cast my love on him?

LUCETTA
Ay, if you thought your love not cast away.

JULIA
Why he, of all the rest, hath never mov'd me.

LUCETTA
Yet he, of all the rest, I think best loves ye.

JULIA
His little speaking shows his love but small.

LUCETTA
Fire that's closest kept burns most of all.

JULIA
They do not love that do not show their love.

LUCETTA
O, they love least that let men know their love.

JULIA
I would I knew his mind.

LUCETTA
Peruse this paper, madam. [*Gives her a letter.*]

JULIA
"To Julia." Say, from whom?

LUCETTA
That the contents will show.

JULIA
Say, say, who gave it thee?

LUCETTA
Sir Valentine's page; and sent, I think, from Proteus.
He would have given it you, but I, being in the way,
Did in your name receive it. Pardon the
fault I pray.

JULIA
Now, by my modesty, a goodly broker!
Dare you presume to harbor wanton lines?
To whisper and conspire against my youth?
Now, trust me, 'tis an office of great worth,
And you an officer fit for the place.
There, take the paper. See it be return'd,
Or else return no more into my sight.

[*Gives the letter back.*]

LUCETTA
To plead for love deserves more fee than hate.

JULIA
Will ye be gone?

LUCETTA
That you may ruminate. [*Exit.*]

JULIA
And yet I would I had o'erlook'd the letter;
It were a shame to call her back again
And pray her to a fault for which I chid her.
What 'fool is she, that knows I am a maid,
And would not force the letter to my view!
Since maids, in modesty, say "no" to that
Which they would have the profferer construe "ay."
Fie, fie, how wayward is this foolish love
That, like a testy babe, will scratch the nurse
And presently, all humbled, kiss the rod!
How churlishly I chid Lucetta hence,

When willingly I would have had her here!
How angerly I taught my brow to frown,
When inward joy enforc'd my heart to smile!
My penance is to call Lucetta back
And ask remission for my folly past.
What ho! Lucetta!

[*Enter Lucetta.*]

LUCETTA
What would your ladyship?

JULIA
Is 't near dinner-time?

LUCETTA
I would it were,
That you might kill your stomach on your meat
And not upon your maid.

[*She drops the letter, and starts to pick it up.*]

JULIA
What is 't that you took up so gingerly?

LUCETTA
Nothing.

JULIA
Why didst thou stoop, then?

LUCETTA
To take a paper up that I let fall.

JULIA
And is that paper nothing?

LUCETTA
Nothing concerning me.

JULIA
Then let it lie for those that it concerns.

LUCETTA
Madam, it will not lie where it concerns,
Unless it have a false interpreter.

JULIA
Some love of yours hath writ to you in rhyme.

LUCETTA
That I might sing it, madam, to a tune.
Give me a note; your ladyship can set.

JULIA
As little by such toys as may be possible.
Best sing it to the tune of "Light o' love."

LUCETTA
It is too heavy for so light a tune.

JULIA
Heavy! Belike it hath some burden then?

LUCETTA
Ay, and melodious were it, would you sing it.

JULIA
And why not you?

LUCETTA
I cannot reach so high.

JULIA
Let's see your song. [*Takes the letter.*] How now, minion?

LUCETTA
Keep tune there still, so you will sing it out.
And yet methinks I do not like this tune.

JULIA
You do not?

LUCETTA
No, madam, 'tis too sharp.

JULIA
You, minion, are too saucy.

LUCETTA
Nay, now you are too flat
And mar the concord with too harsh a descant.
There wanteth but a mean to fill your song.

JULIA
The mean is drown'd with your unruly bass.

LUCETTA
Indeed, I bid the base for Proteus.

JULIA
This babble shall not henceforth trouble me.
Here is a coil with protestation!
[*Tears the letter and scatters the pieces.*]
Go get you gone, and let the papers lie;
You would be fing'ring them, to anger me.

LUCETTA
She makes it strange; but she would be best pleas'd
To be so ang'red with another letter. [*Exit.*]

4 resort group, company **5 parle** talk **8 shallow** slight **simple** plain, undistinguished **10 neat** elegant **16 passion** passionate outburst **17 passing** surpassing **19 censure** pass judgment **27 mov'd** proposed (marriage to) **34 paper** (For the particulars on this letter, see I.i.) **39 being . . . way** i.e., happening to be there **42 broker** go-between, intermediary **49 fee** payment, recompense **51 o'erlook'd** read over **53 pray . . . fault** ask her to commit a wrong **chid** chided, scolded **54 'fool** a fool **58 Fie** (an expression of disgust) **60 presently** immediately thereafter **rod** spanking rod **61 hence** away **63 angerly** angrily **64 enforc'd** urged **66 remission** forgiveness **69 kill your stomach** satisfy your appetite **78 where it concerns** in matters of importance **82 note** musical note (with a punning reference to the letter) **set** set to music (though in the next line Julia takes it in the sense of "setting store," or valuing something) **83 toys** trifles **84 "Light o' love"** (A popular song of the day.) **86 Belike** most likely **burden** (1) bass accompaniment to a melody (2) heavy load **88 reach so high** (1) sing that high a note (2) aspire to be with a person of Proteus' rank **89 minion** hussy (with a play on "minim," or half-note) **91 tune** (1) in tune, pitch (2) an even temper **93 sharp** (1) highly pitched (2) saucy, bitter **95 flat** (1) low pitched (2) blunt, direct **96 concord** harmony **descant** improvised line of musical accompaniment **97 wanteth but** is lacking only **mean** (1) tenor vocalist, i.e., Proteus (2) opportunity **98 unruly bass** (with a play on "base" behavior) **99 bid . . . for** act in behalf of (the image comes from a game called "Prisoner's Base") **101 coil with protestation** fuss over protestations of love (i.e., over Proteus' letter) **103 fing'ring** stealing **104 makes it strange** pretends to be indifferent

(13) Julia and Silvia [IV.iv.107]

The Two Gentlemen of Verona

SCENE: Outside the Duke of Milan's palace.

{Much to her dismay, Julia (currently disguised as a lad named "Sebastian") has been dispatched by Proteus—a man she once called her beau, but now calls her employer—to deliver to Silvia a token of his affection. As if that weren't bad enough, the token in question happens to be the very same ring that Julia had earlier given to Proteus as a symbol of her love for him. But, conflicted as she is, when Julia spots Silvia and her attendants strolling nearby, she somehow manages to gamely step forward and do her duty.}

JULIA
Gentlewoman, good day! I pray you, be my mean
To bring me where to speak with Madam Silvia.

SILVIA
What would you with her, if that I be she?

JULIA
If you be she, I do entreat your patience
To hear me speak the message I am sent on.

SILVIA
From whom?

JULIA
From my master, Sir Proteus, madam.

SILVIA
O, he sends you for a picture?

JULIA
Ay, madam.

SILVIA
[*She gives "Sebastian" a small picture.*]
Go give your master this. Tell him from me,
One Julia, that his changing thoughts forget,
Would better fit his chamber than this shadow.

JULIA
Madam, please you peruse this letter—
[*Starts to give her a letter, takes it back, and offers another instead.*]

Pardon me, madam; I have unadvis'd
Deliver'd you a paper that I should not.
This is the letter to your ladyship.

SILVIA
I pray thee, let me look on that again.

JULIA
It may not be; good madam, pardon me.

SILVIA
There, hold!
I will not look upon your master's lines.
I know they are stuff'd with protestations
And full of new-found oaths, which he will break
As easily as I do tear his paper. [*Tears letter.*]

JULIA
Madam, he sends your ladyship this ring. [*Offers a ring.*]

SILVIA
The more shame for him that he sends it me;
For I have heard him say a thousand times
His Julia gave it him at his departure.
Though his false finger have profan'd the ring,
Mine shall not do his Julia so much wrong.

JULIA
She thanks you.

SILVIA
What say'st thou?

JULIA
I thank you, madam, that you tender her.
Poor gentlewoman! My master wrongs her much.

SILVIA
Dost thou know her?

JULIA
Almost as well as I do know myself.
To think upon her woes I do protest
That I have wept a hundred several times.

SILVIA
Belike she thinks that Proteus hath forsook her.

JULIA
I think she doth, and that's her cause of sorrow.

SILVIA
Is she not passing fair?

JULIA
She hath been fairer, madam, than she is.
When she did think my master lov'd her well,
She, in my judgment, was as fair as you.
But since she did neglect her looking-glass
And threw her sun-expelling mask away,
The air hath starv'd the roses in her cheeks
And pinch'd the lily-tincture of her face,
That now she is become as black as I.

SILVIA
How tall was she?

JULIA
About my stature; for at Pentecost,
When all our pageants of delight were play'd,
Our youth got me to play the woman's part,
And I was trimm'd in Madam Julia's gown,
Which served me as fit, by all men's judgments,
As if the garment had been made for me.
Therefore I know she is about my height.
And at that time I made her weep agood,
For I did play a lamentable part:
Madam, 'twas Ariadne passioning
For Theseus' perjury and unjust flight;
Which I so lively acted with my tears
That my poor mistress, moved therewithal,
Wept bitterly; and would I might be dead
If I in thought felt not her very sorrow!

SILVIA
She is beholding to thee, gentle youth.
Alas, poor lady, desolate and left!
I weep myself to think upon thy words.
Here, youth, there is my purse. [*Gives money.*] I give thee this
For thy sweet mistress' sake, because thou lov'st her.
Farewell.

[*Exit Silvia, with attendants.*]

JULIA
And she shall thank you for 't, if e'er you know her.
A virtuous gentlewoman, mild and beautiful!
I hope my master's suit will be but cold,
Since she respects my mistress' love so much.

[*Exit.*]

1 mean means **11 One** one (who is named) **12 chamber** bedchamber **14 unadvis'd** inadvertently **21 protestations** vows of love **27 departure** (See II.ii.) **28 false** unfaithful **32 tender** feel sympathetically towards **37 several** different **38 Belike** most likely **40 passing** surpassingly **45 sun-expelling mask** mask worn by ladies to protect their face from over-exposure to the sun **46 starv'd** killed, extinguished **47 pinch'd** nipped **48 black** dark-complexioned, tanned **50 Pentecost** Whitsuntide, a time of fun and celebration falling on the seventh Sunday after Easter **51 pageants of delight** delightful entertainments **53 trimm'd** dressed up **57 agood** in earnest **59 Ariadne** (Alludes to the story in which Ariadne, daughter to the King of Crete, falls in love with Theseus, only to be abandoned by him on the island of Naxos.) **passioning** grieving **60 unjust** faithless **62 therewithal** with that indebted **66 left** abandoned **73 but cold** in vain

SCENES FOR TWO ACTORS

(14) CORIN AND TOUCHSTONE [III.II.II]

As You Like It

SCENE: The Forest of Arden.

{Providing something of an unofficial intermission from the play's main story, Corin the shepherd and Touchstone the fool flex their considerable wits.}

CORIN
And how like you this shepherd's life, Master Touchstone?

TOUCHSTONE
Truly, shepherd, in respect of itself, it is a good life; but in respect that it is a shepherd's life, it is naught. In respect that it is solitary, I like it very well; but in respect that it is private, it is a very vile life. Now, in respect it is in the fields, it pleaseth me well; but in respect it is not in the court, it is tedious. As it is a spare life, look you, it fits my humor well; but as there is no more plenty in it, it goes much against my stomach. Hast any philosophy in thee, shepherd?

CORIN
No more but that I know the more one sickens the worse at ease he is; and that he that wants money, means, and content is without three good friends; that the property of rain is to wet and fire to burn; that good pasture makes fat sheep, and that a great cause of the night is lack of the sun; that he that hath learn'd no wit by nature nor art may complain of good breeding, or comes of a very dull kindred.

TOUCHSTONE
Such a one is a natural philosopher. Wast ever in court, shepherd?

CORIN
No, truly.

TOUCHSTONE
Then thou art damn'd.

CORIN
Nay, I hope.

TOUCHSTONE
Truly, thou art damn'd like an ill-roasted egg, all on one side.

CORIN
For not being at court? Your reason.

TOUCHSTONE
Why, if thou never wast at court, thou never saw'st good manners; if thou never saw'st good manners, then thy manners must be wicked; and wickedness is sin, and sin is damnation. Thou art in a parlous state, shepherd.

CORIN
Not a whit, Touchstone. Those that are good manners at the court are as ridiculous in the country as the behavior of the country is most mockable at the court. You told me you salute not at the court but you kiss your hands; that courtesy would be uncleanly if courtiers were shepherds.

TOUCHSTONE
Instance, briefly; come, instance.

CORIN
Why, we are still handling our ewes, and their fells, you know, are greasy.

TOUCHSTONE
Why, do not your courtier's hands sweat? And is not the grease of a mutton as wholesome as the sweat of a man? Shallow, shallow. A better instance, I say; come.

CORIN
Besides, our hands are hard.

TOUCHSTONE
Your lips will feel them the sooner. Shallow again. A more sounder instance, come.

CORIN
And they are often tarr'd over with the surgery of our sheep; and would you have us kiss tar? The courtier's hands are perfum'd with civet.

TOUCHSTONE
Most shallow man! Thou worms-meat, in respect of a good piece of flesh indeed! Learn of the wise, and perpend: civet is of a baser birth than tar, the very uncleanly flux of a cat. Mend the instance, shepherd.

CORIN
You have too courtly a wit for me. I'll rest.

TOUCHSTONE
Wilt thou rest damn'd? God help thee, shallow man! God make incision in thee! Thou art raw.

CORIN
Sir, I am a true laborer: I earn that I eat, get that I wear, owe no man hate, envy no man's happiness, glad of other men's good, content with my harm, and the greatest of my pride is to see my ewes graze and my lambs suck.

TOUCHSTONE
That is another simple sin in you, to bring the ewes and the rams together and to offer to get your living by the copulation of cattle; to be bawd to a bell-wether, and to betray a she-lamb of a twelve-month to a crooked-pated old cuckoldly ram, out of all reasonable match. If thou beest not damn'd for this, the devil himself will have no shepherds; I cannot see else how thou shouldst scape.

2 in . . . itself considered on its own terms **in respect that** considering that worthless **5 spare** frugal **humor** nature, mood **no more plenty** not more of life's comforts **8 wants** lacks **content** pleasure **11 wit** knowledge **art** study **complain of** complain about his lack of **20 manners** (1) etiquette (2) morals **22 parlous** perilous **24 mockable** deserving of ridicule **25 but you kiss** without kissing **27 Instance** proof **briefly** quickly **28 still** always **fells** fleeces **30 Shallow** flimsy, trivial **35 tarr'd over** (Tar was applied to a sheep's wounds to facilitate healing.) **36 civet** perfume derived from the civet cat **37 worms-meat** food fit for worms **respect of** comparison with **38 perpend** consider **39 flux** discharge, secretion **Mend** improve upon **41 God make . . . thee!** i.e., to bleed his folly, just as a physician might make an incision to let out blood **42 raw** green, inexperienced (with a play the word's "sore" sense, and thus needing a physician's care) **43 that** what **owe** bear **44 content . . . harm** untroubled by my misfortune **45 greatest of** greatest source of **47 offer** undertake, strive **get** make **cattle** livestock **bawd** procurer 48 **bell-wether** (The lead sheep of a flock customarily wore a bell around its neck.) **she-lamb . . . twelve-month** one year old lamb **crooked-pated** crooked-horned 49 **cuckoldy** i.e., having a promiscuous mate **out of** contrary to **50 the . . . shepherds** (it is because) the devil himself will brook no shepherds in hell **51 scape** escape

(15) Antipholus of Syracuse and dromio of Ephesus [I.II.33]

The Comedy of Errors

SCENE: A marketplace in Ephesus.

{A bit earlier, Antipholus of Syracuse (who doesn't know his twin brother is in town) dispatched his servant Dromio of Syracuse (who doesn't know his twin brother is in town) back to their inn to deposit their traveling money there for safekeeping. Now, Dromio has returned. Only, unbeknownst to Antipholus, this isn't the same Dromio. This Dromio—of Ephesus—has been sent by his mistress to find the other Antipholus—of Ephesus—and fetch him home to supper. Only, unbeknownst to Dromio, he hasn't found the right Antipholus. Confused? So are they.}

ANTIPHOLUS OF SYRACUSE
I to the world am like a drop of water
That in the ocean seeks another drop,
Who, falling there to find his fellow forth,
Unseen, inquisitive, confounds himself.
So I, to find a mother and a brother,
In quest of them, unhappy, lose myself.

[*Enter Dromio of Ephesus.*]

Here comes the almanac of my true date.
What now? How chance thou art return'd so soon?

DROMIO OF EPHESUS
Return'd so soon! Rather approach'd too late:
The capon burns, the pig falls from the spit,
The clock hath strucken twelve upon the bell;
My mistress made it one upon my cheek.
She is so hot because the meat is cold;
The meat is cold because you come not home;
You come not home because you have no stomach;
You have no stomach having broke your fast.
But we that know what 'tis to fast and pray
Are penitent for your default today.

ANTIPHOLUS OF SYRACUSE
Stop in your wind, sir. Tell me this, I pray:
Where have you left the money that I gave you?

DROMIO OF EPHESUS
O—sixpence that I had a Wednesday last
To pay the saddler for my mistress' crupper?
The saddler had it, sir; I kept it not.

ANTIPHOLUS OF SYRACUSE
I am not in a sportive humor now.
Tell me, and dally not, where is the money?
We being strangers here, how dar'st thou trust
So great a charge from thine own custody?

DROMIO OF EPHESUS
I pray you, jest, sir, as you sit at dinner.
I from my mistress come to you in post;
If I return, I shall be post indeed,
For she will score your fault upon my pate.
Methinks your maw, like mine, should be your clock,
And strike you home without a messenger.

ANTIPHOLUS OF SYRACUSE
Come, Dromio, come, these jests are out of season;
Reserve them till a merrier hour than this.
Where is the gold I gave in charge to thee?

DROMIO OF EPHESUS
To me, sir? Why, you gave no gold to me.

ANTIPHOLUS OF SYRACUSE
Come on, sir knave, have done your foolishness
And tell me how thou hast dispos'd thy charge.

DROMIO OF EPHESUS
My charge was but to fetch you from the mart
Home to your house, the Phoenix, sir, to dinner;
My mistress and her sister stays for you.

ANTIPHOLUS OF SYRACUSE
Now, as I am a Christian, answer me
In what safe place you have bestow'd my money,
Or I shall break that merry sconce of yours
That stands on tricks when I am undispos'd:
Where is the thousand marks thou hadst of me?

DROMIO OF EPHESUS
I have some marks of yours upon my pate,
Some of my mistress' marks upon my shoulders,
But not a thousand marks between you both.

If I should pay your worship those again,
Perchance you will not bear them patiently.

ANTIPHOLUS OF SYRACUSE
Thy mistress' marks? What mistress, slave, hast thou?

DROMIO OF EPHESUS
Your worship's wife, my mistress at the Phoenix;
She that doth fast till you come home to dinner
And prays that you will hie you home to dinner.

ANTIPHOLUS OF SYRACUSE
What, wilt thou flout me thus unto my face,
Being forbid? There, take you that, sir knave. [*Beats him.*]

DROMIO OF EPHESUS
What mean you, sir? For God's sake, hold your hands!
Nay, an you will not, sir, I'll take my heels. [*Exit.*]

ANTIPHOLUS OF SYRACUSE
Upon my life, by some device or other
The villain is o'erraught of all my money.
They say this town is full of cozenage,
As, nimble jugglers that deceive the eye,
Dark-working sorcerers that change the mind,
Soul-killing witches that deform the body,
Disguised cheaters, prating mountebanks,
And many such-like liberties of sin.
If it prove so, I will be gone the sooner.
I'll to the Centaur to go seek this slave;
I greatly fear my money is not safe.

[*Exit.*]

1 to in relation to **3 forth** away **4 confounds himself** loses his identity **6 unhappy** unlucky **7 almanac . . . date** i.e., record of my true birthdate (since he and Dromio were born in the very same hour) **8 How chance** how does it happen **12 My mistress** i.e., Adriana, wife to Antipholus of Ephesus **made it one** i.e., struck once (as a clock would strike one o'clock) **15 stomach** appetite **18 penitent** doing penance **default** fault, sin **19 in your wind** your chatter **22 crupper** leather strap on a saddle that helps secure it to the horse **27 charge** sum of money **from** out of **29 post** haste **30 post** i.e., the doorpost of a tavern on which notches would be made to keep reckonings **31 score** cut, notch **my pate** the top of my head **32 maw** stomach **36 gave in charge** entrusted **39 dispos'd** deposited **40 charge** responsibility **41 the Phoenix** (The dwelling that served as both home and place of business for Antipholus of

Ephesus was called the "Phoenix.") **42 stays** wait **44 bestow'd** stowed away **45 sconce** head **46 stands on** insists upon (playing) **undispos'd** not disposed (toward such tricks), not in a merry mood **51 pay** i.e., repay **52 Perchance** perhaps **56 hie you** hurry **57 flout** mock **60 an** if **take my heels** take to my heels, i.e., run away **62 o'erraught** cheated **63 cozenage** cheating **67 prating mountebanks** quack doctors hawking their curatives **68 liberties of sin** sinful transgressors **70 Centaur** (The name of a popular inn where Antipholus and Dromio of Syracuse are currently staying.)

(16) ANTIPHOLUS OF SYRACUSE AND DROMIO OF SYRACUSE [II.II.1]

The Comedy of Errors

SCENE: A street in Ephesus.

{Mistaken identification continues to run amok (see previous scene) as the same Antipholus as above upbraids the other Dromio for his cavalier attitude toward gold and duty.}

ANTIPHOLUS OF SYRACUSE
The gold I gave to Dromio is laid up
Safe at the Centaur, and the heedful slave
Is wand'red forth, in care to seek me out
By computation and mine host's report.
I could not speak with Dromio since at first
I sent him from the mart. See, here he comes.

[*Enter Dromio of Syracuse.*]

How now, sir, is your merry humor alter'd?
As you love strokes, so jest with me again.
You know no Centaur? You receiv'd no gold?
Your mistress sent to have me home to dinner?
My house was at the Phoenix? Wast thou mad,
That thus so madly thou didst answer me?

DROMIO OF SYRACUSE
What answer, sir? When spake I such a word?

ANTIPHOLUS OF SYRACUSE
Even now, even here, not half an hour since.

DROMIO OF SYRACUSE
I did not see you since you sent me hence,
Home to the Centaur, with the gold you gave me.

ANTIPHOLUS OF SYRACUSE
Villain, thou didst deny the gold's receipt
And told'st me of a mistress and a dinner;
For which, I hope, thou felt'st I was displeas'd.

DROMIO OF SYRACUSE
I am glad to see you in this merry vein.
What means this jest? I pray you, master, tell me.

ANTIPHOLUS OF SYRACUSE
Yea, dost thou jeer and flout me in the teeth?
Think'st thou I jest? Hold, take thou that, and that. [*Beats him.*]

DROMIO OF SYRACUSE
Hold, sir, for God's sake! Now your jest is earnest.
Upon what bargain do you give it me?

ANTIPHOLUS OF SYRACUSE
Because that I familiarly sometimes
Do use you for my fool and chat with you,
Your sauciness will jest upon my love
And make a common of my serious hours.
When the sun shines let foolish gnats make sport,
But creep in crannies when he hides his beams.
If you will jest with me, know my aspect,
And fashion your demeanor to my looks,
Or I will beat this method in your sconce.

DROMIO OF SYRACUSE
Sconce call you it? So you would leave battering, I had rather have it a head. An you use these blows long, I must get a sconce for my head and insconce it too, or else I shall seek my wit in my shoulders. But, I pray, sir why am I beaten?

ANTIPHOLUS OF SYRACUSE
Dost thou not know?

DROMIO OF SYRACUSE
Nothing, sir, but that I am beaten.

ANTIPHOLUS OF SYRACUSE
Shall I tell you why?

DROMIO OF SYRACUSE
Ay, sir, and wherefore; for they say every why hath a wherefore.

ANTIPHOLUS OF SYRACUSE
Why, first—for flouting me; and then, wherefore—for urging it the second time to me.

DROMIO OF SYRACUSE
Was there ever any man thus beaten out of season,
When in the why and the wherefore is neither rhyme nor reason?
Well, sir, I thank you.

ANTIPHOLUS OF SYRACUSE
Thank me, sir, for what?

DROMIO OF SYRACUSE
Marry, sir, for this something that you gave me for nothing.

ANTIPHOLUS OF SYRACUSE
I'll make you amends next, to give you nothing for something. But say, sir, is it dinner-time?

DROMIO OF SYRACUSE
No, sir, I think the meat wants that I have.

ANTIPHOLUS OF SYRACUSE
In good time, sir, what's that?

DROMIO OF SYRACUSE
Basting.

ANTIPHOLUS OF SYRACUSE
Well, sir, then 'twill be dry.

DROMIO OF SYRACUSE
If it be, sir, I pray you, eat none of it.

ANTIPHOLUS OF SYRACUSE
Your reason?

DROMIO OF SYRACUSE
Lest it make you choleric and purchase me another dry basting.

ANTIPHOLUS OF SYRACUSE
Well, sir, learn to jest in good time. There's a time for all things.

DROMIO OF SYRACUSE
I durst have denied that, before you were so choleric.

ANTIPHOLUS OF SYRACUSE
By what rule, sir?

DROMIO OF SYRACUSE
Marry, sir, by a rule as plain as the plain bald pate of father Time himself.

ANTIPHOLUS OF SYRACUSE
Let's hear it.

DROMIO OF SYRACUSE
There's no time for a man to recover his hair that grows bald by nature.

ANTIPHOLUS OF SYRACUSE
May he not do it by fine and recovery?

DROMIO OF SYRACUSE
Yes, to pay a fine for a periwig and recover the lost hair of another man.

ANTIPHOLUS OF SYRACUSE
Why is Time such a niggard of hair, being, as it is, so plentiful an excrement?

DROMIO OF SYRACUSE
Because it is a blessing that he bestows on beasts; and what he hath scanted men in hair he hath given them in wit.

ANTIPHOLUS OF SYRACUSE
Why, but there's many a man hath more hair than wit.

DROMIO OF SYRACUSE
Not a man of those but he hath the wit to lose his hair.

ANTIPHOLUS OF SYRACUSE
Why, thou didst conclude hairy men plain dealers without wit.

DROMIO OF SYRACUSE
The plainer dealer, the sooner lost; yet he loseth it in a kind of jollity.

ANTIPHOLUS OF SYRACUSE
For what reason?

DROMIO OF SYRACUSE
For two; and sound ones too.

ANTIPHOLUS OF SYRACUSE
Nay, not sound, I pray you.

DROMIO OF SYRACUSE
Sure ones, then.

ANTIPHOLUS OF SYRACUSE
Nay, not sure, in a thing falsing.

DROMIO OF SYRACUSE
Certain ones then.

ANTIPHOLUS OF SYRACUSE
Name them.

DROMIO OF SYRACUSE
The one, to save the money that he spends in tiring; the other, that at dinner they should not drop in his porridge.

ANTIPHOLUS OF SYRACUSE
You would all this time have prov'd there is no time for all things.

DROMIO OF SYRACUSE
Marry, and did, sir; namely, e'en no time to recover hair lost by nature.

ANTIPHOLUS OF SYRACUSE
But your reason was not substantial, why there is no time to recover.

DROMIO OF SYRACUSE
Thus I mend it: Time himself is bald and therefore to the world's end will have bald followers.

ANTIPHOLUS OF SYRACUSE
I knew 'twould be a bald conclusion.
But soft, who wafts us yonder?

[*Enter Adriana and Luciana.*]

1 gold I gave (By Antipholus' own account, this scene takes place about a half hour after the end of I.ii. Since that time, Antipholus has apparently gone to the Centaur and been told by the innkeeper ("host") that his money is safe and that Dromio is out searching for him. What puzzles Antipholus, however, is how all of this could have taken place in so short a time, given his own reckoning ("computation") of the time frame and the innkeeper's report of Dromio's activity.) **laid up** stored away **2 Centaur** (The name of a popular inn where Antipholus and Dromio of Syracuse are currently staying.) **6 mart** marketplace (In Ephesus, this would be a large public space dedicated to the buying and selling of all manner of things.) **9 know no Centaur?** (To account for Antipholus' interrogation and Dromio's confusion, see I.ii.) **15 hence** away **22 flout . . . teeth** mock me to my face

23 Hold here (i.e., Here you go!) **24 Hold** stop, wait **earnest** (1) serious (2) down payment on a purchase or bargain **28 jest upon** trifle with **love** i.e., kindness **29 common** public playground **30 make sport** have fun **32 know my aspect** pay attention to my expression **34 sconce** head (though Dromio plays on the meanings "fort" for "battering" and "helmet" for "for my head") **36 An** if **insconce** shelter behind a fortification **37 seek . . . shoulders** i.e., because his head will have been beaten down into his shoulders **49 Marry** (a mild oath uttered to emphasize a point) **nothing** having done nothing **52 wants that** lacks what **53 In good time** indeed **54 basting** beating, thrashing (with a play on the sense "moisten meat when cooking") **58 choleric** hot-tempered (Dry, overdone meat was thought to cause irascibility.) **purchase** gain **60 durst have denied** would have dared to deny **65 fine and recovery** a legal procedure for transferring property ownership **67 niggard** miser **excrement** outgrowth **68 scanted** withheld from **68–69 hath . . . hair** i.e., can manage to contract syphilis (which caused a loss of hair) **72 plain dealers** i.e., men who deal honestly and respectably with women **73 dealer** i.e., dealer with women **kind of jollity** i.e., debauchery, sexual pleasure **75 sound** valid (though Antipholus plays on the sense "healthy") **78 falsing** deceptive **81 tiring** dressing the hair **86 mend** improve, better **87 bald** stupid, senseless **89 soft** wait **wafts** beckons

(17) COMINIUS AND MENENIUS [IV.VI.82]

Coriolanus

SCENE: A public place in Rome.

{Poor Rome. Its greatest general (Coriolanus) has been banished, its fiercest foe (Aufidius) is closing in for the kill, and to top things off, its tribunes (Sicinius and Brutus) appear to be clueless. Solid citizen—and friend to Coriolanus—that he is, Menenius is trying to enlighten the tribunes to the impending doom that hangs over the Eternal City when in bursts an irate general named Cominius to ratchet things up a notch.}

COMINIUS
O, you have made good work!

MENENIUS
What news? What news?

COMINIUS
You have holp to ravish your own daughters and
To melt the city leads upon your pates,
To see your wives dishonor'd to your noses—

MENENIUS
What's the news? What's the news?

COMINIUS
Your temples burned in their cement, and
Your franchises, whereon you stood, confin'd
Into an auger's bore.

MENENIUS
Pray now, your news?—
You have made fair work, I fear me.—Pray, your news?
If Marcius should be join'd wi' th' Volscians—

COMINIUS
If!
He is their god. He leads them like a thing
Made by some other deity than nature,
That shapes man better; and they follow him
Against us brats, with no less confidence
Than boys pursuing summer butterflies,
Or butchers killing flies.

MENENIUS
You have made good work,
You and your apron-men; you that stood so much
Upon the voice of occupation and
The breath of garlic-eaters!

COMINIUS
He'll shake
Your Rome about your ears.

MENENIUS
As Hercules
Did shake down mellow fruit. You have made fair work!

COMINIUS
All the regions
Do smilingly revolt; and who resists
Are mock'd for valiant ignorance,
And perish constant fools. Who is 't can blame him?
Your enemies and his find something in him.

MENENIUS
We are all undone, unless
The noble man have mercy.

COMINIUS
Who shall ask it?
The tribunes cannot do 't for shame; the people
Deserve such pity of him as the wolf
Does of the shepherds. For his best friends, if they
Should say "Be good to Rome," they charg'd him even
As those should do that had deserv'd his hate,
And therein show'd like enemies.

MENENIUS
'Tis true.
If he were putting to my house the brand
That should consume it, I have not the face
To say "Beseech you, cease." You have made fair hands,
You and your crafts! You have crafted fair!

COMINIUS
You have brought
A trembling upon Rome, such as was never
So incapable of help.

MENENIUS
We lov'd him.
But, like beasts and cowardly nobles, we
Gave way unto your clusters, who did
Hoot him out of the city.

COMINIUS
But I fear
They'll roar him in again. Tullus Aufidius,
The second name of men, obeys his points
As if he were his officer. Desperation
Is all the policy, strength, and defense
That Rome can make against them.

[*Enter a troop of Citizens.*]

MENENIUS
Here come the clusters.
And is Aufidius with him? You are they
That made the air unwholesome, when you cast
Your stinking greasy caps in hooting at
Coriolanus' exile. Now he's coming,

And not a hair upon a soldier's head
Which will not prove a whip. As many coxcombs
As you threw caps up will he tumble down,
And pay you for your voices. 'Tis no matter;
If he could burn us all into one coal,
We have deserv'd it.

1 you (Though others are present, Cominius and Menenius direct their remarks exclusively to Sicinius and Brutus.) **2 holp** helped **3 leads** lead roofs **4 to your** before your very **6 burned . . . cement** i.e., burned to the ground **7 franchises** citizen's rights, liberties **whereon you stood** which you insisted upon **7–8 confin'd . . . bore** i.e., restricted and reduced so much they can be contained in the smallest space (such as the tiny hole drilled by an auger) **9 You . . . me** (Menenius directs this comment to Brutus and Sicinius.) **10 Marcius** (Coriolanus was formerly known as Caius Marcius; the title of "Coriolanus" was bestowed upon him only after his resounding victory at Corioles; see I.ix.) **14 brats** worthless creatures **17 apron–men** menial workers, tradesmen (who customarily wore aprons) **18 voice** votes, support **occupation** the workingman **20–21 Hercules . . . fruit** (Refers to the eleventh labor of Hercules, which required him to gather golden apples belonging to Zeus.) **23 smilingly** gladly **who** whoever **25 constant** loyal **26 something in** i.e., reasons to join with **31 For** as for **32 charg'd** would be goading **33 should** would **34 show'd** would appear **35 brand** torch **36 face** audacity, boldness **37 Beseech** I beg of you **made fair hands** done a fine job (Said sarcasticly.) **38 crafts** schemes **crafted fair** (1) plotted well (2) created fine handiwork **40 help** remedy **42 clusters** mobs **43 Hoot** (See III.iii.) **44 roar . . . again** i.e., howl in agony when comes back again **45 second . . . men** the second greatest name among men **his points** Coriolanus' directions **54 coxcombs** fools' heads **56 pay** repay **voices** words (against him)

(18) POSTHUMUS AND IACHIMO [II.iv.26]

Cymbeline

SCENE: A house in Rome.

{Having made a wager that he could seduce Posthumus' wife, Iachimo returns direct from Britain—and the bedchamber of Posthumus' beloved Imogen—with a scandalous progress report.}

POSTHUMUS
Iachimo!

The swiftest harts have posted you by land,
And winds of all the corners kiss'd your sails,
To make your vessel nimble. Welcome, sir.
I hope the briefness of your answer made
The speediness of your return.

IACHIMO

Your lady
Is one of the fairest that I have look'd upon.

POSTHUMUS

And therewithal the best, or let her beauty
Look through a casement to allure false hearts
And be false with them.

IACHIMO

Here are letters for you. [*Gives letters.*]

POSTHUMUS

Their tenor good, I trust.

IACHIMO

'Tis very like.

PHILARIO

Was Caius Lucius in the Britain court
When you were there?

IACHIMO

He was expected then,
But not approach'd.

POSTHUMUS

All is well yet.
Sparkles this stone as it was wont, or is 't not
Too dull for your good wearing? [*Indicates ring.*]

IACHIMO

If I have lost it,
I should have lost the worth of it in gold.
I'll make a journey twice as far, t' enjoy
A second night of such sweet shortness which
Was mine in Britain, for the ring is won.

POSTHUMUS

The stone's too hard to come by.

IACHIMO

Not a whit,
Your lady being so easy.

POSTHUMUS

Make not, sir,
Your loss your sport. I hope you know that we
Must not continue friends.

IACHIMO

Good sir, we must,
If you keep covenant. Had I not brought
The knowledge of your mistress home, I grant
We were to question farther; but I now
Profess myself the winner of her honor,
Together with your ring, and not the wronger
Of her or you, having proceeded but
By both your wills.

POSTHUMUS

If you can make 't apparent
That you have tasted her in bed, my hand
And ring is yours; if not, the foul opinion
You had of her pure honor gains or loses
Your sword or mine, or masterless leaves both
To who shall find them.

IACHIMO

Sir, my circumstances,
Being so near the truth as I will make them,
Must first induce you to believe; whose strength
I will confirm with oath, which I doubt not
You'll give me leave to spare, when you shall find
You need it not.

POSTHUMUS

Proceed.

IACHIMO

First, her bedchamber—
Where, I confess, I slept not, but profess
Had that was well worth watching—it was hang'd
With tapestry of silk and silver; the story
Proud Cleopatra, when she met her Roman,
And Cydnus swell'd above the banks, or for
The press of boats or pride. A piece of work
So bravely done, so rich, that it did strive

In workmanship and value, which I wonder'd
Could be so rarely and exactly wrought,
Since the true life on 't was—

POSTHUMUS

This is true;
And this you might have heard of here, by me,
Or by some other.

IACHIMO

More particulars
Must justify my knowledge.

POSTHUMUS

So they must,
Or do your honor injury.

IACHIMO

The chimney
Is south the chamber, and the chimney-piece
Chaste Dian bathing. Never saw I figures
So likely to report themselves. The cutter
Was as another nature, dumb; outwent her,
Motion and breath left out.

POSTHUMUS

This is a thing
Which you might from relation likewise reap,
Being, as it is, much spoke of.

IACHIMO

The roof o' th' chamber
With golden cherubins is fretted. Her andirons—
I had forgot them—were two winking Cupids
Of silver, each on one foot standing, nicely
Depending on their brands.

POSTHUMUS

This is her honor!
Let it be granted you have seen all this—and praise
Be given to your remembrance—the description
Of what is in her chamber nothing saves
The wager you have laid.

IACHIMO

Then, if you can
Be pale, I beg but leave to air this jewel. See! [*Shows the bracelet.*]

And now 'tis up again. It must be married
To that your diamond; I'll keep them.

POSTHUMUS

Jove!
Once more let me behold it. Is it that
Which I left with her?

IACHIMO

Sir—I thank her—that.
She stripp'd it from her arm; I see her yet;
Her pretty action did outsell her gift,
And yet enrich'd it too. She gave it me,
And said she prized it once.

POSTHUMUS
May be she pluck'd it off
To send it me.

IACHIMO

She writes so to you, doth she?

POSTHUMUS
Render to me some corporal sign about her,
More evident than this; for this was stolen.

IACHIMO
By Jupiter, I had it from her arm.
But if you seek
For further satisfying, under her breast—
Worthy the pressing—lies a mole, right proud
Of that most delicate lodging. By my life,
I kiss'd it; and it gave me present hunger
To feed again, though full. You do remember
This stain upon her?

POSTHUMUS

Ay, and it doth confirm
Another stain, as big as hell can hold,
Were there no more but it.

IACHIMO

Will you hear more?

POSTHUMUS
Spare your arithmetic; never count the turns.
Once, and a million!

IACHIMO

I'll be sworn—

POSTHUMUS

No swearing.
If you will swear you have not done 't, you lie;
And I will kill thee, if thou dost deny
Thou'st made me cuckold.

IACHIMO

I'll deny nothing.

POSTHUMUS

O, that I had her here, to tear her limb-meal!
I will go there and do 't, i' th' court, before
Her father. I'll do something—

[*Exit.*]

2 harts deer **posted** speedily conveyed **3 the corners** four corners of the earth **5 your answer** the answer you received **made** enabled, accounts for **8 therewithal** with that **12 Caius Lucius** (See II.iii.) **14 not approach'd** had not yet arrived **15 All . . . yet** (Posthumus is apparently commenting upon one of the letters given him by Iachimo.) **24 sport** amusement **26 covenant** i.e., your bargain **27 knowledge** carnal knowledge **28 question farther** further dispute the matter, i.e., duel **32 apparent** clear, obvious **37 circumstances** particulars, detailed observations **41 spare** omit, skip **45 that** that which **watching** staying awake for **48 Cydnus** (Cleopatra first met Antony while floating on her barge along the Cydnus River.) **or for** either because of **49 press** swarm, multitude **50 bravely** exquisitely, splendidly **50–51 strive In** excel both in **51 value** material worth **wonder'd** marveled **56 justify** verify, confirm **58 chimney-piece** ornamental sculpture or carving placed over a fireplace **59 Dian** Diana, the moon goddess and goddess of chastity **60 So . . . themselves** so like what they were intended to represent **60–61 The . . . dumb** the sculptor's works rivaled those of nature, except that they uttered no sound **61 outwent** outdid, surpassed **her** i.e., nature **63 relation** hearsay, word of mouth **65 fretted** adorned **66 winking** i.e., blind **68 Depending** leaning **brands** torches **70 remembrance** memory **71 nothing saves** does not at all save **73 pale** unimpressed, unmoved **air** reveal, expose to view **74 up** put away **79 action** gesture **outsell** exceed in value **83 it** it to **84 corporal . . . her** i.e., feature of her body **85 evident** conclusive, indubitable **89 pressing** i.e., of the breast **91 present** immediate, sudden **96 never . . . turns** i.e., do not detail the rest of your sexual activity **101 limb-meal** limb from limb

(19) HAMLET AND HORATIO [I.II.160]

Hamlet

SCENE: A chamber in Elsinore Castle.

{Last evening, Horatio witnessed a familiar looking apparition strolling slowly and stately among the castle walls. Now, a tad unnerved by what he saw, he tracks down his good friend Hamlet to inform him of the eerie encounter.}

[*Enter Horatio.*]

HORATIO
Hail to your lordship!

HAMLET
I am glad to see you well.
Horatio—or I do forget myself.

HORATIO
The same, my lord, and your poor servant ever.

HAMLET
Sir, my good friend; I'll change that name with you.
And what make you from Wittenberg, Horatio?

HORATIO
A truant disposition, good my lord.

HAMLET
I would not hear your enemy say so,
Nor shall you do my ear that violence
To make it truster of your own report
Against yourself: I know you are no truant.
But what is your affair in Elsinore?
We'll teach you to drink deep ere you depart.

HORATIO
My lord, I came to see your father's funeral.

HAMLET
I prithee, do not mock me, fellow-student;
I think it was to see my mother's wedding.

HORATIO
Indeed, my lord, it followed hard upon.

HAMLET
Thrift, thrift, Horatio! The funeral bak'd meats
Did coldly furnish forth the marriage tables.
Would I had met my dearest foe in heaven
Or ever I had seen that day, Horatio!
My father!—Methinks I see my father.

HORATIO
Where, my lord?

HAMLET
In my mind's eye, Horatio.

HORATIO
I saw him once. 'A was a goodly king.

HAMLET
'A was a man, take him for all in all,
I shall not look upon his like again.

HORATIO
My lord, I think I saw him yesternight.

HAMLET
Saw? who?

HORATIO
My lord, the King your father.

HAMLET
The King my father!

HORATIO
Season your admiration for awhile
With an attent ear, till I may deliver
This marvel to you.

HAMLET
For God's love, let me hear.

HORATIO
Two nights together had
Marcellus and Bernardo, on their watch,
In the dead waste and middle of the night,
Been thus encounter'd: A figure like your father,
Armed at point exactly, cap-a-pe,
Appears before them, and with solemn march
Goes slow and stately by them. Thrice he walk'd

By their oppress'd and fear-surprised eyes
Within his truncheon's length, whilst they, distill'd
Almost to jelly with the act of fear,
Stand dumb and speak not to him. This to me
In dreadful secrecy impart they did,
And I with them the third night kept the watch,
Where, as they had delivered, both in time,
Form of the thing, each word made true and good,
The apparition comes. I knew your father;
These hands are not more like.

HAMLET
Did you not speak to it?

HORATIO
My lord, I did;
But answer made it none. Yet once methought
It lifted up it head and did address
Itself to motion, like as it would speak;
But even then the morning cock crew loud,
And at the sound it shrunk in haste away,
And vanish'd from our sight.

HAMLET
'Tis very strange.

HORATIO
As I do live, my honor'd lord, 'tis true;
And I did think it writ down in my duty
To let you know of it.

HAMLET
Indeed, indeed, sir. But this troubles me.
Hold you the watch tonight?

HORATIO
I do, my lord.

HAMLET
Arm'd, say you?

HORATIO
Arm'd, my lord.

HAMLET
From top to toe?

HORATIO
My lord, from head to foot.

HAMLET
Then saw you not his face?

HORATIO
O, yes, my lord; he wore his beaver up.

HAMLET
What, look'd he frowningly?

HORATIO
A countenance more
In sorrow than in anger.

HAMLET
Pale or red?

HORATIO
Nay, very pale.

HAMLET
And fix'd his eyes upon you?

HORATIO
Most constantly.

HAMLET
I would I had been there.

HORATIO
It would have much amaz'd you.

HAMLET
Very like, very like. Stay'd it long?

HORATIO
While one with moderate haste might tell a hundred.

HAMLET
His beard was grizzl'd—no?

HORATIO
It was, as I have seen it in his life,
A sable silver'd.

HAMLET
I will watch tonight.

Perchance 'twill walk again.

HORATIO
I warr'nt it will.

HAMLET
If it assume my noble father's person,
I'll speak to it, though hell itself should gape
And bid me hold my peace. I pray you,
If you have hitherto conceal'd this sight,
Let it be tenable in your silence still;
And whatsoever else shall hap tonight,
Give it an understanding, but no tongue.
I will requite your love. So, fare you well.
Upon the platform,'twixt eleven and twelve,
I'll visit you.

HORATIO
My duty to your honor.

HAMLET
Your loves, as mine to you. Farewell.

[*Exit Horatio.*]

My father's spirit in arms! All is not well.
I doubt some foul play. Would the night were come!
Till then sit still, my soul. Foul deeds will rise,
Though all the earth o'erwhelm them, to men's eyes.

[*Exit.*]

3 poor humble **4 change** exchange **name** i.e., name of "friend" **5 make** brings **6 truant disposition** inclination to neglect my duty **9 truster** a believer **10 truant** shirker, malingerer **14 prithee** pray thee, beg you **16 hard upon** closely thereafter **17 funeral bak'd meats** foods prepared for the funeral **18 coldly** when they were cold **19 dearest** worst, most hated **20 Or** ere, before **23 'A** he **29 Season your admiration** temper your astonishment, tone down your wonder **30 attent** attentive **deliver** report **33 on their watch** i.e., while performing their duties as officers of the watch **34 dead waste** still expanse **36 at point exactly** in precisely the same way **cap-a-pe** from head to toe **39 oppress'd** stunned **fear-surprised** overwhelmed by fear **40 truncheon** baton carried as a symbol of rank or authority **distill'd** melted **41 act** action, effect **43 dreadful** fearful, filled with dread **51 it** its **51–52 address . . . motion** start to gesture **52 like . . . would** as though it were about to

53 even precisely, right **61 Arm'd** (the ghost was) armed **66 beaver** visor or faceguard of a helmet **70 would** would that, wish **73 tell** count to **76 A sable silver'd** black highlighted with white **77 Perchance** perhaps **79 gape** open up **82 tenable** held fast, held tightly **84 Give . . . tongue** i.e., observe it carefully, but do not speak of it **85 requite your love** repay you for your devoted service **91 doubt** suspect **93 o'erwhelm** cover over, obscure

(20) HAMLET AND FIRST CLOWN [V.I.117]

Hamlet

SCENE: A churchyard.

{While strolling around Elsinore with his friend Horatio, Hamlet happens upon a working joe who's obviously up for a bit of verbal byplay. (Here, the term "clown" indicates only that our merry gravedigger resides in the country; it does not imply a penchant for slapstick or colorful makeup.)}

HAMLET
Whose grave's this, sirrah?

FIRST CLOWN
Mine, sir. [*Sings*.]
"O, a pit of clay for to be made
For such a guest is meet."

HAMLET
I think it be thine, indeed, for thou liest in 't.

FIRST CLOWN
You lie out on 't, sir, and therefore 'tis not yours: for my part, I do not lie in 't, yet it is mine.

HAMLET
'Thou dost lie in 't, to be in 't and say it is thine. 'Tis for the dead, not for the quick; therefore thou liest.

FIRST CLOWN
'Tis a quick lie, sir; 'twill away gain from me to you.

HAMLET
What man dost thou dig it for?

FIRST CLOWN
For no man, sir.

HAMLET
What woman, then?

FIRST CLOWN
For none, neither.

HAMLET
Who is to be buried in 't?

FIRST CLOWN
One that was a woman, sir; but, rest her soul, she's dead.

HAMLET
How absolute the knave is! I must speak by the card, or equivocation will undo me. By the Lord, these three years I have taken a note of it: the age is grown so pick'd that the toe of the peasant comes so near the heel of the courtier, he galls his kibe. How long hast thou been grave-maker?

FIRST CLOWN
Of all the days i' th' year, I came to 't that day that our last king Hamlet overcame Fortinbras.

HAMLET
How long is that since?

FIRST CLOWN
Cannot you tell that? Every fool can tell that. It was that very day that young Hamlet was born—he that is mad, and sent into England.

HAMLET
Ay, marry, why was he sent into England?

FIRST CLOWN
Why, because 'a was mad. 'A shall recover his wits there; or if 'a do not, 'tis no great matter there.

HAMLET
Why?

FIRST CLOWN
'Twill not be seen in him there. There the men are as mad as he.

HAMLET
How came he mad?

FIRST CLOWN
Very strangely, they say.

HAMLET
How strangely?

FIRST CLOWN
Faith, e'en with losing his wits.

HAMLET
Upon what ground?

FIRST CLOWN
Why, here in Denmark. I have been sexton here, man and boy, thirty years.

HAMLET
How long will a man lie i' th' earth ere he rot?

FIRST CLOWN
Faith, if 'a be not rotten before 'a die—as we have many pocky corses now-a-days, that will scarce hold the laying in—'a will last you some eight year or nine year. A tanner will last you nine year.

HAMLET
Why he more than another?

FIRST CLOWN
Why, sir, his hide is so tann'd with his trade that 'a will keep out water a great while, and your water is a sore decayer of your whoreson dead body. [*Picks up a skull.*] Here's a skull now hath lain you i' th' earth three and twenty years.

HAMLET
Whose was it?

FIRST CLOWN
A whoreson mad fellow's it was. Whose do you think it was?

HAMLET
Nay, I know not.

FIRST CLOWN
A pestilence on him for a mad rogue! A' pour'd a flagon of Rhenish on my head once. This same skull, sir, was Yorick's skull, the King's jester.

HAMLET
This?

FIRST CLOWN
E'en that.

HAMLET
Let me see. [*Takes the skull.*] Alas, poor Yorick! I knew him; a fellow of infinite jest, of most excellent fancy. He hath borne me on his back a thousand times; and now, how abhorr'd in my imagination it is! My gorge rises at it. Here hung those lips that I have kiss'd I know not how oft. Where be your gibes now? Your gambols? Your songs? Your flashes of merriment that were wont to set the table on a roar? Not one now, to mock your own grinning? Quite chap-fall'n? Now get you to my lady's chamber, and tell her, let her paint an inch thick, to this favor she must come; make her laugh at that.

1 sirrah term used in addressing an inferior **6 out on** outside of **9 quick** alive **17 absolute** precise, strict **by the card** i.e., precisely (A card with compass points on it was used by mariners to make precise directional calculations.) **equivocation** ambiguity, uncertainty **19 pick'd** refined, sophisticated **20 galls his kibe** chafes the sore on his heel **26 marry** indeed **27 'a** he **34 Faith** by my faith (a mild oath) **36 sexton** (The sexton filled many functional roles for the church, sometimes including the digging of graves.) **38 pocky** diseased with the pox **42 with** from practicing **43 sore** severe, strong **whoreson** vile **44 lain you** lain **46 whoreson** (Here, as is often the case, "whoreson" is used in a more light-hearted or affectionate sense.) **48 Rhenish** Rhine wine **51 E'en that** that very one **53 fancy** playfulness, imagination **54 gorge rises at** throat grows tight at the thought of **56 gambols** playful leaps, skipping about **57 roar** i.e., of laughter **58 chap-fall'n** (1) lacking a lower jawbone (2) crestfallen, dejected **59 paint** apply her cosmetics **favor** appearance

(21) CADE AND IDEN [IV.x.1]

Henry VI, Part 2

SCENE: Iden's garden in Kent.

{It's all over but the shouting for rabble-rouser Jack Cade. Famished, fatigued and forsaken by his mob, Cade approaches the grounds of Alexander Iden's estate desperately seeking sustenance. And though Iden is by nature a kind and generous soul, suffering trespasses from the likes of Jack Cade is more than he can stand.}

[*Enter Cade.*]

CADE
Fie on ambition! Fie on myself, that have a sword, and yet am ready to famish! These five days have I hid me in these woods and durst not peep out, for all

the country is laid for me; but now am I so hungry that, if I might have a lease of my life for a thousand years, I could stay no longer. Wherefore, on a brick wall have I climb'd into this garden, to see if I can eat grass, or pick a sallet another while, which is not amiss to cool a man's stomach this hot weather. And I think this word "sallet" was born to do me good; for many a time, but for a sallet, my brain-pan had been cleft with a brown bill; and many a time, when I have been dry and bravely marching, it hath serv'd me instead of a quart pot to drink in; and now the word "sallet" must serve me to feed on.

[*Enter Iden.*]

IDEN
Lord, who would live turmoiled in the court,
And may enjoy such quiet walks as these?
This small inheritance my father left me
Contenteth me, and worth a monarchy.
I seek not to wax great by others' waning,
Or gather wealth, I care not with what envy.
Sufficeth that I have maintains my state
And sends the poor well pleased from my gate.

CADE
[*Aside.*] Here's the lord of the soil come to seize me for a stray, for entering his fee-simple without leave.—Ah, villain, thou wilt betray me, and get a thousand crowns of the King by carrying my head to him; but I'll make thee eat iron like an ostrich, and swallow my sword like a great pin, ere thou and I part.

IDEN
Why, rude companion, whatsoe'er thou be,
I know thee not. Why, then, should I betray thee?
Is 't not enough to break into my garden,
And, like a thief, to come to rob my grounds,
Climbing my walls in spite of me the owner,
But thou wilt brave me with these saucy terms?

CADE
Brave thee! Ay, by the best blood that ever was broach'd, and beard thee too. Look on me well. I have eat no meat these five days; yet, come thou, and if I do not leave you as dead as a doornail, I pray God I may never eat grass more.

IDEN
Nay, it shall ne'er be said, while England stands,
That Alexander Iden, an esquire of Kent,

Took odds to combat a poor famish'd man.
Oppose thy steadfast-gazing eyes to mine,
See if thou canst outface me with thy looks.
Set limb to limb, and thou art far the lesser;
Thy hand is but a finger to my fist,
Thy leg a stick compared with this truncheon;
My foot shall fight with all the strength thou hast;
And if mine arm be heaved in the air,
Thy grave is digg'd already in the earth.
As for words, whose greatness answers words,
Let this my sword report what speech forbears.

CADE
By my valor, the most complete champion that ever I heard! Steel, if thou turn the edge, or cut not out the burly-bon'd clown in chines of beef ere thou sleep in thy sheath, I beseech God on my knees thou mayst be turn'd to hobnails. [*Here they fight. Cade falls.*] O, I am slain! Famine and no other hath slain me. Let ten thousand devils come against me, and give me but the ten meals I have lost, and I'd defy them all. Wither, garden, and be henceforth a burying-place to all that do dwell in this house, because the unconquer'd soul of Cade is fled.

IDEN
Is 't Cade that I have slain, that monstrous traitor?
Sword, I will hallow thee for this thy deed,
And hang thee o'er my tomb when I am dead.
Ne'er shall this blood be wiped from thy point;
But thou shalt wear it as a herald's coat
To emblaze the honor that thy master got.

CADE
Iden, farewell, and be proud of thy victory. Tell Kent from me, she hath lost her best man, and exhort all the world to be cowards; for I, that never fear'd any, am vanquish'd by famine, not by valor. [*Dies.*]

IDEN
How much thou wrong'st me, heaven be my judge.
Die, damned wretch, the curse of her that bare thee!
And as I thrust thy body in with my sword, [*Stabs Cade's body.*]
So wish I, I might thrust thy soul to hell.
Hence will I drag thee headlong by the heels
Unto a dunghill, which shall be thy grave,
And there cut off thy most ungracious head,
Which I will bear in triumph to the King,
Leaving thy trunk for crows to feed upon.

[*Exit.*]

1 Fie (an expression of disgust) **2-3 durst** dared not **laid** laying in wait, set with traps **4 stay** wait **5–6 a sallet** salad greens **8 but . . . sallet** were it not for my helmet ("Sallet" also means "helmet.") **brown bill** brown, long-handled shaft topped with an ax-like head **9 dry** parched, thirsty **10 in** i.e., out of **12 turmoiled** distraught, fraught with worry **13 And may** i.e., when he might **18 Sufficeth . . . state** it suffices that what I have sustains my way of life **19 pleased** i.e., fed **20 stray** trespasser **21 fee-simple** private property **25 rude companion** common rascal, base fellow **30 brave** insult, taunt **saucy** insolent **31 broach'd** shed (By the best blood ever shed, Cade means "by the blood of Christ.") **beard** defy **33 eat** eaten (pronounced "et") **37 odds** advantage **39 outface** stare down, intimidate **42 truncheon** hefty staff, thick pole (i.e., Iden's leg) **44–45 And . . . earth** i.e., and if I should but raise my arm to strike, you are as good as dead **46 words . . . words** my words, whose greatness matches your words **48 complete** accomplished, capable **49 turn the edge** fail to cut **49 cut . . . beef** i.e., do not carve this stout bumpkin into roasts of beef **50 beseech** pray to **50–51 turn'd to hobnails** i.e., melted down and turned into nails **60 herald's coat** i.e., badge of honor **61 emblaze** proclaim **62 Kent** i.e., the county of Kent, where this action takes place **66 bare** bore **69 headlong** stretched out with the head dragging behind **71 ungracious** wicked

(22) CASSIUS AND BRUTUS [IV.ii.37]

Julius Caesar

SCENE: A camp near Sardis, within Brutus' tent.

{Acrimony and accusations abound in the conspiracy's waning days as Cassius and Brutus, chief among those responsible for Caesar's assassination, square off against each other.}

CASSIUS
Most noble brother, you have done me wrong.

BRUTUS
Judge me, you gods! Wrong I mine enemies?
And, if not so, how should I wrong a brother?

CASSIUS
That you have wrong'd me doth appear in this:
You have condemn'd and noted Lucius Pella

For taking bribes here of the Sardians,
Wherein my letters, praying on his side
Because I knew the man, were slighted off.

BRUTUS
You wrong'd yourself to write in such a case.

CASSIUS
In such a time as this it is not meet
That every nice offence should bear his comment.

BRUTUS
Let me tell you, Cassius, you yourself
Are much condemn'd to have an itching palm;
To sell and mart your offices for gold
To undeservers.

CASSIUS
I an itching palm?
You know that you are Brutus that speak this,
Or, by the gods, this speech were else your last.

BRUTUS
The name of Cassius honors this corruption,
And chastisement doth therefore hide his head.

CASSIUS
Chastisement?

BRUTUS
Remember March, the ides of March remember:
Did not great Julius bleed for justice' sake?
What villain touch'd his body that did stab
And not for justice? What, shall one of us,
That struck the foremost man of all this world
But for supporting robbers, shall we now
Contaminate our fingers with base bribes,
And sell the mighty space of our large honors
For so much trash as may be grasped thus?
I had rather be a dog, and bay the moon,
Than such a Roman.

CASSIUS
Brutus, bait not me!
I'll not endure it. You forget yourself
To hedge me in. I am a soldier, I,
Older in practice, abler than yourself

To make conditions.

BRUTUS
Go to! You are not, Cassius.

CASSIUS
I am.

BRUTUS
I say you are not.

CASSIUS
Urge me no more, I shall forget myself.
Have mind upon your health. Tempt me no farther.

BRUTUS
Away, slight man!

CASSIUS
Is 't possible?

BRUTUS
Hear me, for I will speak.
Must I give way and room to your rash choler?
Shall I be frighted when a madman stares?

CASSIUS
O ye gods, ye gods! Must I endure all this?

BRUTUS
All this? Ay, more. Fret till your proud heart break.
Go show your slaves how choleric you are,
And make your bondmen tremble. Must I budge?
Must I observe you? Must I stand and crouch
Under your testy humor? By the gods,
You shall digest the venom of your spleen,
Though it do split you; for, from this day forth,
I'll use you for my mirth, yea, for my laughter,
When you are waspish.

CASSIUS
Is it come to this?

BRUTUS
You say you are a better soldier.
Let it appear so; make your vaunting true,
And it shall please me well. For mine own part,
I shall be glad to learn of noble men.

CASSIUS
You wrong me every way! You wrong me, Brutus.
I said, an elder soldier, not a better.
Did I say "better"?

BRUTUS
If you did, I care not.

CASSIUS
When Caesar liv'd, he durst not thus have mov'd me.

BRUTUS
Peace, peace! You durst not so have tempted him.

CASSIUS
I durst not?

BRUTUS
No.

CASSIUS
What, durst not tempt him?

BRUTUS
For your life you durst not!

CASSIUS
Do not presume too much upon my love.
I may do that I shall be sorry for.

BRUTUS
You have done that you should be sorry for.
There is no terror, Cassius, in your threats,
For I am arm'd so strong in honesty
That they pass by me as the idle wind,
Which I respect not. I did send
To you for gold to pay my legions,
Which you denied me: was that done like Cassius?

CASSIUS
I denied you not.

BRUTUS
You did.

CASSIUS
I did not. He was but a fool that brought
My answer back. Brutus hath riv'd my heart.
A friend should bear his friend's infirmities,

But Brutus makes mine greater than they are.

BRUTUS
I do not, till you practice them on me.

CASSIUS
You love me not.

BRUTUS
I do not like your faults.

CASSIUS
A friendly eye could never see such faults.

BRUTUS
A flatterer's would not, though they do appear
As huge as high Olympus.

CASSIUS
Come, Antony, and young Octavius, come,
Revenge yourselves alone on Cassius,
For Cassius is aweary of the world.
[*Offers his unsheathed dagger.*]
There's my dagger, and here my naked breast;
Strike, as thou didst at Caesar; for, I know,
When thou didst hate him worst, thou lovedst him better
Than ever thou lovedst Cassius.

BRUTUS
Sheathe your dagger:
Be angry when you will, it shall have scope;
Do what you will, dishonor shall be humor.
O Cassius, you are yoked with a lamb
That carries anger as the flint bears fire;
Who, much enforced, shows a hasty spark,
And straight is cold again.

CASSIUS
Hath Cassius liv'd
To be but mirth and laughter to his Brutus,
When grief and blood ill-temper'd vexeth him?

BRUTUS
When I spoke that, I was ill-temper'd too.

CASSIUS
Do you confess so much? Give me your hand.

BRUTUS
And my heart too. [*They embrace.*]

5 noted dishonored, branded with disgrace **7 letters** letter **praying . . . side** asking for consideration on his behalf **8 slighted off** contemptuously disregarded **10 meet** fit, proper **11 nice** trivial **bear his comment** be subject to scrutiny **13 condem'd to have** accused of having **14 mart** market, offer up **offices** services **18 honors** gives an honorable appearance to **19 chastisement . . . head** i.e., authorities are, because of Cassius' reputation, afraid to condemn his actions **21 ides of March** (See III.1.) **26 But** only **robbers** i.e., those who would rob Rome of its liberty (?) **28 mighty . . . honors** the great power and influence of our honorable reputations **31 bait** attack, harass **33 hedge me in** restrict my actions **35 make conditions** manage such matters **38 Urge** goad, push **39 Tempt** provoke **40 slight** insignificant **42 rash choler** impetuous anger **43 stares** glares, stares wildly **47 bondmen** servants **48 observe** defer to **50 digest** swallow (rather than vent) **spleen** foul temper **53 waspish** peevish, bad-tempered **55 vaunting** boasting **57 of** from **61 durst** dared **mov'd** angered **70 honesty** integrity **72 respect not** disregard, pay no attention to **78 riv'd** split **79 infirmities** faults, flaws **85 high Olympus** towering Mount Olympus **86 Antony . . . Octavius** (Mark Antony and Octavius Caesar lead the faction opposing the armies of Cassius and Brutus.) **87 alone** only **93 when . . . scope** whenever you like, your fury will have free rein **94 dishonor . . . humor** your insults will be attributed to your bad temper **95 yoked** allied, paired **lamb** i.e., Brutus **97 enforced** abused, provoked **98 straight** straightaway **cold** collected, calm **100 blood ill-temper'd** bad humor

(23) HUBERT AND ARTHUR [IV.1.8]

King John

SCENE: A room in a castle.

{In thinly veiled terms, King John has instructed Hubert to do away with young Arthur. Although kind Hubert would much prefer to spare the lad, it appears that his allegiance to the King is about to prevail as an unsuspecting Arthur is summoned forth.}

HUBERT
Young lad, come forth; I have to say with you.

ARTHUR
[*Coming forward.*] Good morrow, Hubert.

HUBERT
Good morrow, little prince.

ARTHUR
As little prince, having so great a title
To be more prince, as may be. You are sad.

HUBERT
Indeed, I have been merrier.

ARTHUR
Mercy on me!
Methinks nobody should be sad but I.
Yet I remember, when I was in France,
Young gentlemen would be as sad as night,
Only for wantonness. By my christendom,
So I were out of prison and kept sheep,
I should be as merry as the day is long;
And so I would be here, but that I doubt
My uncle practices more harm to me.
He is afraid of me and I of him.
Is it my fault that I was Geffrey's son?
No, indeed, is 't not; and I would to heaven
I were your son, so you would love me, Hubert.

HUBERT
[*Aside.*] If I talk to him, with his innocent prate
He will awake my mercy, which lies dead.
Therefore I will be sudden and dispatch.

ARTHUR
Are you sick, Hubert? You look pale today.
In sooth, I would you were a little sick,
That I might sit all night and watch with you.
I warrant I love you more than you do me.

HUBERT
[*Aside.*] His words do take possession of my bosom.—
Read here, young Arthur. [*Shows him a paper.*]
[*Aside.*] How now, foolish rheum?
Turning dispiteous torture out of door?
I must be brief, lest resolution drop
Out at mine eyes in tender womanish tears.—
Can you not read it? Is it not fair writ?

ARTHUR
Too fairly, Hubert, for so foul effect.
Must you with hot irons burn out both mine eyes?

HUBERT
Young boy, I must.

ARTHUR
And will you?

HUBERT
And I will.

ARTHUR
Have you the heart? When your head did but ache,
I knit my handercher about your brows—
The best I had, a princess wrought it me—
And I did never ask it you again;
And with my hand at midnight held your head,
And like the watchful minutes to the hour,
Still and anon cheer'd up the heavy time,
Saying, "What lack you?" and "Where lies your grief?"
Or "What good love may I perform for you?"
Many a poor man's son would have lien still
And ne'er have spoke a loving word to you,
But you at your sick service had a prince.
Nay, you may think my love was crafty love
And call it cunning. Do, an if you will.
If heaven be pleas'd that you must use me ill,
Why then you must. Will you put out mine eyes?
These eyes that never did nor never shall
So much as frown on you.

HUBERT
I have sworn to do it,
And with hot irons must I burn them out.

ARTHUR
Ah, none but in this iron age would do it!
The iron of itself, though heat red-hot,
Approaching near these eyes, would drink my tears
And quench his fiery indignation
Even in the matter of mine innocence—
Nay, after that, consume away in rust
But for containing fire to harm mine eye.
Are you more stubborn-hard than hammer'd iron?
An if an angel should have come to me

And told me Hubert should put out mine eyes,
I would not have believed him—no tongue but Hubert's.

HUBERT
Come, boy, prepare yourself.

ARTHUR
Is there no remedy?

HUBERT
None, but to lose your eyes.

ARTHUR
O heaven, that there were but a mote in yours,
A grain, a dust, a gnat, a wandering hair,
Any annoyance in that precious sense!
Then feeling what small things are boisterous there,
Your vile intent must needs seem horrible.

HUBERT
Go to, hold your tongue.

ARTHUR
Hubert, the utterance of a brace of tongues
Must needs want pleading for a pair of eyes.
Let me not hold my tongue, let me not, Hubert;
Or, Hubert, if you will, cut out my tongue,
So I may keep mine eyes. O, spare mine eyes,
Though to no use but still to look on you!
Lo, by my troth, the instrument is cold
And would not harm me.

HUBERT
I can heat it, boy.

ARTHUR
No, in good sooth. The fire is dead with grief,
Being create for comfort, to be us'd
In undeserv'd extremes. See else yourself.
There is no malice in this burning coal;
The breath of heaven has blown his spirit out,
And strew'd repentent ashes on his head.

HUBERT
But with my breath I can revive it, boy.

ARTHUR
An if you do, you will but make it blush

And glow with shame of your proceedings, Hubert.
Nay, it perchance will sparkle in your eyes,
And like a dog that is compell'd to fight,
Snatch at his master that doth tarre him on.
All things that you should use to do me wrong
Deny their office. Only you do lack
That mercy which fierce fire and iron extends,
Creatures of note for mercy-lacking uses.

HUBERT
Well, see to live. I will not touch thine eye
For all the treasure that thine uncle owes.
Yet am I sworn and I did purpose, boy,
With this same very iron to burn them out.

ARTHUR
O, now you look like Hubert! All this while
You were disguis'd.

HUBERT
Peace; no more. Adieu.
Your uncle must not know but you are dead.
I'll fill these dogged spies with false reports.
And, pretty child, sleep doubtless and secure
That Hubert, for the wealth of all the world,
Will not offend thee.

ARTHUR
O heaven! I thank you, Hubert.

HUBERT
Silence, no more. Go closely in with me.
Much danger do I undergo for thee.

[*Exeunt.*]

1 to say something to talk about **2 Good morrow** good morning **3–4 As . . . be** i.e., as little bit a prince, despite being entitled to greater nobility, as I can be **9 for wantonness** on a pretense, affectedly **By my christendom** as am a Christian **10 So** so long as **11 should** would **12 but** except **13 practices** plots **15 Geffrey** King John's deceased elder brother, Geoffrey (See I.i.) **18 prate** chatter, prattle **20 sudden** swift to act **dispatch** deal with this quickly **22 sooth** truth **23 with** over **25 bosom** heart **26 rheum** tears **27 Turning . . . door** i.e., making obvious to all the merciless torture I feel inside **28 brief** quick **30 fair** legibly, clearly **35 knit** tied **36 wrought it** embroidered it for **37 you** from you

39 watchful . . . hour minutes that mark the passing of the hour **40 Still and anon** continually **41 grief** pain **42 love** loving service **43 lien** lain **45 at . . . service** to wait on you when you were sick **47 an if** if **53 iron age** hard, merciless time (with a play on the image of "hot irons") **54 heat** heated **56 his** its **57 the . . . innocence** that which is evidence of my innocence (i.e., his tears) **59 But** merely **66 mote** speck of something **67 wandering** out of place, stray **68 that precious sense** i.e., your sight **69 boisterous** painful **70 must needs** will necessarily **71 Go to** (a common interjection used to convey disapproval or impatience) **72 brace** pair **73 want pleading** plead inadequately **77 Though . . . still to** i.e., even if only to continually **78 by my troth** (a common affirmation of the day on the order of "I swear") **instrument** i.e., hot iron **82 create** created **83 undeserv'd** (inflicting) undeserved **extremes** torments, extreme cruelties **90 sparkle in** blow sparks into **92 tarre** urge **94 Deny their office** refuse to do their duty **95 extends** offer **96 of note** notorious **98 owes** owns, possesses **99 purpose** intend **103 know but** i.e., believe anything other than **104 dogged** malicious, fierce **105 doubtless** fearless **108 closely** secretly

(24) HUBERT AND KING JOHN [IV.II.182]

King John

SCENE: King John's palace.

{Things have gone from bad to worse in a hurry for King John. First his noblemen, suspecting the King of foul play, stormed off after receiving word that young Arthur is dead. Then came news that John's mother has died, followed by reports of growing unrest among the masses. Now, it's all Hubert and the King can do to pause and take stock of this ill-fated series of events.}

HUBERT
My lord, they say five moons were seen tonight;
Four fixed, and the fifth did whirl about
The other four in wondrous motion.

KING JOHN
Five moons!

HUBERT
Old men and bedlams in the streets
Do prophesy upon it dangerously.

Young Arthur's death is common in their mouths,
And when they talk of him, they shake their heads
And whisper one another in the ear;
And he that speaks doth gripe the hearer's wrist,
Whilst he that hears makes fearful action,
With wrinkled brows, with nods, with rolling eyes.
I saw a smith stand with his hammer, thus,
The whilst his iron did on the anvil cool,
With open mouth swallowing a tailor's news;
Who, with his shears and measure in his hand,
Standing on slippers, which his nimble haste
Had falsely thrust upon contrary feet,
Told of a many thousand warlike French
That were embattailed and rank'd in Kent.
Another lean unwash'd artificer
Cuts off his tale and talks of Arthur's death.

KING JOHN
Why seek'st thou to possess me with these fears?
Why urgest thou so oft young Arthur's death?
Thy hand hath murd'red him. I had a mighty cause
To wish him dead, but thou hadst none to kill him.

HUBERT
No had, my lord? Why, did you not provoke me?

KING JOHN
It is the curse of kings to be attended
By slaves that take their humors for a warrant
To break within the bloody house of life,
And on the winking of authority
To understand a law, to know the meaning
Of dangerous majesty, when perchance it frowns
More upon humor than advis'd respect.

HUBERT
Here is your hand and seal for what I did. [*Shows his warrant.*]

KING JOHN
O, when the last account 'twixt heaven and earth
Is to be made, then shall this hand and seal
Witness against us to damnation!
How oft the sight of means to do ill deeds
Make deeds ill done! Hadst not thou been by,
A fellow by the hand of nature mark'd,
Quoted, and sign'd to do a deed of shame,

This murder had not come into my mind.
But, taking note of thy abhorr'd aspect,
Finding thee fit for bloody villany,
Apt, liable to be employ'd in danger,
I faintly broke with thee of Arthur's death;
And thou, to be endeared to a king,
Made it no conscience to destroy a prince.

HUBERT
My lord—

KING JOHN
Hadst thou but shook thy head or made a pause
When I spake darkly what I purposed,
Or turn'd an eye of doubt upon my face,
As bid me tell my tale in express words,
Deep shame had struck me dumb, made me break off,
And those thy fears might have wrought fears in me.
But thou didst understand me by my signs
And didst in signs again parley with sin;
Yea, without stop didst let thy heart consent,
And consequently thy rude hand to act
The deed which both our tongues held vile to name.
Out of my sight, and never see me more!
My nobles leave me, and my state is brav'd,
Even at my gates, with ranks of foreign pow'rs:
Nay, in the body of this fleshly land,
This kingdom, this confine of blood and breath,
Hostility and civil tumult reigns
Between my conscience and my cousin's death.

HUBERT
Arm you against your other enemies,
I'll make a peace between your soul and you.
Young Arthur is alive. This hand of mine
Is yet a maiden and an innocent hand,
Not painted with the crimson spots of blood.
Within this bosom never ent'red yet
The dreadful motion of a murderous thought;
And you have slander'd nature in my form,
Which, howsoever rude exteriorly,
Is yet the cover of a fairer mind
Than to be butcher of an innocent child.

KING JOHN
Doth Arthur live? O, haste thee to the peers,
Throw this report on their incensed rage,
And make them tame to their obedience!
Forgive the comment that my passion made
Upon thy feature; for my rage was blind,
And foul imaginary eyes of blood
Presented thee more hideous than thou art.
O, answer not, but to my closet bring
The angry lords with all expedient haste.
I conjure thee but slowly; run more fast.

[*Exeunt.*]

4 bedlams old women **5 prophesy . . . dangerously** i.e., declare it a dangerous omen **6 common . . . mouths** often spoken of by them **9 gripe** grip **10 fearful action** gestures of apprehension and alarm **16 nimble** quick-moving **17 contrary** i.e., the wrong (right slipper on left foot and vice versa) **19 embattailed** readied for battle **rank'd** positioned in battle lines **20 lean** scrawny **artificer** laborer, artisan **21 Cuts off** breaks off, cuts short **26 No had** did I not have **28 humors** moods, inclinations **for** to be **30 on . . . of** with the slightest nod from **31 understand a law** i.e., surmise what is being ordered **32 perchance** perhaps **33 upon humor** through whim **advis'd respect** careful consideration, deliberate reflection **34 hand** handwriting **37 us** (John is employing the royal plural.) **41 Quoted, and sign'd** designated and assigned **43 abhorr'd aspect** hateful countenance **45 liable** fit **46 faintly broke** indirectly broached the subject **48 conscience** matter of conscience **51 darkly** obscurely of, indirectly of **purposed** proposed **53 As** as if to **express** exact, explicit **54 had** would have **56 signs** subtle indications **59 rude** violent, brutal **act** perform **62 state is brav'd** kingdom is challenged, authority is defied **64 body . . . land** (referring here to his own body) **65 confine** prison **71 a maiden** i.e., free of bloodshed **74 motion** impulse **75 form** outward appearance **76 howsoever rude** however common and unrefined (it may be) **79 haste** hasten **80 report** news **81 tame** submissive to **obedience** (oath of) obedience **83 feature** outward appearance **84 foul . . . blood** i.e., your foul eyes, which I imagined were filled with bloody intentions **86 closet** private chamber **88 conjure** urge

(25) Earl of Gloucester and Edgar [IV.vi.1]

King Lear

SCENE: The fields near Dover.

{It's a sorry scene as Edgar and Gloucester make their way to the pastoral fields of Dover—Edgar, still in the guise of a madman, gently shepherding his aged father, who is now all but helpless after being blinded by the merciless Duke of Corwall.}

GLOUCESTER
When shall I come to th' top of that same hill?

EDGAR
You do climb up it now. Look, how we labor.

GLOUCESTER
Methinks the ground is even.

EDGAR
Horrible steep.
Hark, do you hear the sea?

GLOUCESTER
No, truly.

EDGAR
Why, then, your other senses grow imperfect
By your eyes' anguish.

GLOUCESTER
So may it be, indeed.
Methinks thy voice is alter'd, and thou speak'st
In better phrase and matter than thou didst.

EDGAR
Y' are much deceiv'd. In nothing am I chang'd
But in my garments.

GLOUCESTER
Methinks y' are better spoken.

EDGAR
Come on, sir, here's the place. Stand still. How fearful
And dizzy 'tis, to cast one's eyes so low!

The crows and choughs that wing the midway air
Show scarce so gross as beetles. Half way down
Hangs one that gathers samphire, dreadful trade!
Methinks he seems no bigger than his head.
The fishermen that walk upon the beach
Appear like mice; and yond tall anchoring bark,
Diminish'd to her cock; her cock, a buoy
Almost too small for sight. The murmuring surge,
That on th' unnumb'red idle pebbles chafes,
Cannot be heard so high. I'll look no more,
Lest my brain turn, and the deficient sight
Topple down headlong.

GLOUCESTER
Set me where you stand.

EDGAR
Give me your hand. You are now within a foot
Of th' extreme verge. For all beneath the moon
Would I not leap upright.

GLOUCESTER
Let go my hand.
Here, friend, 's another purse; in it a jewel
Well worth a poor man's taking. Fairies and gods
Prosper it with thee! [*Gives purse.*] Go thou farther off.
Bid me farewell, and let me hear thee going.

EDGAR
[*Moving away.*] Now fare you well, good sir.

GLOUCESTER
With all my heart.

EDGAR
[*Aside.*] Why I do trifle thus with his despair
Is done to cure it.

GLOUCESTER
[*Kneeling.*] O you mighty gods!
This world I do renounce, and, in your sights
Shake patiently my great affliction off.
If I could bear it longer, and not fall
To quarrel with your great opposeless wills,
My snuff and loathed part of nature should
Burn itself out. If Edgar live, O, bless him!
Now, fellow, fare thee well. [*He falls forward.*]

EDGAR

Gone, sir: farewell.—
And yet I know not how conceit may rob
The treasury of life, when life itself
Yields to the theft. Had he been where he thought,
By this had thought been past. Alive or dead?—
Ho, you sir! Friend! Hear you, sir! Speak!—
Thus might he pass indeed; yet he revives.—
What are you, sir?

GLOUCESTER

Away, and let me die.

EDGAR

Hadst thou been aught but gossamer, feathers, air,
So many fathom down precipitating,
Thou'dst shiver'd like an egg; but thou dost breathe,
Hast heavy substance, bleed'st not, speak'st, art sound.
Ten masts at each make not the altitude
Which thou hast perpendicularly fell.
Thy life's a miracle. Speak yet again.

GLOUCESTER

But have I fall'n, or no?

EDGAR

From the dread summit of this chalky bourn.
Look up a-height; the shrill-gorg'd lark so far
Cannot be seen or heard. Do but look up.

GLOUCESTER

Alack, I have no eyes.
Is wretchedness depriv'd that benefit
To end itself by death? 'Twas yet some comfort
When misery could beguile the tyrant's rage,
And frustrate his proud will.

EDGAR

[*Lifting him up.*] Give me your arm.
Up—so. How is 't? Feel you your legs? You stand.

GLOUCESTER

Too well, too well.

EDGAR

This is above all strangeness.
Upon the crown o' th' cliff, what thing was that

Which parted from you?

GLOUCESTER

A poor unfortunate beggar.

EDGAR

As I stood here below, methought his eyes
Were two full moons; he had a thousand noses,
Horns whelk'd and waved like the enridged sea.
It was some fiend. Therefore, thou happy father,
Think that the clearest gods, who make them honors
Of men's impossibilities, have preserved thee.

GLOUCESTER

I do remember now. Henceforth I'll bear
Affliction till it do cry out itself
"Enough, enough," and die. That thing you speak of,
I took it for a man; often 'twould say
"The fiend, the fiend." He led me to that place.

EDGAR

Bear free and patient thoughts.

3 even level **8 than thou didst** (See IV.i.) **12 low** i.e., far below **13 choughs** jackdaws, small crows **14 scarce so gross** barely as large **15 one that** a person who **samphire** herb used in pickling **18 bark** small sailing vessel **19 Diminish'd to** reduced to the size of **cock** cockboat (a small ship's boat) **21 unnumb'red** innumerable, countless **22 so high** this high up **23 the deficient sight** i.e., I, my sight failing me, **26 verge** edge **28 another purse** (Gloucester has already given Edgar one purse; see IV.i.) **37 patiently** calmly, serenely **39 To quarrel with** into rebellion against **opposeless** invincible **40 snuff** exhausted remainder, worthless residue (a "snuff" was the burned–out wick of a candle) **nature** i.e., my life **43 conceit** imagination **45 Yields** consents **48 pass** die **49 What** who (To further his strategy, Edgar now assumes a new persona and speaks in a different voice.) **50 aught** anything **51 precipitating** falling headlong **52 Thou'dst shiver'd** you would have shattered **54 at each** end to end **58 this chalky bourn** i.e., these cliffs of chalk that bound the sea **59 a-height** on high **shrill-gorg'd** shrill-throated **64 beguile** outsmart, cheat **65 proud** arrogant **68 crown** top **72 whelk'd** twisted **enridged** furrowed (by the wind) **73 thou happy father** you lucky old man **74 clearest** most glorious **74–75 who . . . impossibilities** who gain our reverence by performing deeds that are impossible for men to do **81 free** carefree, serene,

(26) LUCIO AND DUKE VINCENTIO [III.ii.85]

Measure For Measure

SCENE: A prison cell in Vienna.

{Since Duke Vincentio has of late been gadding about town in the guise of a friar, a local eccentric named Lucio has no idea who it really is he's talking to when he starts popping off about the failings of both the Duke and his deputy, Lord Angelo.}

LUCIO
What news, friar, of the Duke?

DUKE
I know none. Can you tell me of any?

LUCIO
Some say he is with the Emperor of Russia; other some, he is in Rome. But where is he, think you?

DUKE
I know not where; but wheresoever, I wish him well.

LUCIO
It was a mad fantastical trick of him to steal from the state, and usurp the beggary he was never born to. Lord Angelo dukes it well in his absence; he puts transgression to 't.

DUKE
He does well in 't.

LUCIO
A little more lenity to lechery would do no harm in him. Something too crabbed that way, friar.

DUKE
It is too general a vice, and severity must cure it.

LUCIO
Yes, in good sooth, the vice is of a great kindred; it is well allied. But it is impossible to extirp it quite, friar, till eating and drinking be put down. They say this Angelo was not made by man and woman after this downright way of creation. Is it true, think you?

DUKE
How should he be made, then?

LUCIO
Some report a sea-maid spawn'd him; some, that he was begot between two stock-fishes. But it is certain that when he makes water his urine is congeal'd ice; that I know to be true. And he is a motion ungenerative, that's infallible.

DUKE
You are pleasant, sir, and speak apace.

LUCIO
Why, what a ruthless thing is this in him, for the rebellion of a codpiece to take away the life of a man! Would the Duke that is absent have done this? Ere he would have hang'd a man for the getting a hundred bastards, he would have paid for the nursing a thousand. He had some feeling of the sport; he knew the service, and that instructed him to mercy.

DUKE
I never heard the absent Duke much detected for women. He was not inclin'd that way.

LUCIO
O, sir, you are deceiv'd.

DUKE
'Tis not possible.

LUCIO
Who, not the Duke? Yes, your beggar of fifty; and his use was to put a ducat in her clack-dish. The Duke had crotchets in him. He would be drunk too, that let me inform you.

DUKE
You do him wrong, surely.

LUCIO
Sir, I was an inward of his. A shy fellow was the Duke, and I believe I know the cause of his withdrawing.

DUKE
What, I prithee, might be the cause?

LUCIO
No, pardon. 'Tis a secret must be lock'd within the teeth and the lips. But this I can let you understand, the greater file of the subject held the Duke to be wise.

DUKE
Wise? Why, no question but he was.

LUCIO
A very superficial, ignorant, unweighing fellow.

DUKE
Either this is envy in you, folly, or mistaking. The very stream of his life and the business he hath helm'd must, upon a warranted need, give him a better proclamation. Let him be but testimonied in his own bringings-forth, and he shall appear to the envious a scholar, a statesman, and a soldier. Therefore you speak unskilfully; or if your knowledge be more, it is much dark'ned in your malice.

LUCIO
Sir, I know him, and I love him.

DUKE
Love talks with better knowledge, and knowledge with dearer love.

LUCIO
Come, sir, I know what I know.

DUKE
I can hardly believe that, since you know not what you speak. But, if ever the Duke return, as our prayers are he may, let me desire you to make your answer before him. If it be honest you have spoke, you have courage to maintain it. I am bound to call upon you; and, I pray you, your name?

LUCIO
Sir, my name is Lucio; well known to the Duke.

DUKE
He shall know you better, sir, if I may live to report you.

LUCIO
I fear you not.

DUKE
O, you hope the Duke will return no more, or you imagine me too unhurtful an opposite. But indeed I can do you little harm; you'll forswear this again.

LUCIO
I'll be hanged first. Thou art deceiv'd in me, friar. But no more of this. Farewell, good friar. I prithee, pray for me. The Duke, I say to thee again,

would eat mutton on Fridays. He's now past it, yet, and I say to thee, he would mouth with a beggar, though she smelt brown bread and garlic. Say that I said so. Farewell. [*Exit.*]

DUKE

No might nor greatness in mortality
Can censure scape; back-wounding calumny
The whitest virtue strikes. What king so strong
Can tie the gall up in the slanderous tongue?

6 steal . . . state sneak away from his responsibilities as Duke **7 dukes it** assumes the role of Duke **8 puts transgression to 't** extends severe penalties to lawbreaking **10–11 Something too crabbed** a bit too harsh **12 general** widespread **13 in good sooth** in truth, that is true **great kindred** large family **well allied** i.e., found in the best of families **14 extirp it quite** completely eradicate it **put down** abolished **15–16 after . . . creation** in the usual manner of procreation **18 sea-maid** mermaid **19 stock-fishes** dried codfish **19-20 congeal'd** solid **20 motion ungenerative** puppet that is incapable of reproducing **21 infallible** certain **22 pleasant** comical **apace** (1) rapidly (2) carelessly **23 codpiece** a flap or pouch covering the crotch of a man's trousers (with a bawdy reference to that which lies beneath) **25 getting** begetting **26 nursing a** rearing of a **27 service** profession of prostitution **mercy** i.e., be merciful **28 detected for** suspected of (chasing) **32 ducat** coin **33 clack-dish** wooden bowl with a lid that was "clacked" by beggars to attract attention (here the term is probably meant to suggest the female genitalia) **crotchets** eccentric ways **36 inward** intimate acquaintance **38 prithee** pray you, ask you **40 greater . . . subject** majority of his subjects **43 unweighing** inconsiderate, imprudent **44 envy** malice **45 helm'd** steered, overseen **upon . . . need** if a warrant were needed **45–46 give . . . proclamation** proclaim him a better person (than you claim he is) **46 testimonied** proved, attested to **in . . . bringings-forth** by his own actions **47 to the envious** (even) to the malicious **48 unskillfully** ignorantly **54 desire** ask **55 make your answer** be answerable **56 bound** duty-bound, obliged **60–61 unhurtful** harmless **61 opposite** opponent, adversary **forswear** deny under oath **65 eat mutton** eat forbidden meat, i.e., engage in relations with a prostitute ("mutton" was slang for "whore") **66 mouth with** kiss **smelt** smelled of **brown bread** coarse bran bread **68 mortality** humankind **69 scape** escape, avoid **back-wounding calumny** back–biting slander **70 whitest** purest **71 tie . . . in** restrain the malice of

(27) FORD AND FALSTAFF [II.ii.147]

The Merry Wives of Windsor

SCENE: A room in the Garter Inn.

{Ford suspects Mistress Ford of being unfaithful to him, and so has devised a plot to catch the little woman red-handed. Phase one of his curious plan involves arriving here at the Garter disguised as "Master Brook" in order to hire Falstaff to seduce his wife. The fat knight, of course, seems more than up to the challenge.}

[*Enter Ford, disguised.*]

FORD
Bless you, sir!

FALSTAFF
And you, sir! Would you speak with me?

FORD
I make bold to press with so little preparation upon you.

FALSTAFF
You're welcome. What's your will?

FORD
Sir, I am a gentleman that have spent much; my name is Brook.

FALSTAFF
Good Master Brook, I desire more acquaintance of you.

FORD
Good Sir John, I sue for yours—not to charge you, for I must let you understand I think myself in better plight for a lender than you are, the which hath something embold'ned me to this unseason'd intrusion; for they say, if money go before, all ways do lie open.

FALSTAFF
Money is a good soldier, sir, and will on.

FORD
Troth, and I have a bag of money here troubles me. If you will help to bear it, Sir John, take all, or half, for easing me of the carriage. [*Gives money.*]

FALSTAFF
Sir, I know not how I may deserve to be your porter.

FORD
I will tell you, sir, if you will give me the hearing.

FALSTAFF
Speak, good Master Brook. I shall be glad to be your servant.

FORD
Sir, I hear you are a scholar—I will be brief with you—and you have been a man long known to me, though I had never so good means, as desire, to make myself acquainted with you. I shall discover a thing to you, wherein I must very much lay open mine own imperfection. But, good Sir John, as you have one eye upon my follies, as you hear them unfolded, turn another into the register of your own, that I may pass with a reproof the easier, sith you yourself know how easy it is to be such an offender.

FALSTAFF
Very well, sir; proceed.

FORD
There is a gentlewoman in this town; her husband's name is Ford.

FALSTAFF
Well, sir.

FORD
I have long lov'd her, and, I protest to you, bestow'd much on her; follow'd her with a doting observance, engross'd opportunities to meet her, fee'd every slight occasion that could but niggardly give me sight of her; not only bought many presents to give her, but have given largely to many to know what she would have given. Briefly, I have pursu'd her as love hath pursu'd me, which hath been on the wing of all occasions. But whatsoever I have merited, either in my mind or in my means, meed I am sure I have receiv'd none, unless experience be a jewel—that I have purchas'd at an infinite rate, and that hath taught me to say this:
"Love like a shadow flies when substance love pursues,
Pursuing that that flies, and flying what pursues."

FALSTAFF
Have you receiv'd no promise of satisfaction at her hands?

FORD
Never.

FALSTAFF
Have you importun'd her to such a purpose?

FORD
Never.

FALSTAFF
Of what quality was your love, then?

FORD
Like a fair house built on another man's ground; so that I have lost my edifice by mistaking the place where I erected it.

FALSTAFF
To what purpose have you unfolded this to me?

FORD
When I have told you that, I have told you all. Some say that, though she appear honest to me, yet in other places she enlargeth her mirth so far that there is shrewd construction made of her. Now, Sir John, here is the heart of my purpose: you are a gentleman of excellent breeding, admirable discourse, of great admittance, authentic in your place and person, generally allow'd for your many war-like, court-like, and learned preparations.

FALSTAFF
O, sir!

FORD
Believe it, for you know it. [*Offers money.*] There is money; spend it, spend it; spend more; spend all I have. Only give me so much of your time in exchange of it, as to lay an amiable siege to the honesty of this Ford's wife. Use your art of wooing; win her to consent to you. If any man may, you may as soon as any.

FALSTAFF
Would it apply well to the vehemency of your affection, that I should win what you would enjoy? Methinks you prescribe to yourself very preposterously.

FORD
O, understand my drift. She dwells so securely on the excellency of her honor, that the folly of my soul dares not present itself; she is too bright to be look'd against. Now, could I could come to her with any detection in my hand, my desires had instance and argument to commend themselves. I could drive her then from the ward of her purity, her reputation, her marriage-vow, and a thousand other her defenses, which now are too too strongly embattled against me. What say you to 't, Sir John?

FALSTAFF
Master Brook, I will first make bold with your money; next, give me your hand; and last, as I am a gentleman, you shall, if you will, enjoy Ford's wife.

FORD
O good sir!

FALSTAFF
I say you shall.

FORD
Want no money, Sir John; you shall want none.

FALSTAFF
Want no Mistress Ford, Master Brook; you shall want none. I shall be with her, I may tell you, by her own appointment; even as you came in to me, her assistant or go-between parted from me. I say I shall be with her between ten and eleven; for at that time the jealous rascally knave her husband will be forth. Come you to me at night; you shall know how I speed.

FORD
I am blest in your acquaintance. Do you know Ford, sir?

FALSTAFF
Hang him, poor cuckoldly knave! I know him not. Yet I wrong him to call him poor. They say the jealous wittolly knave hath masses of money; for the which his wife seems to me well-favor'd. I will use her as the key of the cuckoldly rogue's coffer, and there's my harvest–home.

FORD
I would you knew Ford, sir, that you might avoid him if you saw him.

FALSTAFF
Hang him, mechanical salt-butter rogue! I will stare him out of his wits. I will awe him with my cudgel; it shall hang like a meteor o'er the cuckold's horns. Master Brook, thou shalt know I will predominate over the peasant, and thou shalt lie with his wife. Come to me soon at night. Ford's a knave, and I will aggravate his style; thou, Master Brook, shalt know him for knave and cuckold. Come to me soon at night!

[*Exit.*]

3 I . . . you i.e., it is presumptuous of me to intrude upon you with so little advance notice **7 charge you** burden you with an expense **8 plight for** shape to be **9 something** somewhat **unseason'd** untimely, inconvenient **11 on** march on, advance (a cause) **12 Troth** (An abbreviated form of "by my troth," an affirmation of one's honesty.) **19 discover** reveal **22 register** record **sith** since **28 engross'd** made the most of, seized **fee'd** employed, made use of **30 largely** generously **31 what . . . given** what she would like to have given to her **32 on . . . occasions** i.e., on the move at every opportunity **33 meed**

reward **34 an infinite** the highest possible **37 flying** fleeing from **42 quality** nature, form **43 fair** fine **ground** property **47 honest** virtuous **enlargeth** extends the limits, widens the scope **mirth** merrymaking **48 shrewd** malicious **50 of great admittance** i.e., readily admitted into high society **authentic** admired, recognized **place** position in society **person** appearance **51 allow'd** acknowledged **preparations** accomplishments **55 amiable** amorous **honesty** honor, virtue **58 apply well** be well suited **vehemency** vehemence, passion **59 would** wish to **61 securely** confidently **62 folly** wantonness, lust **63 look'd against** looked at directly (i.e., she is as dazzling as the sun) **63 detection** i.e., accusation or exposure of her infidelity **had** would have **64 instance** precedent **argument** proof **65 ward** defensive posture (a term from fencing) **67 embattled** readied for battle **69 will** wish to **72 Want** lack **74 appointment** (See II.i.) **77 forth** away (from home) **how I speed** what progress I've made **80 wittolly** cuckoldy **80–81 for the which** for which reason **82 harvest-home** culmination of the harvest, i.e., time to reap a profit **84 mechanical** base, common (literally, refers to a manual laborer) **salt-butter** of unrefined taste (?) foul-smelling (?) **86 predominate** ascend (a term from astrology) **88 aggravate his style** expand his title (i.e., by adding the term "cuckold")

(28) IAGO AND CASSIO [II.iii.253]

Othello

SCENE: A room in Othello's castle.

{Imagine if, shortly after getting that really big promotion, you find yourself on the job in the midst of a drunken brawl when in walks your boss. Well thanks to Iago's scheming, that's pretty much how things stand at the moment for poor Cassio. The boss in question—Othello—was so disappointed in his lieutenant that he summarily discharged Cassio and marched off. Now, among the rubble of Cassio's career, Iago stands ready to take his plot of revenge one step further.}

IAGO
What, are you hurt, lieutenant?

CASSIO
Ay, past all surgery.

IAGO
Marry, God forbid!

CASSIO
Reputation, reputation, reputation! O, I have lost my reputation! I have lost the immortal part of myself, and what remains is bestial. My reputation, Iago, my reputation!

IAGO
As I am an honest man, I thought you had receiv'd some bodily wound; there is more sense in that than in reputation. Reputation is an idle and most false imposition: oft got without merit, and lost without deserving. You have lost no reputation at all, unless you repute yourself such a loser. What, man, there are ways to recover the general again. You are but now cast in his mood, a punishment more in policy than in malice, even so as one would beat his offenseless dog to affright an imperious lion. Sue to him again, and he's yours.

CASSIO
I will rather sue to be despis'd than to deceive so good a commander with so slight, so drunken, and so indiscreet an officer. Drunk? And speak parrot? And squabble? Swagger? Swear? And discourse fustian with one's own shadow? O thou invisible spirit of wine, if thou hast no name to be known by, let us call thee devil!

IAGO
What was he that you follow'd with your sword? What had he done to you?

CASSIO
I know not.

IAGO
Is 't possible?

CASSIO
I remember a mass of things, but nothing distinctly; a quarrel, but nothing wherefore. O God, that men should put an enemy in their mouths to steal away their brains! That we should, with joy, pleasance, revel, and applause, transform ourselves into beasts!

IAGO
Why, but you are now well enough. How came you thus recover'd?

CASSIO
It hath pleas'd the devil drunkenness to give place to the devil wrath. One unperfectness shows me another, to make me frankly despise myself.

IAGO
Come, you are too severe a moraler. As the time, the place, and the condition of this country stands, I could heartily wish this had not befall'n; but since it is as it is, mend it for your own good.

CASSIO
I will ask him for my place again; he shall tell me I am a drunkard! Had I as many mouths as Hydra, such an answer would stop them all. To be now a sensible man, by and by a fool, and presently a beast! O strange! Every inordinate cup is unbless'd, and the ingredient is a devil.

IAGO
Come, come, good wine is a good familiar creature, if it be well us'd. Exclaim no more against it. And, good lieutenant, I think you think I love you.

CASSIO
I have well approv'd it, sir. I drunk!

IAGO
You or any man living may be drunk at a time, man. I'll tell you what you shall do. Our general's wife is now the general—I may say so in this respect, for that he hath devoted and given up himself to the contemplation, mark, and denotement of her parts and graces. Confess yourself freely to her; importune her help to put you in your place again. She is of so free, so kind, so apt, so bless'd a disposition, she holds it a vice in her goodness not to do more than she is requested. This broken joint between you and her husband entreat her to splinter; and, my fortunes against any lay worth naming, this crack of your love shall grow stronger than it was before.

CASSIO
You advise me well.

IAGO
I protest, in the sincerity of love and honest kindness.

CASSIO
I think it freely; and betimes in the morning I will beseech the virtuous Desdemona to undertake for me. I am desperate of my fortunes if they check me here.

IAGO
You are in the right. Good night, lieutenant; I must to the watch.

CASSIO: Good night, honest Iago.

[*Exeunt.*]

3 Marry (a mild oath used to emphasize an assertion) **8 that than in** i.e., crying out over a physical wound than there is in bemoaning a loss of reputation **idle** empty, useless **9 imposition** thing artificially imposed and of no inherent value **10 repute** regard, consider **11 recover** regain favor with **general** i.e., Othello **11–12 cast . . . mood** dismissed in his fit of anger **12 in . . . in malice** to do with official business than with personal hostility **12–13 as . . . lion** (Refers to a proverbial saying of the day.) **13 Sue . . . again** i.e., humbly beg his forgiveness **16 slight** worthless **speak parrot** talk nonsense **17 discourse fustian** converse in gibberish **20 follow'd** pursued **24 wherefore** as to why (we were quarreling) **25 pleasance** delight **28 give place to** make way for **30 moraler** moralizer **31 befall'n** happened, come to pass **33 place** official position **34 Hydra** many-headed monster slain by Hercules **35 sensible man** man in possession of his senses **35–36 inordinate cup** intemperate cup, i.e., cup of wine **37 familiar** kindly **38 I think . . . love you** I believe you know that I hold you in high regard **39 approv'd** proved, demonstrated **40 at a time** at some time, on a given occasion **42 mark** observation **43 denotement** noting **parts** outstanding qualities **44 free** generous **45 apt** willing **vice** defect **46 she is requested** is requested of her **47 splinter** bind up and heal with splints **lay** wager, bet **50 protest** declare (that which is true) **51 think it freely** believe it wholeheartedly **betimes** early **52 desperate of** in despair over **check** spurn, repulse **54 watch** night watch

(29) IAGO AND OTHELLO [III.iii.95]

Othello

SCENE: A garden outside Othello's castle.

{One can't help but appreciate the sinuous and skillful way in which Iago goes about his evil work. Witness for example the following exchange, in which Iago ever-so-subtly corrupts Othello's opinion of the honorable Cassio.}

IAGO
My noble lord—

OTHELLO
What dost thou say, Iago?

IAGO
Did Michael Cassio, when you woo'd my lady,
Know of your love?

OTHELLO
He did, from first to last. Why dost thou ask?

IAGO
But for a satisfaction of my thought;
No further harm.

OTHELLO
Why of thy thought, Iago?

IAGO
I did not think he had been acquainted with her.

OTHELLO
O, yes, and went between us very oft.

IAGO
Indeed?

OTHELLO
Indeed? Ay, indeed. Discern'st thou aught in that?
Is he not honest?

IAGO
Honest, my lord?

OTHELLO
Honest. Ay, honest.

IAGO
My lord, for aught I know.

OTHELLO
What dost thou think?

IAGO
Think, my lord?

OTHELLO
Think, my lord? By heaven, he echoes me,
As if there were some monster in his thought
Too hideous to be shown. Thou dost mean something.
I heard thee say even now, thou lik'st not that,
When Cassio left my wife. What didst not like?
And when I told thee he was of my counsel
In my whole course of wooing, thou criedst "Indeed!"
And didst contract and purse thy brow together,
As if thou then hadst shut up in thy brain
Some horrible conceit. If thou dost love me,
Show me thy thought.

IAGO
My lord, you know I love you.

OTHELLO
I think thou dost;
And, for I know thou 'rt full of love and honesty,
And weigh'st thy words before thou giv'st them breath,
Therefore these stops of thine fright me the more.
For such things in a false disloyal knave
Are tricks of custom, but in a man that's just
They're close dilations, working from the heart
That passion cannot rule.

IAGO
For Michael Cassio,
I dare be sworn I think that he is honest.

OTHELLO
I think so too.

IAGO
Men should be what they seem;
Or those that be not, would they might seem none!

OTHELLO
Certain, men should be what they seem.

IAGO
Why, then, I think Cassio's an honest man.

OTHELLO
Nay, yet there's more in this.
I prithee speak to me as to thy thinkings,
As thou dost ruminate, and give thy worst of thoughts
The worst of words.

IAGO
Good my lord, pardon me.
Though I am bound to every act of duty,
I am not bound to that all slaves are free to.
Utter my thoughts? Why, say they are vile and false,
As where's that palace whereinto foul things
Sometimes intrude not? Who has a breast so pure
But some uncleanly apprehensions
Keep leets and law-days and in sessions sit
With meditations lawful?

OTHELLO
By heaven, I'll know thy thoughts.

IAGO
You cannot, if my heart were in your hand;
Nor shall not, whilst 'tis in my custody.

OTHELLO
Ha?

IAGO
O, beware, my lord, of jealousy!
It is the green-ey'd monster which doth mock
The meat it feeds on. That cuckold lives in bliss
Who, certain of his fate, loves not his wronger;
But, O, what damned minutes tells he o'er
Who dotes, yet doubts, suspects, yet strongly loves!

OTHELLO
O misery!

IAGO
Poor and content is rich, and rich enough,
But riches fineless is as poor as winter
To him that ever fears he shall be poor.
Good God, the souls of all my tribe defend
From jealousy!

OTHELLO
Why, why is this?
Think'st thou I'd make a life of jealousy,
To follow still the changes of the moon
With fresh suspicions? No, Iago,
I'll see before I doubt; when I doubt, prove;
And on the proof, there is no more but this—
Away at once with love or jealousy!

IAGO
I am glad of this, for now I shall have reason
To show the love and duty that I bear you
With franker spirit. Therefore, as I am bound,
Receive it from me. I speak not yet of proof.
Look to your wife; observe her well with Cassio.
Wear your eye thus, not jealous nor secure.
I would not have your free and noble nature,
Out of self-bounty, be abus'd. Look to 't.
I know our country disposition well;

In Venice they do let God see the pranks
They dare not show their husbands; their best conscience
Is not to leave 't undone, but keep 't unknown.

OTHELLO
Dost thou say so?

IAGO
She did deceive her father, marrying you;
And when she seem'd to shake and fear your looks,
She lov'd them most.

OTHELLO
And so she did.

IAGO
Why, go to then!
She that, so young, could give out such a seeming
To seel her father's eyes up close as oak—
He thought 'twas witchcraft—but I am much to blame;
I humbly do beseech you of your pardon
For too much loving you.

OTHELLO
I am bound to thee forever.

IAGO
I see this hath a little dash'd your spirits.

OTHELLO
Not a jot, not a jot.

IAGO
I' faith, I fear it has.
I hope you will consider what is spoke
Comes from my love. But I do see y' are mov'd.
I am to pray you not to strain my speech
To grosser issues nor to larger reach
Than to suspicion.

OTHELLO
I will not.

IAGO
Should you do so, my lord,
My speech should fall into such vile success
As my thoughts aim'd not. Cassio's my worthy friend—
My lord, I see y' are mov'd.

OTHELLO

No, not much mov'd.
I do not think but Desdemona's honest.

IAGO

Long live she so! And long live you to think so!

OTHELLO

And yet, how nature erring from itself—

IAGO

Ay, there's the point! As—to be bold with you—
Not to affect many proposed matches
Of her own clime, complexion, and degree,
Whereto we see in all things nature tends—
Foh! One may smell in such a will most rank,
Foul disproportion, thoughts unnatural.
But pardon me; I do not in position
Distinctly speak of her; though I may fear
Her will, recoiling to her better judgment,
May fall to match you with her country forms,
And happily repent.

OTHELLO

Farewell, farewell!
If more thou dost perceive, let me know more;
Set on thy wife to observe. Leave me, Iago.

IAGO

My lord, I take my leave. [*Exit.*]

8 went between us i.e., served as our go-between **10 aught** anything **20 I . . . that** (See III.iii.35.) **26 conceit** understanding, thought **30 weigh'st** carefully consider **31 stops** pauses in speaking, hesitations **33 tricks of custom** (his) usual tricks **34 close dilations** revelations of secret thoughts **35 that . . . rule** i.e., these "close dilations" are so passionately strong they cannot be restrained **42 prithee** pray thee, beg of you **46 that** that which **free to** free with respect to **50 uncleanly** improper, indecent **apprehensions** ideas, notions **51 Keep . . . law-days** hold court sessions **52 With** along with **meditations lawful** innocent thoughts **56 Ha** (An exclamation of annoyance.) **58 green-ey'd** jealous **60 his wronger** i.e., his faithless wife **61 tells he o'er** he counts over and over **65 fineless** endless, boundless **71 still** always, continually **81 not** neither **secure** unsuspicious **83 self-bounty** innate goodness **91 go to** (An exclamation of impatience or exasperation.) **92 seeming** misleading appearance **93 seel...up** sew up, i.e., blind, her fathers eyes (The term comes from falconry.) **oak** (Oak being a tight-grained wood.) **99 I' faith** in good faith, in truth (A mild oath.) **103 grosser issues** greater significance **reach** meaning scope **109 honest** virtuous **113 affect** desire, choose (from) **114 clime** land, region **116 will** lust **117 disproportion** abnormality, unfitness **118 position** assertion **120 recoiling** reverting **121 fall . . . forms** set about comparing you with Venetian standards of handsomeness **122 happily repent** will perhaps repent (her marriage) **124 Set on** urge

(30) IAGO AND OTHELLO [III.iii.330]

Othello

SCENE: A garden outside Othello's castle.

{Iago's scheme to smear Desdemona and Cassio—and destroy Othello in the process—has nearly reached fruition. Here, the tormented Moor lashes out at Iago as he grapples with both his need to know the truth and his desire to remain blissfully ignorant.}

IAGO
The Moor already changes with my poison.
Dangerous conceits are, in their natures, poisons,
Which at the first are scarce found to distaste,
But with a little act upon the blood
Burn like the mines of sulphur. I did say so.
Look, where he comes!
[*Enter Othello.*]

Not poppy, nor mandragora,
Nor all the drowsy syrups of the world,
Shall ever medicine thee to that sweet sleep
Which thou ow'dst yesterday.

OTHELLO
Ha, ha, false to me?

IAGO
Why, how now, general? No more of that.

OTHELLO
Avaunt! Be gone! Thou hast set me on the rack:

I swear 'tis better to be much abus'd
Than but to know 't a little.

IAGO

How now, my lord?

OTHELLO

What sense had I of her stol'n hours of lust?
I saw 't not, thought it not, it harm'd not me.
I slept the next night well, fed well, was free and merry;
I found not Cassio's kisses on her lips.
He that is robb'd, not wanting what is stol'n,
Let him not know 't, and he's not robb'd at all.

IAGO

I am sorry to hear this.

OTHELLO

I had been happy if the general camp,
Pioners and all, had tasted her sweet body,
So I had nothing known. O, now, forever
Farewell the tranquil mind! Farewell content!

IAGO

Is 't possible, my lord?

OTHELLO

Villain, be sure thou prove my love a whore!
Be sure of it. Give me the ocular proof,
Or by the worth of mine eternal soul,
Thou hadst been better have been born a dog
Than answer my wak'd wrath!

IAGO

Is 't come to this?

OTHELLO

Make me to see 't; or, at the least, so prove it
That the probation bear no hinge nor loop
To hang a doubt on; or woe upon thy life!

IAGO

My noble lord—

OTHELLO

If thou dost slander her and torture me,
Never pray more; abandon all remorse;
On horror's head horrors accumulate;

Do deeds to make heaven weep, all earth amaz'd;
For nothing canst thou to damnation add
Greater than that.

IAGO
O grace! O heaven forgive me!
Are you a man? Have you a soul or sense?
God buy you; take mine office. O wretched fool,
That liv'st to make thine honesty a vice!
O monstrous world! Take note, take note, O world,
To be direct and honest is not safe.
I thank you for this profit, and from hence
I'll love no friend, sith love breeds such offense.

OTHELLO
Nay, stay. Thou shouldst be honest.

IAGO
I should be wise, for honesty's a fool
And loses that it works for.

OTHELLO
By the world,
I think my wife be honest and think she is not;
I think that thou art just and think thou art not.
I'll have some proof. Would I were satisfied!

IAGO
But how? How satisfied, my lord?
Would you, the supervisor, grossly gape on?
Behold her topp'd?

OTHELLO
Death and damnation! O!

IAGO
It were a tedious difficulty, I think,
To bring them to that prospect; damn them, then,
If ever mortal eyes do see them bolster
More than their own. What then? How then?
What shall I say? Where's satisfaction?

OTHELLO
Give me a living reason she's disloyal.

IAGO
I do not like the office:
But, sith I am ent'red in this cause so far,

Prick'd to 't by foolish honesty and love,
I will go on. I lay with Cassio lately,
And, being troubled with a raging tooth,
I could not sleep. There are a kind of men
So loose of soul that in their sleeps will mutter
Their affairs. One of this kind is Cassio.
In sleep I heard him say, "Sweet Desdemona,
Let us be wary, let us hide our loves."
And then, sir, would he gripe and wring my hand,
Cry "O sweet creature!" and then kiss me hard,
As if he pluck'd up kisses by the roots
That grew upon my lips; then laid his leg
Over my thigh, and sigh'd, and kiss'd; and then
Cried, "Cursed fate that gave thee to the Moor!"

OTHELLO
O monstrous! Monstrous!

IAGO
Nay, this was but his dream.

OTHELLO
But this denoted a foregone conclusion.
'Tis a shrewd doubt, though it be but a dream.

IAGO
And this may help to thicken other proofs
That do demonstrate thinly.

OTHELLO
I'll tear her all to pieces.

IAGO
Nay, but be wise. Yet we see nothing done;
She may be honest yet. Tell me but this;
Have you not sometimes seen a handkerchief
Spotted with strawberries in your wife's hand?

OTHELLO
I gave her such a one; 'twas my first gift.

IAGO
I know not that; but such a handkerchief—
I am sure it was your wife's—did I today
See Cassio wipe his beard with.

OTHELLO
If it be that—

IAGO
If it be that, or any that was hers,
It speaks against her with the other proofs.

OTHELLO
O, that the slave had forty thousand lives!
One is too poor, too weak for my revenge.

IAGO
Yet be content; your mind perhaps may change.

OTHELLO
Never, Iago. Like to the Pontic Sea,
Whose icy current and compulsive course
Nev'r feels retiring ebb, but keeps due on
To the Propontic and the Hellespont,
Even so my bloody thoughts, with violent pace,
Shall nev'r look back, nev'r ebb to humble love,
Till that a capable and wide revenge
Swallow them up. [*He kneels.*] Now, by yond marble heaven,
In the due reverence of a sacred vow
I here engage my words.

IAGO
Do not rise yet. [*Kneels.*]
Witness, you ever-burning lights above,
You elements that clip us round about,
Witness that here Iago doth give up
The execution of his wit, hands, heart,
To wrong'd Othello's service! Let him command,
And to obey shall be in me remorse,
What bloody business ever. [*They rise.*]

OTHELLO
I greet thy love,
Not with vain thanks, but with acceptance bounteous,
And will upon the instant put thee to 't.
Within these three days let me hear thee say
That Cassio's not alive.

IAGO
My friend is dead;
'Tis done at your request. But let her live.

OTHELLO

Damn her, lewd minx! O, damn her, damn her!
Come, go with me apart. I will withdraw
To furnish me with some swift means of death
For the fair devil. Now art thou my lieutenant.

IAGO

I am your own for ever.

[*Exeunt.*]

2 conceits ideas, thoughts **3 scarce** rarely **distaste** taste foul **4 with . . . act** after they acted for a little while **blood** emotion (The blood was considered to be the seat of one's emotions.) **6 mandragora** opiate made from the mandrake root **7 drowsy** sleep-inducing **8 medicine thee** act as a medicine to bring you **9 ow'dst** owned, had **11 Avaunt** away **14 stol'n** secret, furtive **16 free** carefree **18 wanting** missing **21 the general** i.e., every soldier in **22 Pioners** the lowest grade of soldiers, employed primarily in jobs such as digging and mining **27 ocular** visible **32 probation** proof **36 remorse** compassion **37 horrors accumulate** heap on even more atrocities **38 all** i.e., all those inhabiting **39 to** to your **42 God buy you** God be with you, i.e., goodbye **office** assigned position **43 a vice** your failing **46 profit** profitable instruction, valuable lesson **47 sith** since **offense** injustice (to the one who loves) **48 stay** wait **Thou shouldst be** it appears that you are honest (In reply to which Iago then uses "should be" in its "ought to be" sense.) **52 just** honorable, loyal **55 supervisor** spectator **grossly** blatantly **56 topp'd** copulated with **59 prospect** scene, situation **59–61 damn . . . own** i.e., to condemn them only if human eyes other than their own see them in bed together **64 office** assignment **70 loose** undisciplined, lacking in restraint **74 gripe** grab, grip **81 a foregone conclusion** an act already committed **82 shrewd doubt** compelling reason to suspect **83 thicken** strengthen **98 Pontic** Black Sea **99 compulsive** propulsive **100 retiring** receding, subsiding **101 Propontic** small sea between the Bosporus and Hellespont straits into which the Black Sea flows **103 ebb** fade, retreat **104 capable** capacious, huge **105 marble** shining like marble (?) enduring (?) **109 clip** enclose **111 execution** action **wit** mind **113 remorse** compassion, pity (for "wrong'd Othello") **115 vain** empty **120 minx** hussy, wanton **121 apart** to another place, somewhere

(31) IAGO AND OTHELLO [IV.1.1]

Othello

SCENE: Before Othello's castle.

{Yet another of Iago's deliciously sinister machinations, this one focused on further poisoning Othello's mind against Cassio and Desdemona.}

[*Enter Othello and Iago.*]

IAGO
Will you think so?

OTHELLO
Think so, Iago?

IAGO
What,
To kiss in private?

OTHELLO
An unauthoriz'd kiss!

IAGO
Or to be naked with her friend in bed
An hour or more, not meaning any harm?

OTHELLO
Naked in bed, Iago, and not mean harm?
It is hypocrisy against the devil.
They that mean virtuously, and yet do so,
The devil their virtue tempts, and they tempt heaven.

IAGO
If they do nothing, 'tis a venial slip.
But if I give my wife a handkerchief—

OTHELLO
What then?

IAGO
Why, then, 'tis hers, my lord; and, being hers,
She may, I think, bestow 't on any man.

OTHELLO
She is protectress of her honor too;
May she give that?

IAGO
Her honor is an essence that's not seen;
They have it very oft that have it not.
But, for the handkerchief—

OTHELLO
By heaven, I would most gladly have forgot it.
Thou said'st—O, it comes o'er my memory,
As doth the raven o'er the infectious house,
Boding to all—he had my handkerchief.

IAGO
Ay, what of that?

OTHELLO
That's not so good now.

IAGO
What
If I had said I had seen him do you wrong?
Or heard him say—as knaves be such abroad,
Who having, by their own importunate suit,
Or voluntary dotage of some mistress,
Convinced or supplied them, cannot choose
But they must blab—

OTHELLO
Hath he said anything?

IAGO
He hath, my lord; but be you well assur'd,
No more than he'll unswear.

OTHELLO
What hath he said?

IAGO
Faith, that he did—I know not what he did.

OTHELLO
What? What?

IAGO
Lie—

OTHELLO

With her?

IAGO

With her, on her; what you will.

OTHELLO

Lie with her? Lie on her? We say lie on her, when they belie her. Lie with her! 'Zounds, that's fulsome.—Handkerchief—confessions—handkerchief!—To confess, and be hang'd for his labor—first, to be hang'd, and then to confess.—I tremble at it. Nature would not invest herself in such shadowing passion without some instruction. It is not words that shakes me thus. Pish! Noses, ears, and lips.—Is 't possible?—Confess—handkerchief!—O devil! [*Falls in a trance.*]

IAGO

Work on,
My medicine, work! Thus credulous fools are caught;
And many worthy and chaste dames even thus,
All guiltless, meet reproach.

9 venial slip minor sin **10 handkerchief** (See III.iii.290.) **17 They . . . not** i.e., often, people are given credit for having honor when in fact they do not have it **21 raven . . . house** (Some believed that the raven hovered over a home stricken with an infectious disease.) **28 Convinced** seduced, conquered **supplied** satisfied the desires of **31 unswear** disavow **32 Faith** by my faith (a mild oath) **36 'Zounds** a contraction of the popular interjection, "God's Wounds" **fulsome** filthy, disgusting **38–39 Nature . . . instruction** i.e., without some basis in fact (i.e., Desdemona's infidelity) for doing so, Nature would not present herself in me as such an overwhelming fit of emotion **42 medicine** i.e., machinations

(32) Iago and Roderigo [IV.ii.174]

Othello

SCENE: A room in Othello's castle.

{Iago takes time out from tormenting Othello (see prior entries) to work his black magic on an unwitting and witless Roderigo. Seems that the would-be suitor to Desdemona is not entirely satisfied with Iago's performance as a go-between.}

[*Enter Roderigo.*]

IAGO
How now, Roderigo?

RODERIGO
I do not find that thou deal'st justly with me.

IAGO
What in the contrary?

RODERIGO
Every day thou daff'st me with some device, Iago, and rather, as it seems to me now, keep'st from me all conveniency than suppliest me with the least advantage of hope. I will indeed no longer endure it, nor am I yet persuaded to put up in peace what already I have foolishly suff'red.

IAGO
Will you hear me, Roderigo?

RODERIGO
Faith, I have heard too much, for your words and performances are no kin together.

IAGO
You charge me most unjustly.

RODERIGO
With nought but truth. I have wasted myself out of my means. The jewels you have had from me to deliver to Desdemona would half have corrupted a votarist. You have told me she hath receiv'd them and return'd me expectations and comforts of sudden respect and acquaintance, but I find none.

IAGO
Well, go to; very well.

RODERIGO
Very well! Go to! I cannot go to, man, nor 'tis not very well. By this hand, I think it is scurvy, and begin to find myself fopp'd in it.

IAGO
Very well.

RODERIGO
I tell you 'tis not very well. I will make myself known to Desdemona. If she will return me my jewels, I will give over my suit and repent my unlawful solicitation; if not, assure yourself I will seek satisfaction of you.

IAGO
You have said now.

RODERIGO
Ay, and said nothing but what I protest intendment of doing.

IAGO
Why, now I see there's mettle in thee, and even from this instant do build on thee a better opinion than ever before. Give me thy hand, Roderigo. Thou hast taken against me a most just exception; but yet I protest I have dealt most directly in thy affair.

RODERIGO
It hath not appear'd.

IAGO
I grant indeed it hath not appear'd, and your suspicion is not without wit and judgment. But, Roderigo, if thou hast that in thee indeed which I have greater reason to believe now than ever—I mean purpose, courage, and valor—this night show it. If thou the next night following enjoy not Desdemona, take me from this world with treachery and device engines for my life.

RODERIGO
Well, what is it? Is it within reason and compass?

IAGO
Sir, there is especial commission come from Venice to depute Cassio in Othello's place.

RODERIGO
Is that true? Why, then Othello and Desdemona return again to Venice.

IAGO
O, no; he goes into Mauritania and taketh away with him the fair Desdemona, unless his abode be ling'red here by some accident; wherein none can be so determinate as the removing of Cassio.

RODERIGO
How do you mean, removing him?

IAGO
Why, by making him uncapable of Othello's place; knocking out his brains.

RODERIGO
And that you would have me to do?

IAGO

Ay, if you dare do yourself a profit and a right. He sups tonight with a harlotry, and thither will I go to him. He knows not yet of his honorable fortune. If you will watch his going thence, which I will fashion to fall out between twelve and one, you may take him at your pleasure. I will be near to second your attempt, and he shall fall between us. Come, stand not amaz'd at it, but go along with me; I will show you such a necessity in his death that you shall think yourself bound to put it on him. It is now high supper-time, and the night grows to waste. About it.

RODERIGO

I will hear further reason for this.

IAGO

And you shall be satisfied.

[*Exeunt.*]

3 What . . . contrary i.e., in what way have I dealt with you unjustly **4 daff'st me** put me off **device** ploy **5 conveniency** opportunity (to meet with Desdemona) **7 put . . . peace** meekly accept, peacefully tolerate **9 Faith** by my faith (a mild oath) **12 wasted . . . of** i.e., spent beyond **14 votarist** nun **return'd** in return given **15 sudden respect** immediate consideration **16 go to** (a common interjection on the order of "come now," used to convey disapproval or impatience) **18 fopp'd** made a fool of, duped **21 give over** give up on, abandon **22 of** from **24 said** had your say **intendment** intention **27 exception** objection **30 wit** reason **34 engines for** plots against **36 compass** reach, feasibility **37 depute** appoint **41 abode be ling'red** stay be extended **42 determinate** decisive, effective **44 uncapable of** i.e., incapable of assuming **46–47 harlotry** harlot **48 thence** from there **fashion . . . out** see to it happens, contrive to take place **50 he . . . us** between the two of us, he will die **53 grows to waste** i.e., wastes away **About it** (an exhortation similar to "let's go" or "get moving") **54 will** want to **reason** argument

(33) SECOND MURDERER AND FIRST MURDERER [I.IV.100]

Richard III

SCENE: The Tower of London.

{Richard has commissioned these two swords for hire to assassinate his brother, the Duke of Gloucester. But no sooner does the odd couple enter the Duke's cell than second thoughts start flying.}

SECOND MURDERER
What, shall we stab him as he sleeps?

FIRST MURDERER
No. He'll say 'twas done cowardly, when he wakes.

SECOND MURDERER
Why, he shall never wake till the Judgment Day.

FIRST MURDERER
Why, then he'll say we stabb'd him sleeping.

SECOND MURDERER
The urging of that word "judgment" hath bred a kind of remorse in me.

FIRST MURDERER
What, art thou afraid?

SECOND MURDERER
Not to kill him, having a warrant; but to be damn'd for killing him, from the which no warrant can defend me.

FIRST MURDERER
I thought thou hadst been resolute.

SECOND MURDERER
So I am—to let him live.

FIRST MURDERER
I'll back to the Duke of Gloucester, and tell him so.

SECOND MURDERER
Nay, I prithee, stay a little. I hope this passionate humor of mine will change. It was wont to hold me but while one tells twenty.

FIRST MURDERER
How dost thou feel thyself now?

SECOND MURDERER
Faith, some certain dregs of conscience are yet within me.

FIRST MURDERER
Remember our reward when the deed's done.

SECOND MURDERER
'Zounds, he dies! I had forgot the reward.

FIRST MURDERER
Where's thy conscience now?

SECOND MURDERER
O, in the Duke of Gloucester's purse.

FIRST MURDERER
When he opens his purse to give us our reward, thy conscience flies out.

SECOND MURDERER
'Tis no matter, let it go. There's few or none will entertain it.

FIRST MURDERER
What if it come to thee again?

SECOND MURDERER
I'll not meddle with it; it makes a man a coward. A man cannot steal, but it accuseth him; a man cannot swear, but it checks him; a man cannot lie with his neighbor's wife, but it detects him. 'Tis a blushing shamefac'd spirit that mutinies in a man's bosom. It fills a man full of obstacles. It made me once restore a purse of gold that by chance I found. It beggars any man that keeps it. It is turn'd out of towns and cities for a dangerous thing, and every man that means to live well endeavors to trust to himself and live without it.

FIRST MURDERER
'Zounds, 'tis even now at my elbow, persuading me not to kill the Duke.

SECOND MURDERER
Take the devil in thy mind, and believe him not. He would insinuate with thee but to make thee sigh.

FIRST MURDERER
I am strong-fram'd; he cannot prevail with me.

SECOND MURDERER
Spoke like a tall man that respects thy reputation. Come, shall we fall to work?

FIRST MURDERER
Take him on the costard with the hilts of thy sword, and then throw him into the malmsey-butt in the next room.

SECOND MURDERER
O excellent device! And make a sop of him.

FIRST MURDERER
Soft, he wakes.

SECOND MURDERER
Strike!

5 urging mention **remorse** compassion **12 prithee** pray thee, beg you **stay** wait **passionate humor** compassionate mood **13 wont . . . twenty** in the habit of keeping a hold on me only as long as it takes to count to twenty **15 Faith** by my faith (a mild oath) **dregs** last bits **17 'Zounds** a contraction of the popular interjection, "God's Wounds" **21 entertain it** welcome it as a guest **24 checks** reprimands **27 beggars** makes a beggar of **31 Take** suppress, check **the . . . mind** i.e., your devilish conscience **insinuate** ingratiate himself, curry favor **32 but** only **34 tall** brave **fall to** begin **35 Take** strike **costard** apple, i.e., head **hilts** hilt, handle **36 malmsey-butt** wine cask (Malmsey is a strong, sweet wine.) **37 device** plan **sop** piece of bread or other food soaked in wine before being eaten **38 Soft** wait, hold on

(34) ALCIBIADES AND TIMON [IV.III.49]

Timon of Athens

SCENE: Before Timon's cave.

{With the fast life and false friends of Athens far behind him, Timon now contents himself with a solitary existence out here in the woods. Which explains why an unexpected (and unappreciated) drop-in by Alcibiades garners the banished captain little but scorn for his trouble.}

[*Enter Alcibiades.*]

ALCIBIADES
What art thou there? Speak.

TIMON
A beast, as thou art. The canker gnaw thy heart
For showing me again the eyes of man!

ALCIBIADES
What is thy name? Is man so hateful to thee,
That art thyself a man?

TIMON
I am Misanthropos, and hate mankind.
For thy part, I do wish thou wert a dog,
That I might love thee something.

ALCIBIADES
I know thee well,
But in thy fortunes am unlearn'd and strange.

TIMON
I know thee too; and more than that I know thee
I not desire to know. Follow thy drum;
With man's blood paint the ground, gules, gules:
Religious canons, civil laws are cruel;
Then what should war be?

ALCIBIADES
How came the noble Timon to this change?

TIMON
As the moon does, by wanting light to give.
But then renew I could not, like the moon;
There were no suns to borrow of.

ALCIBIADES
Noble Timon,
What friendship may I do thee?

TIMON
None, but to
Maintain my opinion.

ALCIBIADES
What is it, Timon?

TIMON
Promise me friendship, but perform none. If thou wilt not promise, the gods plague thee, for thou art a man! If thou dost perform, confound thee, for thou art a man!

ALCIBIADES
I have heard in some sort of thy miseries;
How cursed Athens, mindless of thy worth,
Forgetting thy great deeds, when neighbor states,
But for thy sword and fortune, trod upon them—

TIMON
I prithee beat thy drum and get thee gone.

ALCIBIADES
I am thy friend, and pity thee, dear Timon.

TIMON
How dost thou pity him whom thou dost trouble?
I had rather be alone.

ALCIBIADES
Why, fare thee well. Here is some gold for thee. [*Offers gold.*]

TIMON
Keep it; I cannot eat it.

ALCIBIADES
When I have laid proud Athens on a heap—

TIMON
Warr'st thou 'gainst Athens?

ALCIBIADES
Ay, Timon, and have cause.

TIMON
The gods confound them all in thy conquest;
And thee after, when thou hast conquer'd!

ALCIBIADES
Why me, Timon?

TIMON
That by killing of villains
Thou wast born to conquer my country.
Put up thy gold: go on—here's gold—go on; [*Offers gold.*]
Be as a planetary plague, when Jove
Will o'er some high-vic'd city hang his poison
In the sick air. Let not thy sword skip one.
Make large confusion; and, thy fury spent,
Confounded be thyself! Speak not, be gone.

ALCIBIADES
Hast thou gold yet? I'll take the gold thou givest me,
Not all thy counsel.

TIMON
Dost thou, or dost thou not, heaven's curse upon thee!

ALCIBIADES
Farewell, Timon.
If I thrive well, I'll visit thee again.

TIMON
If I hope well, I'll never see thee more.

ALCIBIADES
I never did thee harm.

TIMON
Yes, thou spokest well of me.

ALCIBIADES
Call'st thou that harm?

TIMON
Men daily find it. Get thee away.

[*Exit Alcibiades.*]

2 The canker gnaw a malignant sore eat away at **6 Misanthropos** hater of mankind **8 something** somewhat, a bit **9 unlearn'd** uninformed **strange** ignorant **11 not** do not **drum** (The drum was a symbol of war.) **12 gules** a term from heraldry meaning the color of red **16 wanting** lacking **21–23 If . . . man!** i.e., if you will not falsely promise friendship, damn you anyway just for being a man; if you promise friendship and keep your word, damn you still—because you are still a man **24 in . . . of** a little about, something of **27 But** were it not **trod** (would have) trod **28 prithee** pray thee, beg of you **38 That** in that, because **40 planetary plague** (Some believed that the planets could exert a malicious influence upon earthly matters.) **42 high-vic'd** extremely wicked **43 one** i.e., citizen of Athens **44 large confusion** widespread ruin, wholesale destruction **47 Not** but not **48 Dost . . . not** whether you do or do not (take my counsel) **51 If . . . well** If I hope successfully, i.e., if my dreams come true **54 daily find it** i.e., discover every day that it is harmful to be wished well

(35) Speed and Proteus [I.i.71]

The Two Gentlemen of Verona

SCENE: A street in Verona.

{The fact that he's frantically searching for his master, Valentine, who is about to set sail for Milan, seems neither here nor there for the quick-witted Speed—at least not when he has a chance to crack wise with the equally-clever Proteus.}

[*Enter Speed.*]

SPEED
Sir Proteus, save you! Saw you my master?

PROTEUS
But now he parted hence, to embark for Milan.

SPEED
Twenty to one then he is shipp'd already,
And I have play'd the sheep in losing him.

PROTEUS
Indeed, a sheep doth very often stray,
An if the shepherd be a while away.

SPEED
You conclude that my master is a shepherd, then, and I a sheep?

PROTEUS
I do.

SPEED
Why then, my horns are his horns, whether I wake or sleep.

PROTEUS
A silly answer, and fitting well a sheep.

SPEED
This proves me still a sheep.

PROTEUS
True; and thy master a shepherd.

SPEED
Nay, that I can deny by a circumstance.

PROTEUS
It shall go hard but I'll prove it by another.

SPEED
The shepherd seeks the sheep, and not the sheep the shepherd; but I seek my master, and my master seeks not me. Therefore I am no sheep.

PROTEUS
The sheep for fodder follow the shepherd; the shepherd for food follows not the sheep. Thou for wages followest thy master; thy master for wages follows not thee. Therefore thou art a sheep.

SPEED
Such another proof will make me cry "baa."

PROTEUS
But, dost thou hear? Gav'st thou my letter to Julia?

SPEED
Ay sir. I, a lost mutton, gave your letter to her, a lac'd mutton; and she, a lac'd mutton, gave me, a lost mutton, nothing for my labor.

PROTEUS
Here's too small a pasture for such store of muttons.

SPEED
If the ground be overcharg'd, you were best stick her.

PROTEUS
Nay, in that you are astray, 'twere best pound you.

SPEED
Nay, sir, less than a pound shall serve me for carrying your letter.

PROTEUS
You mistake; I mean the pound—a pinfold.

SPEED
From a pound to a pin? Fold it over and over, 'Tis threefold too little for carrying a letter to your lover.

PROTEUS
But what said she?

SPEED
[*Nodding.*] Ay.

PROTEUS
Nod—Ay—why, that's "noddy."

SPEED
You mistook, sir. I say, she did nod; and you ask me if she did nod, and I say, "Ay."

PROTEUS
And that set together is "noddy."

SPEED
Now you have taken the pains to set it together, take it for your pains.

PROTEUS
No, no, you shall have it for bearing the letter.

SPEED
Well, I perceive I must be fain to bear with you.

PROTEUS
Why, sir, how do you bear with me?

SPEED
Marry, sir, the letter, very orderly; having nothing but the word "noddy" for my pains.

PROTEUS
Beshrew me, but you have a quick wit.

SPEED
And yet it cannot overtake your slow purse.

PROTEUS
Come, come, open the matter in brief: what said she?

SPEED
Open your purse, that the money and the matter may be both at once deliver'd.

PROTEUS
[*Gives him money.*] Well, sir, here is for your pains. What said she?

SPEED
Truly, sir, I think you'll hardly win her.

PROTEUS
Why, couldst thou perceive so much from her?

SPEED
Sir, I could perceive nothing at all from her; no, not so much as a ducat for delivering your letter. And being so hard to me that brought your mind, I fear she'll prove as hard to you in telling your mind. Give her no token but stones, for she's as hard as steel.

PROTEUS
What said she? Nothing?

SPEED
No, not so much as "Take this for thy pains." To testify your bounty, I thank you, you have testern'd me; in requital whereof, henceforth carry your letters yourself. And so, sir, I'll commend you to my master.

PROTEUS
Go, go, be gone, to save your ship from wrack,
Which cannot perish having thee aboard,
Being destin'd to a drier death on shore.

[*Exit Speed.*]
I must go send some better messenger.
I fear my Julia would not deign my lines,
Receiving them from such a worthless post.

[*Exit.*]

1 save you may God save you (a common greeting of the day) **2 But** just **hence** away from this place **3, 4 shipp'd, sheep** (These two words made for a nice pun to Elizabethan ears, in that they were pronounced almost identically.) **6 An if** if **9 my . . . horns** he owns my horns, i.e., he is a cuckold (which, according to tradition, sprouted horns) **13 circumstance** process of reasoning **14 It . . . I'll** i.e., I'll be in serious trouble if I cannot **20 "baa"** (with a play on "bah, humbug") **22 lost, lac'd** (another play on words that sounded alike to Elizabethan audiences) **lac'd mutton** ("mutton" was also slang for "whore;" "lac'd" refers to the laces of her bodice or corset) **24 store** an abundance **25 overcharg'd** overcrowded **stick** stab (with a bawdy pun), slaughter **26 astray** (1) wandering off like a lost sheep (2) beyond the bounds of propriety, going too far **pound you** (1) close you up in a pound (an enclosure for stray animals) (2) beat on you **27 pound** 20 shillings in English currency **28 pinfold** pen for stray animals **29 pin** i.e., an object of little worth **Fold** multiply **33 "noddy"** a blockhead, simpleton **37 taken . . . to** carefully and thoughtfully **your pains** your efforts **39 fain** obliged, content **bear with** (1) put up with (2) act as carrier for **41 Marry** (a mild oath uttered to emphasize a point) **very orderly** as expected, according to form **43 Beshrew me** (a mild oath on the order of "curse me") **44 slow** slow to appear, reluctant **45 open** lay out, disclose **49 hardly win** have a hard time winning **50 perceive** receive **ducat** coin worth about 1/3 of a pound **51 mind** intentions, thoughts of her **52 in telling** when you tell her **53 stones** jewels **55 testify** demonstrate, provide proof of **bounty** generosity **56 testern'd** given me a tester (a coin worth just sixpence) **57 commend you** deliver your greetings **58 wrack** shipwreck **59–60 Which . . . shore** (Alludes to the saying, "He that is born to be hanged shall never be drowned.") **60 Being** since you are **62 deign** lower herself (to accept) **63 post** (1) messenger (2) blockhead

(36) SPEED AND LAUNCE [II.v.1]

The Two Gentlemen of Verona

SCENE: A street in Milan.

{Here on the streets of Milan, a pair of old friends from Verona flex their wits just for the heck of it.}

[*Enter Speed and Launce, from different directions.*]

SPEED
Launce! By mine honesty, welcome to Milan!

LAUNCE
Forswear not thyself, sweet youth, for I am not welcome. I reckon this always, that a man is never undone till he be hang'd, nor never welcome to a place till some certain shot be paid and the hostess say "Welcome!"

SPEED
Come on, you madcap, I'll to the alehouse with you presently; where, for one shot of five pence, thou shalt have five thousand welcomes. But, sirrah, how did thy master part with Madam Julia?

LAUNCE
Marry, after they clos'd in earnest, they parted very fairly in jest.

SPEED
But shall she marry him?

LAUNCE
No.

SPEED
How then? Shall he marry her?

LAUNCE
No, neither.

SPEED
What, are they broken?

LAUNCE
No, they are both as whole as a fish.

SPEED
Why, then, how stands the matter with them?

LAUNCE
Marry, thus: when it stands well with him, it stands well with her.

SPEED
What an ass art thou! I understand thee not.

LAUNCE
What a block art thou, that thou canst not! My staff understands me.

SPEED
What thou say'st?

LAUNCE
Ay, and what I do too. Look thee, I'll but lean, and my staff understands me.

SPEED
It stands under thee, indeed.

LAUNCE
Why, stand-under and under-stand is all one.

SPEED
But tell me true, will 't be a match?

LAUNCE
Ask my dog. If he say ay, it will; if he say no, it will; if he shake his tail and say nothing, it will.

SPEED
The conclusion is then that it will.

LAUNCE
Thou shalt never get such a secret from me but by a parable.

SPEED
'Tis well that I get it so. But, Launce, how say'st thou, that my master is become a notable lover?

LAUNCE
I never knew him otherwise.

SPEED
Than how?

LAUNCE
A notable lubber, as thou reportest him to be.

SPEED
Why, thou whoreson ass, thou mistak'st me.

LAUNCE
Why, fool, I meant not thee; I meant thy master.

SPEED
I tell thee, my master is become a hot lover.

LAUNCE
Why, I tell thee, I care not though he burn himself in love. If thou wilt, with me to the alehouse; if not, thou art an Hebrew, a Jew, and not worth the name of a Christian.

SPEED
Why?

LAUNCE
Because thou hast not so much charity in thee as to go to the ale with a Christian. Wilt thou go?

SPEED
At thy service.

[*Exeunt.*]

1 By mine honesty (a mild oath affirming one's sincerity) **3 undone** doomed, ruined **4 some certain shot** his bar tab, his tavern bill **6 pence** pennies, cents **sirrah** (A form of address often used between servants of equal standing.) **8 Marry** (a mild oath uttered to emphasize a point) **clos'd** (1) embraced (2) came to an agreement **fairly** warmly, gently **12 broken** estranged, no longer together (though Launce proceeds to play on the sense "broken into pieces") **16 when . . . well** (with a bawdy reference to male genitalia) **20 staff** walking stick **27 a parable** i.e., roundabout fashion, indirect route **28 how say'st thou** what do you say to this **32 lubber** oaf, clumsy fool **33 whoreson** bastard, detestable (used here in a friendly manner) **36–37 go . . . alehouse** i.e., go to a church-ale (a festival at which ale was sold to raise money for the church)

(37) CLOWN AND SHEPHERD [III.iii.58]

The Winter's Tale

SCENE: A deserted area near the Bohemian seacoast.

{By command of King Leontes, Queen Hermione's newborn babe has been abandoned here on the desolate shores of Bohemia. With a storm rising and ravenous bears on the prowl, it looks like it's curtains for the little girl. But then along comes this kindly old shepherd...}

[*Enter a Shepherd.*]

SHEPHERD

I would there were no age between ten and three-and-twenty, or that youth would sleep out the rest; for there is nothing in the between but getting wenches with child, wronging the ancientry, stealing, fighting—Hark you now! Would any but these boil'd brains of nineteen and two-and-twenty hunt this weather? They have scar'd away two of my best sheep, which I fear the wolf will sooner find than the master. If anywhere I have them, 'tis by the seaside, browsing of ivy. Good luck, an 't be thy will! [*Sees the infant.*] What have we here? Mercy on 's, a barne, a very pretty barne! A boy or a child, I wonder? A pretty one, a very pretty one. Sure, some scape. Though I am not bookish, yet I can read waiting-gentlewoman in the scape. This has been some stair-work, some trunk-work, some behind-door-work. They were warmer that got this than the poor thing is here. I'll take it up for pity. Yet I'll tarry till my son come; he halloo'd but even now. Whoa, ho, hoa!

[*Enter Clown.*]

CLOWN

Hilloa, loa!

SHEPHERD

What, art so near? If thou'lt see a thing to talk on when thou art dead and rotten, come hither. What ail'st thou, man?

CLOWN

I have seen two such sights, by sea and by land! But I am not to say it is a sea, for it is now the sky; betwixt the firmament and it you cannot thrust a bodkin's point.

SHEPHERD

Why, boy, how is it?

CLOWN

I would you did but see how it chafes, how it rages, how it takes up the shore! But that's not the point. O, the most piteous cry of the poor souls! Sometimes to see 'em, and not to see 'em; now the ship boring the moon with her main-mast, and anon swallow'd with yest and froth, as you'd thrust a cork into a hogshead. And then for the land-service, to see how the bear tore out his shoulder-bone; how he cried to me for help and said his name was Antigonus, a nobleman. But to make an end of the ship, to see how the sea flap-dragon'd it; but, first, how the poor souls roar'd, and the sea mock'd them; and how the poor gentleman roar'd and the bear mock'd him, both roaring louder than the sea or weather.

SHEPHERD

Name of mercy, when was this, boy?

CLOWN
Now, now. I have not wink'd since I saw these sights. The men are not yet cold under water, nor the bear half din.d on the gentleman. He's at it now.

SHEPHERD
Would I had been by, to have help'd the old man!

CLOWN
I would you had been by the ship side, to have help'd her. There your charity would have lack'd footing.

SHEPHERD
Heavy matters, heavy matters! But look thee here, boy. Now bless thyself. Thou mett'st with things dying, I with things new-born. Here's a sight for thee; look thee, a bearing-cloth for a squire's child! Look thee here; take up, take up, boy; open 't. So, let's see. It was told me I should be rich by the fairies. This is some changeling. Open 't. What's within, boy?

CLOWN
[*He opens the bundle.*] You're a made old man. If the sins of your youth are forgiven you, you're well to live. Gold, all gold!

SHEPHERD
This is fairy gold, boy, and 'twill prove so. Up with 't, keep it close. Home, home, the next way. We are lucky, boy; and to be so still requires nothing but secrecy. Let my sheep go. Come, good boy, the next way home.

CLOWN
Go you the next way with your findings. I'll go see if the bear be gone from the gentleman and how much he hath eaten. They are never curst but when they are hungry. If there be any of him left, I'll bury it.

SHEPHERD
That's a good deed. If thou mayest discern by that which is left of him what he is, fetch me to th' sight of him.

CLOWN
Marry, will I; and you shall help to put him i' th' ground.

SHEPHERD
'Tis a lucky day, boy, and we'll do good deeds on 't.

[*Exeunt.*]

I would wish that **3 ancientry** elders **4 boil'd brains** hot-headed creatures **nineteen . . . twenty** (Apparently two young hunters, ages nineteen and twenty-two, have managed to frighten away a pair of the shepherd's sheep.)

5 this in this **7 browsing of** grazing on **an . . . will** if it be God's will **8 barne** child **9 child** female infant **scape** transgression, escapade (of a sexual nature) **11 stair, trunk, behind-door** (Shepherd is referring to a few of the more likely spots for an impromptu sexual liaison.) **12 warmer** (with a play on hot-blooded, i.e., passionate) **got** begot **13 my son** (The shepherd's son is known here only as "Clown," a term that merely pegs him as a country-dweller.) **15 art** are you **18 now the sky** i.e., rages so violently that it seems to touch the sky **betwixt . . . it** i.e., between the sky and the sea **19 bodkin's** needle's **21 takes up** contends with, rebukes **24 anon** soon thereafter **yest** foam **25 hogshead** large oak barrel **land-service** events on land **27 Antigonus** (For an account of Antigonus' presence in the area, see III.iii.) **make an end** i.e., conclude my tale **28 flap-dragon'd it** swallowed it as one would a "flapdragon" (which was a flaming raisin afloat in a glass of burning liquor) **36 footing** a firm foothold (with a play on the word's "foundation" sense, as in "charity without funding") **39 bearing-cloth** fine cloth in which a child was carried to its baptism **41 changeling** child left by fairies **43 well to live** well to do **44 close** secret **45 next** quickest, shortest **be so still** go on being so **48 curst** ferocious, vicious **52 Marry** (a mild oath uttered to emphasize a point)

(38) CLOWN AND AUTOLYCUS [IV.III.32]

The Winter's Tale

SCENE: A road in the Bohemian countryside.

{Autolycus is a peddler, rogue and small-time thief who is particularly adept at fleecing country bumpkins. Right on cue, enter Clown—a simple soul on his way to purchase supplies for a sheep-shearing festival, and just made to order for the likes of Autolycus.}

[*Enter Clown.*]

CLOWN

Let me see: every 'leven wether tods; every tod yields pound and odd shilling; fifteen hundred shorn, what comes the wool to?

AUTOLYCUS

[*Aside.*] If the springe hold, the cock's mine.

CLOWN
I cannot do 't without counters. Let me see; what am I to buy for our sheep-shearing feast? Three pound of sugar, five pound of currants, rice—what will this sister of mine do with rice? But my father hath made her mistress of the feast, and she lays it on. She hath made me four and twenty nosegays for the shearers—three-man-song-men all, and very good ones, but they are most of them means and bases; but one puritan amongst them, and he sings psalms to hornpipes. I must have saffron to color the warden pies; mace; dates?—none, that's out of my note; nutmegs, seven; a race or two of ginger, but that I may beg; four pound of prunes, and as many of raisins o' th' sun.

AUTOLYCUS
O that ever I was born! [*Groveling on the ground.*]

CLOWN
I' th' name of me—

AUTOLYCUS
O, help me, help me! Pluck but off these rags; and then, death, death!

CLOWN
Alack, poor soul! Thou hast need of more rags to lay on thee, rather than have these off.

AUTOLYCUS
O sir, the loathsomeness of them offends me more than the stripes I have receiv'd, which are mighty ones and millions.

CLOWN
Alas, poor man! A million of beating may come to a great matter.

AUTOLYCUS
I am robb'd, sir, and beaten; my money and apparel ta'en from me, and these detestable things put upon me.

CLOWN
What, by a horseman, or a footman?

AUTOLYCUS
A footman, sweet sir, a footman.

CLOWN
Indeed, he should be a footman by the garments he has left with thee. If this be a horseman's coat, it hath seen very hot service. Lend me thy hand, I'll help thee. Come, lend me thy hand. [*Helps him up.*]

AUTOLYCUS
O, good sir, tenderly, O!

CLOWN
Alas, poor soul!

AUTOLYCUS
O, good sir, softly, good sir! I fear, sir, my shoulder-blade is out.

CLOWN
How now? Canst stand?

AUTOLYCUS
[*Picking Clown's pocket.*] Softly, dear sir; good sir, softly. You ha' done me a charitable office.

CLOWN
Dost lack any money? I have a little money for thee.

AUTOLYCUS
No, good sweet sir; no, I beseech you, sir. I have a kinsman not past three quarters of a mile hence, unto whom I was going. I shall there have money, or any thing I want. Offer me no money, I pray you; that kills my heart.

CLOWN
What manner of fellow was he that robb'd you?

AUTOLYCUS
A fellow, sir, that I have known to go about with troll-my-dames. I knew him once a servant of the Prince. I cannot tell, good sir, for which of his virtues it was, but he was certainly whipp'd out of the court.

CLOWN
His vices, you would say; there's no virtue whipp'd out of the court. They cherish it to make it stay there; and yet it will no more but abide.

AUTOLYCUS
Vices, I would say, sir. I know this man well. He hath been since an ape-bearer, then a process-server, a bailiff. Then he compass'd a motion of the Prodigal Son, and married a tinker's wife within a mile where my land and living lies; and, having flown over many knavish professions, he settled only in rogue. Some call him Autolycus.

CLOWN
Out upon him! Prig, for my life, prig! He haunts wakes, fairs and bear-baitings.

AUTOLYCUS
Very true, sir; he, sir, he. That's the rogue that put me into this apparel.

CLOWN
Not a more cowardly rogue in all Bohemia If you had but look'd big and spit at him, he'd have run.

AUTOLYCUS
I must confess to you, sir, I am no fighter. I am false of heart that way, and that he knew, I warrant him.

CLOWN
How do you now?

AUTOLYCUS
Sweet sir, much better than I was; I can stand and walk. I will even take my leave of you, and pace softly towards my kinsman's.

CLOWN
Shall I bring thee on the way?

AUTOLYCUS
No, good-fac'd sir; no, sweet sir.

CLOWN
Then fare thee well. I must go buy spices for our sheep-shearing. [*Exit.*]

AUTOLYCUS
Prosper you, sweet sir! Your purse is not hot enough to purchase your spice. I'll be with you at your sheep-shearing too. If I make not this cheat bring out another, and the shearers prove sheep, let me be unroll'd and my name put in the book of virtue! [*Singing.*]

Jog on, jog on, the foot-path way,
  And merrily hent the stile-a;
A merry heart goes all the day,
  Your sad tires in a mile-a.

[*Exit.*]

1 every 'leven wether every eleven sheep produce **tods** a tod (i.e., 28 pounds of wool) **1–2 yields . . . shilling** will bring in currency a pound and a shilling **3 springe** snare used to trap birds **cock** woodcock (thought to be a particularly stupid bird) **4 counters** coin-like metal discs used in reckoning **7 lays it on** does it up big, does it well **8 nosegays** small bouquets of flowers **three-man-song-men** male singers of three-part songs **9 means** tenors **but** only **puritan** male singer with a very high voice **10 to hornpipes** i.e., to the music of dance tunes **10–11 warden pies** pies made of warden, or winter, pears **11 mace** spice made from the nutmeg seed **out . . . note** not on my list **race** root **13 o' th' sun** sun dried **16 Pluck but off** just strip off **19 stripes** i.e., wounds from whipping **24 horseman . . . footman** i.e., mounted robber or one traveling on foot **25 footman** (Here, Clown uses the word in its "servant" sense, in that a common servant might well have shoddy garments.) **27 hot** intense, severe **31 softly** gently **40 go . . . troll-my-dames** i.e., play troll-my-dames, a game involving balls and hoops **44 abide** stay briefly **45–46 ape-bearer** performer who employs a tame monkey as part of his act **46 compass'd** came up with (?) toured about with (?) **motion** puppet show **50 Out upon** (A common exclamation, expressing indignation or disgust.) **Prig** thief **wakes** village festivals **51 bear-baiting** a "sport" in which vicious dogs attacked a chained bear **53 big** menacing **60 bring . . . way** accompany you part of the way **61 good-fac'd** handsome **63 hot** potent (with a play on the sense "spicy") **64–65 cheat bring out** thievery bring about **65 me be unroll'd** i.e., my name be removed from the register ("roll") of theives **68 hent** grasp (in order to leap over) **stile** set of steps that enable one to climb over a fence or wall

SCENES FOR ONE ACTRESS AND ONE ACTOR

(39) DIANA AND BERTRAM [IV.II.1]

All's Well That Ends Well

SCENE: The Widow Capilet's house.

{Being married off to Helena against his will hasn't stopped Bertram from pursuing his heart's desire—which at the moment happens to be the fair Diana. What Bertram doesn't realize, however, is that this rendezvous at Diana's home is all part of a plot cooked up by Diana, her mother and Helena to secure both Bertram's ring and his eventual return to Helena.}

BERTRAM
They told me that your name was Fontibell.

DIANA
No, my good lord, Diana.

BERTRAM
Titled goddess,
And worth it, with addition! But, fair soul,
In your fine frame hath love no quality?
If the quick fire of youth light not your mind,
You are no maiden, but a monument.
When you are dead, you should be such a one
As you are now; for you are cold and stern,
And now you should be as your mother was
When your sweet self was got.

DIANA
She then was honest.

BERTRAM
So should you be.

DIANA

No.
My mother did but duty—such, my lord,
As you owe to your wife.

BERTRAM

No more o' that;
I prithee, do not strive against my vows.
I was compell'd to her; but I love thee
By love's own sweet constraint, and will for ever
Do thee all rights of service.

DIANA

Ay, so you serve us
Till we serve you; but when you have our roses,
You barely leave our thorns to prick ourselves
And mock us with our bareness.

BERTRAM

How have I sworn!

DIANA

'Tis not the many oaths that makes the truth,
But the plain single vow that is vow'd true.
What is not holy, that we swear not by,
But take the High'st to witness. Then pray you tell me,
If I should swear by Jove's great attributes
I lov'd you dearly, would you believe my oaths
When I did love you ill? This has no holding,
To swear by Him whom I protest to love,
That I will work against Him. Therefore your oaths
Are words and poor conditions, but unseal'd—
At least in my opinion.

BERTRAM

Change it, change it;
Be not so holy-cruel. Love is holy,
And my integrity ne'er knew the crafts
That you do charge men with. Stand no more off,
But give thyself unto my sick desires,
Who then recover. Say thou art mine, and ever
My love as it begins shall so persever.

DIANA

I see that men may rope 's in such a snare
That we'll forsake ourselves. Give me that ring.

BERTRAM
I'll lend it thee, my dear, but have no power
To give it from me.

DIANA
Will you not, my lord?

BERTRAM
It is an honor 'longing to our house,
Bequeathed down from many ancestors,
Which were the greatest obloquy i' th' world
In me to lose.

DIANA
Mine honor's such a ring.
My chastity's the jewel of our house,
Bequeathed down from many ancestors;
Which were the greatest obloquy i' th' world
In me to lose. Thus your own proper wisdom
Brings in the champion Honor on my part,
Against your vain assault.

BERTRAM
Here, take my ring!
My house, mine honor, yea, my life, be thine,
And I'll be bid by thee. [*Gives her the ring.*]

DIANA
When midnight comes, knock at my chamber-window.
I'll order take my mother shall not hear.
Now will I charge you in the band of truth,
When you have conquer'd my yet maiden bed,
Remain there but an hour, nor speak to me.
My reasons are most strong, and you shall know them
When back again this ring shall be deliver'd.
And on your finger in the night I'll put
Another ring, that what in time proceeds
May token to the future our past deeds.
Adieu, till then; then, fail not. You have won
A wife of me, though there my hope be done.

BERTRAM
A heaven on earth I have won by wooing thee.

[*Exit.*]

DIANA
For which live long to thank both heaven and me!
You may so in the end.
My mother told me just how he would woo,
As if she sat in 's heart. She says all men
Have the like oaths. He had sworn to marry me
When his wife's dead; therefore I'll lie with him
When I am buried. Since Frenchmen are so braid,
Marry that will, I live and die a maid.
Only in this disguise I think 't no sin
To cozen him that would unjustly win.

[*Exit.*]

2–3 Titled . . . addition you, bearing a goddess' name, and worthy of that honor and more **4 quality** position, rank **5 quick** invigorating **10 got** begotten **11 honest** virtuous (Bertram, in turn, opts to play on the word's "frank" meaning.) **14 vows** i.e., vows to live apart from Helena **18 serve you** i.e., sexually (The bawdy wordplay continues with "roses" and "prick.") **19 barely** bare, exposed **20 our bareness** i.e., the loss of our virginity ("roses") **24 pray you** I beg you **27 ill** wickedly, in ways unsanctioned by religion **has no holding** makes no sense, has no consistency **28 protest** profess **29 work against Him** i.e., act in defiance of God's prohibition of illicit sex **30 words** mere words **poor . . . unseal'd** poorly drawn contracts lacking the official seal that would make them legally binding **32 holy-cruel** cruelly adherent to your religious scruples **33 crafts** schemes **36 Who** which **37 persever** persevere **38 rope 's** rope us, entrap us **39 Give . . . ring** (For background on the ring's significance, see III.ii and III.vii.) **44 obloquy** disgrace **45 honor's** virtue is **50 part** side **53 bid** commanded **54 chamber** bedchamber **55 order take** take care that **56 band** bond **58 but** only **62 that . . . proceeds** which, whatever happens **63 token** symbolize, indicate **65 of** in **though . . . done** even though my hope for a legitimate marriage is there by destroyed **71 like** same **had** has(?) would have (?) **73 braid** devious **74 Marry that** let those marry who **76 cozen** cheat

(40) CLEOPATRA AND ANTONY [I.III.13]

Antony and Cleopatra

SCENE: Cleopatra's palace.

{Unrest back home means that Antony must immediately return to Rome, leaving behind both Egypt and his indulgent lifestyle with Cleopatra. This

sudden turn of events does not sit well with the Queen, and she lets Antony know as much.}

CLEOPATRA
I am sick and sullen.

ANTONY
I am sorry to give breathing to my purpose—

CLEOPATRA
Pray you stand farther from me.

ANTONY
What's the matter?

CLEOPATRA
I know by that same eye there's some good news.
What, says the married woman you may go?
Would she had never given you leave to come!
Let her not say 'tis I that keep you here.
I have no power upon you; hers you are.

ANTONY
The gods best know—

CLEOPATRA
O, never was there queen
So mightily betray'd! Yet at the first
I saw the treasons planted.

ANTONY
Cleopatra—

CLEOPATRA
Why should I think you can be mine, and true,
Though you in swearing shake the throned gods,
Who have been false to Fulvia? Riotous madness,
To be entangled with those mouth-made vows,
Which break themselves in swearing!

ANTONY
Most sweet queen—

CLEOPATRA
Nay, pray you, seek no color for your going,
But bid farewell, and go. When you sued staying,
Then was the time for words. No going then;

Eternity was in our lips and eyes,
Bliss in our brows' bent; none our parts so poor
But was a race of heaven. They are so still,
Or thou, the greatest soldier of the world,
Art turn'd the greatest liar.

ANTONY

How now, lady?

CLEOPATRA
I would I had thy inches; thou shouldst know
There were a heart in Egypt.

ANTONY

Hear me, Queen:
The strong necessity of time commands
Our services awhile, but my full heart
Remains in use with you. Our Italy
Shines o'er with civil swords; Sextus Pompeius
Makes his approaches to the port of Rome;
Equality of two domestic powers
Breed scrupulous faction; the hated, grown to strength,
Are newly grown to love; the condemn'd Pompey,
Rich in his father's honor, creeps apace
Into the hearts of such as have not thrived
Upon the present state, whose numbers threaten;
And quietness, grown sick of rest, would purge
By any desperate change. My more particular,
And that which most with you should safe my going,
Is Fulvia's death.

CLEOPATRA
Though age from folly could not give me freedom,
It does from childishness. Can Fulvia die?

ANTONY
She's dead, my queen.
Look here, and at thy sovereign leisure read
The garboils she awak'd. At the last, best,
See when and where she died. [*Offers letters.*]

CLEOPATRA

O most false love!
Where be the sacred vials thou shouldst fill
With sorrowful water? Now I see, I see,
In Fulvia's death, how mine receiv'd shall be.

ANTONY
Quarrel no more, but be prepar'd to know
The purposes I bear; which are, or cease,
As you shall give th' advice. By the fire
That quickens Nilus' slime, I go from hence
Thy soldier, servant, making peace or war
As thou affects.

CLEOPATRA
I am quickly ill, and well,
So Antony loves.

ANTONY
My precious queen, forbear,
And give true evidence to his love which stands
An honorable trial.

CLEOPATRA
So Fulvia told me.
I prithee, turn aside and weep for her;
Then bid adieu to me, and say the tears
Belong to Egypt. Good now, play one scene
Of excellent dissembling; and let it look
Life perfect honor.

ANTONY
You'll heat my blood; no more.

CLEOPATRA
You can do better yet; but this is meetly.

ANTONY
Now, by my sword—

CLEOPATRA
And target. Still he mends.
But this is not the best. Look, prithee,
How this Herculean Roman does become
The carriage of his chafe.

ANTONY
I'll leave you, lady.

CLEOPATRA
Courteous lord, one word.
Sir, you and I must part, but that's not it;
Sir, you and I have lov'd, but there's not it;

That you know well. Something it is I would—
O, my oblivion is a very Antony,
And I am all forgotten.

ANTONY

But that your royalty
Holds idleness your subject, I should take you
For idleness itself.

CLEOPATRA

'Tis sweating labor
To bear such idleness so near the heart
As Cleopatra this. But, sir, forgive me,
Since my becomings kill me when they do not
Eye well to you. Your honor calls you hence;
Therefore be deaf to my unpitied folly,
And all the gods go with you! Upon your sword
Sit laurel victory, and smooth success
Be strew'd before your feet!

ANTONY

Let us go. Come;
Our separation so abides and flies,
That thou, residing here, goes yet with me,
And I, hence fleeting, here remain with thee. Away!

[*Exeunt.*]

1 sullen depressed **2 breathing** voice, utterance **3 Pray you** I beg you **5 married woman** i.e., Antony's wife, Fulvia **15 mouth-made** insincere **16 break . . . swearing** are broken as soon as they are sworn **17 color** pretext **18 sued staying** begged to stay **20 our** (Cleopatra is using the royal plural) **21 bent** arch **22 was . . . heaven** it was of heavenly origin **25 inches** height, manly proportions **26 were . . . Egypt** was courage in the Queen of Egypt **28 Our** my **30 civil swords** i.e., swords wielded in civil unrest **Sextus Pompeius** (a leader of the revolt against Rome) **32 Equality . . . powers** (Refers to the power sharing arrangement agreed to by Octavius Caesar and Antony.) **33 scrupulous faction** political factions uncertain in their allegiance **34 Are . . . love** have recently risen in esteem **35 apace** quickly **36–37 thrived . . . state** prospered under the present government **38 purge** heal itself (The thinking was that an extended peace ("quietness") bred disease in the body politic that could only be purged by war.) **39 particular** personal reason **40 most . . . safe** should reassure you most about **46 garboils** commotions, disturbances **best** best of all **48 sacred vials** (Alludes to the supposed custom of putting tear-filled vials in the tombs of the departed.) **52–53 which . . . advice** which will proceed, or not, as you shall determine **53 the fire** i.e., the sun **54 quickens** brings to life **54 Nilus' slime** sediment deposited by the Nile river **hence** this place **56 affects** desires **57 So** so long as (?) **58 give true evidence** bear true witness **stands** will withstand **60 prithee** pray thee, beg thee **62 Belong to Egypt** are shed for Cleopatra **65 meetly** not bad, pretty good **66 target** shield **mends** improves (i.e., his "scene of excellent dissembling") **68–69 How . . . chafe** how handsomely Antony (who claims Hercules as an ancestor) bears his rage **74 oblivion . . . Antony** forgetfulness is like Antony himself (who will forget me) **75 am all forgotten** (1) forgot was I was about to say (2) am entirely forgotten by Antony **But** were it not **76 idleness** absurd banter, frivolity **77 sweating labor** difficult work **78 such idleness** such apparent frivolity **80 my becomings** even those qualities that become me **81 Eye** appear **84 laurel** wreathed with laurel **86 abides and flies** stays and goes

(41) IMOGEN AND IACHIMO [I.vi.11]

Cymbeline

SCENE: Cymbeline's palace.

{Back in Italy, Iachimo made a wager with Posthumus that he would have no problem seducing Posthumus' wife, Imogen. Now, having completed the arduous journey to Britain, Iachimo arrives at Imogen's home to try and make good on his boast.}

IACHIMO
Change you, madam;
The worthy Leonatus is in safety
And greets your highness dearly.

IMOGEN
Thanks, good sir.
You're kindly welcome. Continues well my lord?
His health, beseech you?

IACHIMO
Well, madam.

IMOGEN
Is he dispos'd to mirth? I hope he is.

IACHIMO
Exceeding pleasant; none a stranger there
So merry and so gamesome. He is call'd
The Britain reveler.

IMOGEN
When he was here,
He did incline to sadness, and oft-times
Not knowing why.

IACHIMO
I never saw him sad.
There is a Frenchman his companion, one
An eminent monsieur that, it seems, much loves
A Gallian girl at home. He furnaces
The thick sighs from him, whiles the jolly Britain—
Your lord, I mean—laughs from 's free lungs, cries "O,
Can my sides hold, to think that man, who knows
By history, report, or his own proof,
What woman is, yea, what she cannot choose
But must be, will 's free hours languish for
Assured bondage?"

IMOGEN
Will my lord say so?

IACHIMO
Ay, madam, with his eyes in flood with laughter.
It is a recreation to be by
And hear him mock the Frenchman. But, heavens know,
Some men are much to blame.

IMOGEN
Not he, I hope.

IACHIMO
Not he; but yet heaven's bounty towards him might
Be us'd more thankfully. In himself, 'tis much;
In you, which I account his, beyond all talents.
Whilst I am bound to wonder, I am bound
To pity too.

IMOGEN
What do you pity, sir?

IACHIMO
Two creatures heartily.

IMOGEN

Am I one, sir?
You look on me. What wrack discern you in me
Deserves your pity?

IACHIMO

Lamentable! What,
To hide me from the radiant sun and solace
I' th' dungeon by a snuff?

IMOGEN

I pray you, sir,
Deliver with more openness your answers
To my demands. Why do you pity me?

IACHIMO

That others do—
I was about to say—enjoy your—But
It is an office of the gods to venge it,
Not mine to speak on 't.

IMOGEN

You do seem to know
Something of me, or what concerns me. Pray you—
Since doubting things go ill often hurts more
Than to be sure they do; for certainties
Either are past remedies, or, timely knowing,
The remedy then born—discover to me
What both you spur and stop.

IACHIMO

Had I this cheek
To bathe my lips upon; this hand, whose touch,
Whose every touch, would force the feeler's soul
To th' oath of loyalty; this object, which
Takes prisoner the wild motion of mine eye,
Fixing it only here; should I, damn'd then,
Slaver with lips as common as the stairs
That mount the Capitol; join gripes with hands
Made hard with hourly falsehood—falsehood, as
With labor; then by-peeping in an eye
Base and illustrous as the smoky light
That's fed with stinking tallow; it were fit
That all the plagues of hell should at one time
Encounter such revolt.

IMOGEN

My lord, I fear,
Has forgot Britain.

IACHIMO

And himself. Not I,
Inclin'd to this intelligence, pronounce
The beggary of his change; but 'tis your graces
That from my mutest conscience to my tongue
Charms this report out.

IMOGEN

Let me hear no more.

IACHIMO

O dearest soul, your cause doth strike my heart
With pity that doth make me sick. A lady
So fair, and fasten'd to an empery
Would make the great'st king double—to be partner'd
With tomboys hir'd with that self exhibition
Which your own coffers yield; with diseas'd ventures
That play with all infirmities for gold
Which rottenness can lend nature; such boil'd stuff
As well might poison poison! Be reveng'd;
Or she that bore you was no queen, and you
Recoil from your great stock.

IMOGEN

Reveng'd?
How should I be reveng'd? If this be true—
As I have such a heart that both mine ears
Must not in haste abuse—if it be true,
How should I be reveng'd?

IACHIMO

Should he make me
Live, like Diana's priest, betwixt cold sheets,
Whiles he is vaulting variable ramps,
In your despite, upon your purse? Revenge it.
I dedicate myself to your sweet pleasure,
More noble than that runagate to your bed,
And will continue fast to your affection,
Still close as sure.

IMOGEN

What, ho, Pisanio!

IACHIMO
Let me my service tender on your lips.

IMOGEN
Away! I do condemn mine ears that have
So long attended thee. If thou wert honorable,
Thou wouldst have told this tale for virtue, not
For such an end thou seek'st—as base as strange.
Thou wrong'st a gentleman who is as far
From thy report as thou from honor, and
Solicit here a lady that disdains
Thee and the devil alike. What ho, Pisanio!
The King my father shall be made acquainted
Of thy assault. If he shall think it fit
A saucy stranger in his court to mart
As in a Romish stew, and to expound
His beastly mind to us, he hath a court
He little cares for and a daughter who
He not respects at all. What, ho, Pisanio!

IACHIMO
O happy Leonatus! I may say
The credit that thy lady hath of thee
Deserves thy trust, and thy most perfect goodness
Her assur'd credit. Blessed live you long,
A lady to the worthiest sir that ever
Country call'd his, and you his mistress, only
For the most worthiest fit! Give me your pardon.
I have spoke this to know if your affiance
Were deeply rooted, and shall make your lord,
That which he is, new o'er; and he is one
The truest manner'd, such a holy witch
That he enchants societies into him.
Half all men's hearts are his.

IMOGEN
You make amends.

IACHIMO
He sits 'mongst men like a descended god.
He hath a kind of honor sets him off,
More than a mortal seeming. Be not angry,
Most mighty Princess, that I have adventur'd
To try your taking of a false report, which hath
Honor'd with confirmation your great judgment
In the election of a sir so rare,

Which you know cannot err. The love I bear him
Made me to fan you thus, but the gods made you,
Unlike all others, chaffless. Pray, your pardon.

IMOGEN
All's well, sir. Take my pow'r i' th' court for yours.

IACHIMO
My humble thanks.

1 Change you change your mood, cheer up **2 Leonatus** (Posthumus' full name is Posthumus Leonatus.) **8 none a stranger** no other foreigner **11 sadness** seriousness **15 Gallian** French **furnaces** exhales, gives forth (like a furnace) **16 thick** frequent **17 from . . . lungs** unrestrained **19 proof** experience **21 languish** pine **22 Assured bondage** i.e., bonds of matrimony **23 in flood with** flooding with tears of **24 by** nearby **27 heaven's . . . him** the qualities bestowed on him by heaven **28 In . . . much** i.e., insofar as his own qualities go, heaven has given much **29 In you** i.e., heaven's generosity in giving him you **talents** riches **32 heartily** earnestly **33 wrack** wreckage, ruin **35 hide me** hide **solace** take pleasure **36 snuff** burned-out candlewick **41 office** task, duty **43 Pray you** I beg you **44 doubting** fearing that, suspecting **46 timely knowing** if one knows in time **47 then** is then **discover** reveal **48 What . . . stop** what you both goad yourself to say and then stop yourself from saying it **51 object** one who, upon being scene, excites great love or other emotion **54 Slaver** give slobbery kisses **common** base, lowly **55 gripes** grips **56–57 as With labor** as if made by hard labor **57 by-peeping** glancing sideways **58 illustrous** dull, lacking luster **61 Encounter** do battle with **revolt** faithlessness **62–63 Not . . . pronounce** not through any inclination to reveal this information do I report **64 beggary . . . change** his fall into degradation **65 mutest conscience** most silent inner knowledge **69 empery** empire **70 double** twice as powerful **70–71 partner'd With** put on a level with **71 tomboys** harlots **self exhibition** very same allowance (of money) **72 ventures** risks for commercial gain **73–74 That . . . nature** who for money risk all the infirmities which venereal disease ("rottenness") inflicts on the body and mind ("nature") **74 boil'd stuff** i.e., women who had undergone the "sweating" cure for venereal disease **77 Recoil** degenerate, regress from **83 Diana** goddess of chastity **priest** priestess **84 vaulting variable ramps** mounting various harlots **85 your despite** contempt of you **87 runagate** renegade **88 fast** true, firm **89 Still** ever **close** secret **sure** trustworthy, loyal **What, ho, Pisanio!** (Imogen calls for help from Pisanio, Posthumus' servant, who left a few moments earlier to run an errand.) **92 attended** listened to **94 as strange** as it is strange **101 mart** haggle, bargain **102 Romish** Roman **stew** brothel **106 Leonatus** (Posthumus' proper name is Posthumus Leonatus.) **107 credit . . . of** faith . . . in **109 credit**

trust **111 Country call'd his** a country called its own **113 affiance** trust **115 new o'er** renewed, made over again **115–116 one . . . manner'd** above all others well behaved **116 witch** charmer **117 societies into** entire groups of people to **122 adventur'd** dared **123 try** test **127 fan** test **128 chaffless** faultless **129 pow'r** influence, standing

(42) IMOGEN AND PISANIO [III.IV.I]

Cymbeline

SCENE: The Welsh countryside near Milford-Haven.

{When Imogen received word from her banished husband, Posthumus, that he was longing to meet with her out here in the Welsh countryside, she was understandably overjoyed. Little did she suspect that the good news was part of a plot—hatched by Posthumus and executed by his servant, Pisanio—to take her life.}

IMOGEN
Thou told'st me, when we came from horse, the place
Was near at hand. Ne'er long'd my mother so
To see me first, as I have now. Pisanio, man,
Where is Posthumus? What is in thy mind
That makes thee stare thus?

PISANIO
[*Offering her a letter.*] Please you, read,
And you shall find me, wretched man, a thing
The most disdain'd of fortune.

IMOGEN
[*Reads the letter.*] "Thy mistress, Pisanio, hath play'd the strumpet in my bed; the testimonies whereof lie bleeding in me. I speak not out of weak surmises, but from proof as strong as my grief and as certain as I expect my revenge. That part thou, Pisanio, must act for me, if thy faith be not tainted with the breach of hers. Let thine own hands take away her life. I shall give thee opportunity at Milford-Haven—she hath my letter for the purpose—where, if thou fear to strike and to make me certain it is done, thou art the pander to her dishonor and equally to me disloyal."

PISANIO
What shall I need to draw my sword? The paper
Hath cut her throat already.

IMOGEN
False to his bed? What is it to be false?
To lie in watch there and to think on him?
To weep 'twixt clock and clock? If sleep charge nature,
To break it with a fearful dream of him
And cry myself awake? That's false to 's bed, is it?

PISANIO
Alas, good lady!

IMOGEN
I false? Thy conscience witness! Iachimo,
Thou didst accuse him of incontinency.
Thou then look'dst like a villain; now methinks
Thy favor's good enough.
[*Draws sword and offers it to him.*]
Come, do thou thy master's bidding. When thou see'st him,
A little witness my obedience. Look,
I draw the sword myself. Take it, and hit
The innocent mansion of my love, my heart.
Fear not; 'tis empty of all things but grief.
Thy master is not there, who was indeed
The riches of it. Do his bidding, strike.
Thou mayst be valiant in a better cause,
But now thou seem'st a coward.

PISANIO
[*He rejects the sword.*] Hence, vile instrument!
Thou shalt not damn my hand.

IMOGEN
Why, I must die;
And if I do not by thy hand, thou art
No servant of thy master's. Against self-slaughter
There is a prohibition so divine
That cravens my weak hand. Come, here's my heart;
The lamb entreats the butcher. Where's thy knife?
Thou art too slow to do thy master's bidding,
When I desire it too.

PISANIO
O gracious lady,
Since I receiv'd command to do this business
I have not slept one wink.

IMOGEN
Do 't, and to bed then.

PISANIO
I'll wake mine eyeballs blind first.

IMOGEN
Wherefore then
Didst undertake it? Why hast thou gone so far,
To be unbent when thou hast ta'en thy stand,
The elected deer before thee?

PISANIO
But to win time
To lose so bad employment, in the which
I have consider'd of a course. Good lady,
Hear me with patience.

IMOGEN
Talk thy tongue weary, speak.
I have heard I am a strumpet, and mine ear,
Therein false struck, can take no greater wound,
Nor tent to bottom that. But speak.

PISANIO
Then, madam,
I thought you would not back again.

IMOGEN
Most like,
Bringing me here to kill me.

PISANIO
Not so, neither.
But if I were as wise as honest, then
My purpose would prove well. It cannot be
But that my master is abus'd. Some villain,
Ay, and singular in his art, hath done
You both this cursed injury.

IMOGEN
Some Roman courtezan.

PISANIO
No, on my life.
I'll give but notice you are dead, and send him
Some bloody sign of it, for 'tis commanded
I should do so. You shall be miss'd at court,
And that will well confirm it.

IMOGEN

Why, good fellow,
What shall I do the while? Where bide? How live?
Or in my life what comfort, when I am
Dead to my husband?

PISANIO

If you'll back to th' court—

IMOGEN

No court, no father, nor no more ado
With that harsh, noble, simple nothing,
That Cloten, whose love-suit hath been to me
As fearful as a siege.

PISANIO

If not at court,
Then not in Britain must you bide.

IMOGEN

Where then?
Hath Britain all the sun that shines? Day, night,
Are they not but in Britain? I' th' world's volume
Our Britain seems as of it, but not in 't;
In a great pool a swan's nest. Prithee think
There's livers out of Britain.

PISANIO

I am most glad
You think of other place. The ambassador,
Lucius the Roman, comes to Milford-Haven
Tomorrow. Now, if you could wear a mind
Dark as your fortune is, and but disguise
That which, t' appear itself, must not yet be
But by self-danger, you should tread a course
Pretty and full of view.

IMOGEN

O, for such means!
Though peril to my modesty, not death on 't,
I would adventure.

PISANIO

Well, then, here's the point:
You must forget to be a woman; change
Command into obedience, fear and niceness

Into a waggish courage; ready in gibes,
Quick-answer'd, saucy and as quarrelous
As the weasel. Nay, you must—

IMOGEN

Nay, be brief.
I see into thy end, and am almost
A man already.

PISANIO

First, make yourself but like one.
Forethinking this, I have already fit—
'Tis in my cloak-bag—doublet, hat, hose, all
That answer to them. Would you in their serving,
And with what imitation you can borrow
From youth of such a season, 'fore noble Lucius
Present yourself, desire his service, tell him
Wherein you're happy—which will make him know,
If that his head have ear in music—doubtless
With joy he will embrace you, for he's honorable,
And doubling that, most holy. Your means abroad,
You have me, rich; and I will never fail
Beginning nor supplyment.

IMOGEN

Thou art all the comfort
The gods will diet me with. Prithee, away.
There's more to be consider'd, but we'll even
All that good time will give us. This attempt
I am soldier to, and will abide it with
A prince's courage. Away, I prithee.

[*Exeunt, severally.*]

1 came from horse dismounted our horses **3 have now** i.e., now long to see Posthumus **11 expect** expect (will be) **12 That part** (i.e., of avenger) **21 'twixt . . . and clock** hour after hour **charge nature** overcome wakefulness **22 break it** cut it short **fearful . . . him** i.e., dream in which I was full of fear for his safety **25–26 Iachimo . . . incontinency** (In his attempt to corrupt Imogen, Iachimo falsely claimed that Posthumus was back in Italy indulging himself in all manner of wanton behaviors; see I.vi.) **28 favor's** countenance, appearance **30 A little witness** testify a little to **35 riches** most precious thing **37 Hence** away from here **42 cravens** it makes cowardly **48 wake . . . blind** stay awake until I go blind **50 be unbent** unbend your bow (i.e., refuse to kill your prey) **51 elected** chosen **52 the which** which time **56 take** receive, suffer **57 tent . . . that** probe that wound to its bottom (A tent was a roll of cloth used to probe and cleanse a wound; to apply a tent, then, was to "tent" a wound.) **58 like** likely **62 abus'd** deceived **63 singular** unmatched, without peer **74 noble** of a noble family (Cloten is the Queen's son by a former husband.) **79 Are . . . but** do they exist only in **80 as . . . 't** i.e., a part of it, but only a small and removed part **81 Prithee** I pray thee, I beg you **83 livers** living persons, human beings **84–85 Lucius . . . Tomorrow** (See II.iii.) **86 Dark** lowly (?) obscure (?) **87 That** i.e., the fact that you are a woman **appear itself** show itself undisguised **89 Pretty . . . view** advantageous and promising **92–93 change . . . obedience** i.e., change from one who commands (Imogen being a queen's daughter) to one who obeys **94 waggish** masculine, roguish **95 Quick-answer'd** sharp in reply **quarrelous** quarrelsome **99 Forethinking** anticipating **fit** ready **101 answer to** go along with **in their serving** aided by them **103 season** age **'fore** before **104 desire his service** request employment in service to him **105 happy** gifted, accomplished **make him know** convince him **106 If . . . music** i.e., if he has an ear for music **107 embrace** happily receive you into his service **108 Your means abroad** as for your financial needs while you're abroad **110 supplyment** continuing support **111 diet** nourish **112 even** profit by, take advantage of **114 soldier to** committed to **abide** bear

(43) OPHELIA AND HAMLET [III.i.89]

Hamlet

SCENE: A chamber in Elsinore Castle.

{While wandering the castle and contemplating the rotten state of Denmark, Hamlet spies fair Ophelia quietly reading a book. What begins as a friendly exchange between the two soon turns dark—so dark in fact that one has to wonder if Hamlet might have detected Polonius and Claudius lurking nearby, eavesdropping on every word.}

HAMLET

Soft you now,
The fair Ophelia. Nymph, in thy orisons
Be all my sins rememb'red.

OPHELIA

Good my lord,
How does your honor for this many a day?

HAMLET
I humbly thank you; well, well, well.

OPHELIA
My lord, I have remembrances of yours
That I have longed long to re-deliver.
I pray you, now receive them. [*Offers tokens.*]

HAMLET
No, not I; I never gave you aught.

OPHELIA
My honor'd lord, you know right well you did,
And with them words of so sweet breath compos'd
As made the things more rich. Their perfume lost,
Take these again, for to the noble mind
Rich gifts wax poor when givers prove unkind.
There, my lord. [*Gives tokens.*]

HAMLET
Ha, ha! Are you honest?

OPHELIA
My lord?

HAMLET
Are you fair?

OPHELIA
What means your lordship?

HAMLET
That if you be honest and fair, your honesty should admit no discourse to your beauty.

OPHELIA
Could beauty, my lord, have better commerce than with honesty?

HAMLET
Ay, truly; for the power of beauty will sooner transform honesty from what it is to a bawd than the force of honesty can translate beauty into his likeness This was sometime a paradox, but now the time gives it proof. I did love you once.

OPHELIA
Indeed, my lord, you made me believe so.

HAMLET

You should not have believ'd me, for virtue cannot so inoculate our old stock but we shall relish of it. I lov'd you not.

OPHELIA

I was the more deceiv'd.

HAMLET

Get thee to a nunn'ry Why wouldst thou be a breeder of sinners? I am myself indifferent honest; but yet I could accuse me of such things that it were better my mother had not borne me: I am very proud, revengeful, ambitious, with more offences at my beck than I have thoughts to put them in, imagination to give them shape, or time to act them in. What should such fellows as I do crawling between earth and heaven? We are arrant knaves, all; believe none of us. Go thy ways to a nunn'ry. Where's your father?

OPHELIA

At home, my lord.

HAMLET

Let the doors be shut upon him, that he may play the fool no where but in 's own house. Farewell.

OPHELIA

O, help him, you sweet heavens!

HAMLET

If thou dost marry, I'll give thee this plague for thy dowry: be thou as chaste as ice, as pure as snow, thou shalt not escape calumny. Get thee to a nunn'ry, farewell. Or, if thou wilt needs marry, marry a fool; for wise men know well enough what monsters you make of them. To a nunn'ry, go, and quickly too. Farewell.

OPHELIA

Heavenly powers, restore him!

HAMLET

I have heard of your paintings too, well enough. God hath given you one face, and you make yourselves another. You jig, you amble, and you lisp; you nickname God's creatures and make your wantonness your ignorance. Go to, I'll no more on 't; it hath made me mad. I say we will have no moe marriage. Those that are married already—all but one—shall live; the rest shall keep as they are. To a nunn'ry, go.

[*Exit.*]

OPHELIA
O, what a noble mind is here o'erthrown!
The courtier's, soldier's, scholar's, eye, tongue, sword,
Th' expectancy and rose of the fair state,
The glass of fashion and the mold of form,
Th' observ'd of all observers, quite, quite down!
And I, of ladies most deject and wretched,
That suck'd the honey of his music vows,
Now see that noble and most sovereign reason,
Like sweet bells jangled, out of time and harsh;
That unmatch'd form and feature of blown youth
Blasted with ecstasy. O, woe is me,
T' have seen what I have seen, see what I see!

1 Soft you now ("Soft" being short for "go softly," this mild exclamation is akin to today's "Wait a minute" or "Hold on.") **2 orisons** prayers **16 honest** (1) truthful (2) chaste **18 fair** (1) beautiful (2) virtuous **20 admit no discourse** permit no familiar behavior **22 commerce** dealings, interaction **25 sometime** at one time **paradox** view contrary to popular opinion **time** current age **28–29 inoculate . . . stock** virtue cannot be so deftly grafted to our long-standing sinful nature **29 relish of it** keep our taste for it (i.e., the sinfulness) **31 nunn'ry** convent **32 indifferent honest** moderately virtuous, somewhat decent **33 proud** vain, haughty **34 beck** beckoning, command **36 arrant** out and out **42 plague** curse **43 calumny** malicious slander **44 wilt needs** must **45 monsters** i.e., cuckolds **you** you women **48 paintings** use of cosmetics **49–50 You jig . . . creatures** i.e., you walk and speak in an affected manner **50 make . . . ignorance** excuse your affections as being part of your simpleness **on** of **51 moe** more in number **56 expectancy** source of hope (as the "fair state's" heir apparent) **57 glass** mirror **mold of form** model of courtly behavior **58 observ'd** one most attentively watched and honored **63 blown** in full bloom **64 ecstasy** madness

(44) MARGARET AND EARL OF SUFFOLK [V.III.45]

Henry VI, Part 1

SCENE: The fields before Angiers.

{It's not the best of times for the French. Their forces have been routed in the field, Joan of Arc is off to meet her fiery end, and noblewoman Margaret of Anjou has been taken prisoner by the Earl of Suffolk. There is at least one

bright spot, though: Suffolk seems far more interested in wooing the lovely Margaret than he is in her value as a spoil of war.}

[*Enter Suffolk, with Margaret in hand.*]

SUFFOLK
Be what thou wilt, thou art my prisoner.
[*Gazes on her.*]
O fairest beauty, do not fear nor fly,
For I will touch thee but with reverent hands.
I kiss these fingers for eternal peace,
And lay them gently on thy tender side.
Who art thou? Say, that I may honor thee.

MARGARET
Margaret my name, and daughter to a king,
The King of Naples, whosoe'er thou art.

SUFFOLK
An earl I am, and Suffolk am I call'd.
Be not offended, nature's miracle,
Thou art allotted to be ta'en by me.
So doth the swan her downy cygnets save,
Keeping them prisoner underneath her wings.
Yet, if this servile usage once offend.
Go and be free again as Suffolk's friend.
[*She starts to go.*]
O, stay! [*Aside.*] I have no power to let her pass;
My hand would free her, but my heart says no.
As plays the sun upon the glassy streams,
Twinkling another counterfeited beam,
So seems this gorgeous beauty to mine eyes.
Fain would I woo her, yet I dare not speak.
I'll call for pen and ink, and write my mind.
Fie, de la Pole, disable not thyself.
Hast not a tongue? Is she not here?
Wilt thou be daunted at a woman's sight?
Ay, beauty's princely majesty is such,
Confounds the tongue and makes the senses rough.

MARGARET
Say, Earl of Suffolk—if thy name be so—
What ransom must I pay before I pass?
For I perceive I am thy prisoner.

SUFFOLK
[*Aside.*] How canst thou tell she will deny thy suit,
Before thou make a trial of her love?

MARGARET
Why speak'st thou not? What ransom must I pay?

SUFFOLK
[*Aside.*] She's beautiful, and therefore to be woo'd;
She is a woman, therefore to be won.

MARGARET
Wilt thou accept of ransom, yea or no?

SUFFOLK
[*Aside.*] Fond man, remember that thou hast a wife.
Then how can Margaret be thy paramour?

MARGARET
I were best to leave him, for he will not hear.

SUFFOLK
[*Aside.*] There all is marr'd; there lies a cooling card.

MARGARET
He talks at random; sure the man is mad.

SUFFOLK
[*Aside.*] And yet a dispensation may be had.

MARGARET
And yet I would that you would answer me.

SUFFOLK
[*Aside.*] I'll win this Lady Margaret. For whom?
Why, for my king. Tush, that's a wooden thing!

MARGARET
He talks of wood; it is some carpenter.

SUFFOLK
[*Aside.*] Yet so my fancy may be satisfied,
And peace established between these realms.
But there remains a scruple in that too;
For though her father be the King of Naples,
Duke of Anjou and Maine, yet is he poor,
And our nobility will scorn the match.

MARGARET
Hear ye, captain, are you not at leisure?

SUFFOLK
[*Aside.*] It shall be so, disdain they ne'er so much.
Henry is youthful and will quickly yield.—
Madam, I have a secret to reveal.

MARGARET
[*Aside.*] What though I be enthrall'd? He seems a knight,
And will not any way dishonor me.

SUFFOLK
Lady, vouchsafe to listen what I say.

MARGARET
[*Aside.*] Perhaps I shall be rescu'd by the French,
And then I need not crave his courtesy.

SUFFOLK
Sweet madam, give me a hearing in a cause—

MARGARET
[*Aside.*] Tush, women have been captivate ere now.

SUFFOLK
Lady, wherefore talk you so?

MARGARET
I cry you mercy, 'tis but quid for quo.

SUFFOLK
Say, gentle Princess, would you not suppose
Your bondage happy, to be made a queen?

MARGARET
To be a queen in bondage is more vile
Than is a slave in base servility;
For princes should be free.

SUFFOLK
And so shall you,
If happy England's royal king be free.

MARGARET
Why, what concerns his freedom unto me?

SUFFOLK
I'll undertake to make thee Henry's queen,
To put a golden scepter in thy hand,
And set a precious crown upon thy head,
If thou wilt condescend to be my—

MARGARET
What?

SUFFOLK
His love.

MARGARET
I am unworthy to be Henry's wife.

SUFFOLK
No, gentle madam. I unworthy am
To woo so fair a dame to be his wife
And have no portion in the choice myself.
How say you, madam, are ye so content?

MARGARET
An if my father please, I am content.

SUFFOLK
Then call our captains and our colors forth.
And, madam, at your father's castle walls
We'll crave a parley, to confer with him.

4 for in token of **11 allotted** destined **14 servile** slave-like **19 Twinkling** causing to twinkle **counterfeited** i.e., reflected **21 Fain** gladly **23 Fie** (an expression of disgust) **de la Pole** (Suffolk's given name is William de la Pole.) **disable** belittle **27 Confounds** that it confounds **rough** dull **37 Fond** foolish **40 marr'd** ruined, spoiled **cooling card** card played by an opponent that spoils one's chance to win **42 dispensation** permission from the Pope to do that which would normally be forbidden by the Church's edicts **45 Tush** (an exclamation of contempt) **wooden** stupid **49 scruple** problem, objection **55 Henry** i.e., King Henry VI **57 enthrall'd** captured, taken prisoner **59 vouchsafe** be so kind as to **61 crave** require **63 captivate** taken captive **65 cry you mercy** beg your pardon **72 concerns** concern is **76 condescend** agree, consent **83 An if** if **84 colors** banners of an army **86 crave** request

(45) Lady Grey and King Edward IV [III.ii.36]

Henry VI, Part 3

SCENE: The royal palace in London.

{The recently-widowed Lady Grey has come before King Edward to beg that her family's lands be restored to her and her children. The King seems amenable to the idea, but his largess comes with a price tag.}

KING EDWARD
Widow, we will consider of your suit;
And come some other time to know our mind.

LADY GREY
Right gracious lord, I cannot brook delay.
May it please your Highness to resolve me now;
And what your pleasure is, shall satisfy me.

KING EDWARD IV
How many children hast thou, widow? Tell me.

LADY GREY
Three, my most gracious lord.

KING EDWARD IV
'Twere pity they should lose their father's lands.

LADY GREY
Be pitiful, dread lord, and grant it then.

KING EDWARD
Tell me, madam, do you love your children?

LADY GREY
Ay, full as dearly as I love myself.

KING EDWARD
And would you not do much to do them good?

LADY GREY
To do them good, I would sustain some harm.

KING EDWARD
Then get your husband's lands, to do them good.

LADY GREY
Therefore I came unto your Majesty.

KING EDWARD
I'll tell you how these lands are to be got.

LADY GREY
So shall you bind me to your Highness' service.

KING EDWARD
What service wilt thou do me if I give them?

LADY GREY
What you command, that rests in me to do.

KING EDWARD
But you will take exceptions to my boon.

LADY GREY
No, gracious lord, except I cannot do it.

KING EDWARD
Ay, but thou canst do what I mean to ask.

LADY GREY
Why, then I will do what your Grace commands.

KING EDWARD
'Tis an easy task; 'tis but to love a king.

LADY GREY
That's soon perform'd, because I am a subject.

KING EDWARD
Why, then, thy husband's lands I freely give thee.

LADY GREY
I take my leave with many thousand thanks. [*Starts to go.*]

KING EDWARD
But stay thee. 'Tis the fruits of love I mean.

LADY GREY
The fruits of love I mean, my loving liege.

KING EDWARD
Ay, but, I fear me, in another sense.
What love, think'st thou, I sue so much to get?

LADY GREY
My love till death, my humble thanks, my prayers—
That love which virtue begs and virtue grants.

KING EDWARD
No, by my troth, I did not mean such love.

LADY GREY
Why then you mean not as I thought you did.

KING EDWARD
But now you partly may perceive my mind.

LADY GREY
My mind will never grant what I perceive
Your Highness aims at, if I aim aright.

KING EDWARD
To tell thee plain, I aim to lie with thee.

LADY GREY
To tell you plain, I had rather lie in prison.

KING EDWARD
Why then thou shalt not have thy husband's lands.

LADY GREY
Why then mine honesty shall be my dower;
For by that loss I will not purchase them.

KING EDWARD
Therein thou wrong'st thy children mightily.

LADY GREY
Herein your Highness wrongs both them and me.
But, mighty lord, this merry inclination
Accords not with the sadness of my suit.
Please you dismiss me, either with "ay" or "no."

KING EDWARD
Ay, if thou wilt say "ay" to my request;
No, if thou dost say "no" to my demand.

LADY GREY
Then, no, my lord. My suit is at an end.

KING EDWARD
[*Aside.*] Her looks doth argue her replete with modesty;
Her words doth show her wit incomparable;
All her perfections challenge sovereignty.
One way or other, she is for a king,

And she shall be my love, or else my queen.—
Say that King Edward take thee for his queen?

LADY GREY
'Tis better said than done, my gracious lord.
I am a subject fit to jest withal,
But far unfit to be a sovereign.

KING EDWARD
Sweet widow, by my state I swear to thee
I speak no more than what my soul intends;
And that is, to enjoy thee for my love.

LADY GREY
And that is more than I will yield unto.
I know I am too mean to be your queen,
And yet too good to be your concubine.

KING EDWARD
You cavil, widow: I did mean my queen.

LADY GREY
'Twill grieve your grace my sons should call you father.

KING EDWARD
No more than when my daughters call thee mother.
Thou art a widow, and thou hast some children;
And, by God's mother, I, being but a bachelor,
Have other some. Why, 'tis a happy thing
To be the father unto many sons.
Answer no more, for thou shalt be my queen.

3 brook tolerate **4 resolve me** answer me, end my worrying **9 dread** deeply revered **17 bind me** make me beholden, obligate me **20 my boon** the favor I ask **21 except** unless **31 sue so much** seek so earnestly **34 by my troth** (a mild oath affirming one's truthfulness) **38 aims** guesses **aright** correctly **40 plain** frankly, straightforwardly **42 honesty** chastity **dower** dowry **46 merry inclination** i.e., high spirited exchange of ours **47 sadness** seriousness **52 argue her** show her to be **54 challenge** lay claim to **59 withal** with **61 state** i.e., exalted position in the world, kingship **65 mean** lowly, common **67 cavil** object without cause **68 grieve** annoy, irritate **72 other some** some others

(46) LADY MACBETH AND MACBETH [II.II.1]

Macbeth

SCENE: An inner courtyard of Macbeth's castle.

{The die is cast, and King Duncan is no more. Lady Macbeth anxiously awaits the return of her murderous husband, who has just struck the crowning blow in a horrific night's work.}

LADY MACBETH
That which hath made them drunk hath made me bold;
What hath quench'd them hath given me fire. Hark! Peace!
It was the owl that shriek'd, the fatal bellman,
Which gives the stern'st good-night. He is about it.
The doors are open; and the surfeited grooms
Do mock their charge with snores. I have drugg'd their possets,
That death and nature do contend about them
Whether they live or die.

MACBETH
[*Within.*] Who's there? What, ho!

LADY MACBETH
Alack, I am afraid they have awak'd,
And 'tis not done. Th' attempt and not the deed
Confounds us. Hark! I laid their daggers ready;
He could not miss 'em. Had he not resembled
My father as he slept, I had done 't.
[*Enter Macbeth, bearing bloody daggers.*]
My husband!

MACBETH
I have done the deed. Didst thou not hear a noise?

LADY MACBETH
I heard the owl scream and the crickets cry.
Did you not speak?

MACBETH
When?

LADY MACBETH
Now.

MACBETH
As I descended?

LADY MACBETH
Ay.

MACBETH
Hark! Who lies i' th' second chamber?

LADY MACBETH
Donalbain.

MACBETH
This is a sorry sight. [*Looks at his hands.*]

LADY MACBETH
A foolish thought, to say a sorry sight.

MACBETH
There's one did laugh in 's sleep, and one cried "Murder!"
That they did wake each other. I stood and heard them.
But they did say their prayers, and address'd them
Again to sleep.

LADY MACBETH
There are two lodg'd together.

MACBETH
One cried "God bless us!" and "Amen!" the other,
As they had seen me with these hangman's hands.
List'ning their fear, I could not say "Amen,"
When they did say "God bless us!"

LADY MACBETH
Consider it not so deeply.

MACBETH
But wherefore could not I pronounce "Amen"?
I had most need of blessing, and "Amen"
Stuck in my throat.

LADY MACBETH
These deeds must not be thought
After these ways; so, it will make us mad.

MACBETH
Methought I heard a voice cry "Sleep no more!
Macbeth does murder sleep"—the innocent sleep,
Sleep that knits up the ravel'd sleave of care,
The death of each day's life, sore labor's bath,

Balm of hurt minds, great nature's second course,
Chief nourisher in life's feast.

LADY MACBETH

What do you mean?

MACBETH

Still it cried "Sleep no more!" to all the house;
"Glamis hath murder'd sleep, and therefore Cawdor
Shall sleep no more; Macbeth shall sleep no more."

LADY MACBETH

Who was it that thus cried? Why, worthy thane,
You do unbend your noble strength, to think
So brainsickly of things. Go get some water,
And wash this filthy witness from your hand.
Why did you bring these daggers from the place?
They must lie there. Go carry them, and smear
The sleepy grooms with blood.

MACBETH

I'll go no more.
I am afraid to think what I have done.
Look on 't again I dare not.

LADY MACBETH

Infirm of purpose!
Give me the daggers. The sleeping and the dead
Are but as pictures. 'Tis the eye of childhood
That fears a painted devil. If he do bleed,
I'll gild the faces of the grooms withal,
For it must seem their guilt.
[*She takes the daggers and exits. There is a knock within.*]

MACBETH

Whence is that knocking?
How is 't with me, when every noise appalls me?
What hands are here? Ha! They pluck out mine eyes.
Will all great Neptune's ocean wash this blood
Clean from my hand? No, this my hand will rather
The multitudinous seas incarnadine,
Making the green one red.

[*Enter Lady Macbeth.*]

LADY MACBETH
My hands are of your color; but I shame
To wear a heart so white. [*Knock within.*] I hear a knocking
At the south entry. Retire we to our chamber.
A little water clears us of this deed.
How easy is it, then! Your constancy
Hath left you unattended. [*Knock within.*] Hark! More knocking.
Get on your nightgown, lest occasion calls us
And show us to be watchers. Be not lost
So poorly in your thoughts.

MACBETH
To know my deed, 'twere best not know myself. [*Knock within.*]
Wake Duncan with thy knocking! I would thou couldst!

[*Exeunt.*]

3 bellman watchman (It was the night watchman who rang a bell—"the stern'st goodnight"—outside the cell of a prisoner condemned to die the following morning) **5 surfeited grooms** servants sated with drink and food **6 charge** duty, responsibility **possets** a hot, spiced drink commonly taken at bedtime **7 That** so that **11 Confounds** destroys, ruins **12 He** i.e., Macbeth **19 Donalbain** (One of Duncan's two sons.) **24 address'd them** prepared themselves **28 hangman's hands** bloody hands (The second part of the hangman's bloody job was to draw and quarter the condemned.) **29 their** to their **34 thought** dwelled upon **38 knits up** ties up in knots **ravel'd sleave** tangled thread (A "sleave" was a filament of fine silk.) **40 second course** (Feasts of the day customarily had two courses, the second of which was the larger and "chief nourisher.") **42 Still** on and on, continually **43 Glamis, Cawdor** (Macbeth is Thane of Glamis and of Cawdor, titles roughly equivalent to that of Earl.) **46 unbend** weaken, make slack **47 brainsickly** foolishly, madly **48 filthy witness** i.e., blood (and the deed it "testifies" to) **57 gild** smear with blood (The colors "red" and "gold" were often used interchangeably.) **59 appalls me** fills me with fear, disconcerts me **63 incarnadine** turn red **66 white** pale (with fear) **69 constancy** resolve, firmness of mind **70 left you unattended** deserted you **71 nightgown** a type of dressing gown worn at night **72 watchers** those who remain awake **73 poorly** unworthily **75 would** wish

(47) Isabella and Angelo [II.ii.29]

Measure For Measure

SCENE: Angelo's house.

{Isabella has temporarily shelved her plans to enter a nunnery in order to come to the aid of her incarcerated brother, Claudio. Though Claudio's transgression seems a minor one, he's been sentenced to pay for it with his life. Which explains why Isabella now comes before Vienna's deputy, Angelo, to plead for mercy and her brother's life.}

ANGELO
Y' are welcome. What's your will?

ISABELLA
I am a woeful suitor to your honor,
Please but your honor hear me.

ANGELO
Well; what's your suit?

ISABELLA
There is a vice that most I do abhor,
And most desire should meet the blow of justice,
For which I would not plead, but that I must;
For which I must not plead, but that I am
At war 'twixt will and will not.

ANGELO
Well; the matter?

ISABELLA
I have a brother is condemn'd to die.
I do beseech you, let it be his fault,
And not my brother.

ANGELO
Condemn the fault, and not the actor of it?
Why, every fault's condemn'd ere it be done.
Mine were the very cipher of a function,
To fine the faults whose fine stands in record,
And let go by the actor.

ISABELLA
O just but severe law!
I had a brother, then. Heaven keep your honor!

ANGELO
Maiden, no remedy.

ISABELLA
Yes; I do think that you might pardon him,
And neither heaven nor man grieve at the mercy.

ANGELO
I will not do 't.

ISABELLA
But can you, if you would?

ANGELO
Look what I will not, that I cannot do.

ISABELLA
But might you do 't, and do the world no wrong,
If so your heart were touch'd with that remorse
As mine is to him?

ANGELO
He's sentenc'd; 'tis too late.

ISABELLA
Too late? Why, no; I, that do speak a word.
May call it back again. Well, believe this,
No ceremony that to great ones 'longs,
Not the king's crown, nor the deputed sword,
The marshal's truncheon, nor the judge's robe,
Become them with one half so good a grace
As mercy does.
If he had been as you and you as he,
You would have slipp'd like him; but he, like you,
Would not have been so stern.

ANGELO
Pray you be gone.

ISABELLA
I would to heaven I had your potency,
And you were Isabel! Should it then be thus?
No; I would tell what 'twere to be a judge,
And what a prisoner.

ANGELO
Your brother is a forfeit of the law,
And you but waste your words.

ISABELLA

Alas, alas!
Why, all the souls that were were forfeit once;
And He that might the vantage best have took
Found out the remedy. How would you be,
If He, which is the top of judgment, should
But judge you as you are? O, think on that;
And mercy then will breathe within your lips,
Like man new made.

ANGELO

Be you content, fair maid.
It is the law, not I, condemn your brother.
Were he my kinsman, brother, or my son,
It should be thus with him. He must die tomorrow.

ISABELLA

Tomorrow? O, that's sudden! Spare him, spare him!
He's not prepar'd for death. Even for our kitchens
We kill the fowl of season. Shall we serve heaven
With less respect than we do minister
To our gross selves? Good, good my lord, bethink you:
Who is it that hath died for this offence?
There's many have committed it.

ANGELO

The law hath not been dead, though it hath slept.
Those many had not dar'd to do that evil
If the first that did th' edict infringe
Had answer'd for his deed. Now 'tis awake,
Takes note of what is done, and like a prophet
Looks in a glass that shows what future evils,
Either now, or by remissness new-conceiv'd,
And so in progress to be hatch'd and born,
Are now to have no successive degrees,
But here they live, to end.

ISABELLA

Yet show some pity.

ANGELO

I show it most of all when I show justice;
For then I pity those I do not know,
Which a dismiss'd offence would after gall,
And do him right that, answering one foul wrong,
Lives not to act another. Be satisfied;
Your brother dies tomorrow. Be content.

ISABELLA
So you must be the first that gives this sentence,
And he, that suffers. O, it is excellent
To have a giant's strength; but it is tyrannous
To use it like a giant. Could great men thunder
As Jove himself does, Jove would never be quiet,
For every pelting, petty officer
Would use his heaven for thunder,
Nothing but thunder! Merciful Heaven,
Thou rather with thy sharp and sulphurous bolt
Splits the unwedgeable and gnarled oak
Than the soft myrtle; but man, proud man,
Dress'd in a little brief authority,
Most ignorant of what he's most assur'd,
His glassy essence, like an angry ape,
Plays such fantastic tricks before high heaven
As make the angels weep; who, with our spleens,
Would all themselves laugh mortal.
We cannot weigh our brother with ourself.
Great men may jest with saints; 'tis wit in them,
But in the less foul profanation.
That in the captain's but a choleric word,
Which in the soldier is flat blasphemy.

ANGELO
Why do you put these sayings upon me?

ISABELLA
Because authority, though it err like others,
Hath yet a kind of medicine in itself,
That skins the vice o' th' top. Go to your bosom;
Knock there, and ask your heart what it doth know
That's like my brother's fault. If it confess
A natural guiltiness such as is his,
Let it not sound a thought upon your tongue
Against my brother's life.

ANGELO
[*Aside.*] She speaks, and 'tis such sense
That my sense breeds with it.—Fare you well. [*He starts to go.*]

ISABELLA
Gentle my lord, turn back.

ANGELO
I will bethink me. Come again tomorrow.

ISABELLA
Hark how I'll bribe you. Good my lord, turn back.

ANGELO
How? Bribe me?

ISABELLA
Ay, with such gifts that heaven shall share with you.
Not with fond sicles of the tested gold,
Or stones whose rate are either rich or poor
As fancy values them, but with true prayers
That shall be up at heaven and enter there
Ere sunrise; prayers from preserved souls,
From fasting maids whose minds are dedicate
To nothing temporal.

ANGELO
Well, come to me tomorrow.

ISABELLA
Heaven keep your honor safe!

ANGELO
[*Aside.*] Amen:
For I am that way going to temptation,
Where prayers cross.

ISABELLA
At what hour tomorrow
Shall I attend your lordship?

ANGELO
At any time 'fore noon.

ISABELLA
'Save your honor!

[*Exeunt Isabella.*]

6 would not do not wish to **10 let . . . fault** (i.e., let it be his crime that is to be condemned) **14 Mine . . . function** my function here would be totally worthless **15 fine . . . fine** punish . . . penalty **18 I had** (at least) I would have a **19 no** there is no **23 Look what** whatever **25 remorse** pity **29 ceremony** symbol of authority **'longs** belongs **30 deputed sword** the sword of justice **31 truncheon** staff borne by military officers **35 like you** in your position (of authority) **37 potency** power, authority **39 tell** know **41 forfeit** person condemned to death **44–45 He . . . remedy** (Refers to the biblical Redemption.) **44 vantage** advantage **46 top of judgment** supreme judge **49 Like . . . made** as if you were a new and different man **53 sudden** too soon, rash **55 of season** in season, i.e., that has sufficiently matured **56 respect** thoughtful care, consideration **57 gross** material, corporeal **bethink you** think about it **62 edict infringe** violate the law **65 glass** crystal ball **66 Either . . . new-conceiv'd** i.e., both evils already afoot, and those yet to be conceived under lax enforcement of the law ("remissness") **67 in progress** as time goes on **68 successive degrees** successors **69 here** i.e., in potential offenders **72 dismiss'd** forgiven **gall** injure **73 right** justice **answering** answering for **78 giant's** (The giants of Greek mythology were notable for both their extraordinary strength and their lack of wisdom and compassion.) **80 be quiet** have any peace **81 pelting** paltry **officer** official **84 sulpherous** having the qualities of burning sulpher **86 proud** arrogant **87 brief** short-lived **88 assur'd** assured of (i.e., his "glassy essence") **89 glassy essence** i.e., frail and mirror-like (in that it reflects his godlike soul) essential being **like . . . ape** (The sense here is that when a man attempts to play the role of a god, he is as pitiful and ridiculous as the ape who tries to imitate a man.) **91 with our spleens** if they had temperaments like ours (The spleen was thought to be the seat of emotions.) **92 themselves laugh mortal** laugh as if they were mortals **93 weigh . . . ourself** judge others by the same standards as we judge ourself **94 jest with** make jokes about **95 the less** lesser men (it is) **97 flat** outright **98 put . . . upon** apply . . . to **101 skins . . . top** covers the sore with skin (i.e., hides, but does not redress, transgressions it has committed) **107 'tis such sense** its import is such **108 sense** sensual appetite **109 Gentle my lord** my noble lord **113 that** as **114 fond** foolishly overvalued **sicles** shekels, i.e., coins **tested** purest **115 rate** values **118 preserved souls** souls protected from the world **119 dedicate** dedicated **120 temporal** worldly, secular **124 cross** are at cross purposes

(48) Isabella and Claudio [III.i.53]

Measure For Measure

SCENE: The prison.

{As if sitting here behind bars awaiting execution isn't bad enough for Claudio, in comes his sister Isabella bearing even more bad tidings. Her attempt to win a reprieve from the governor (see preceding entry) has failed.}

CLAUDIO
Now, sister, what's the comfort? 1

ISABELLA
Why,
As all comforts are; most good, most good indeed.
Lord Angelo, having affairs to heaven,
Intends you for his swift ambassador,
Where you shall be an everlasting leiger.
Therefore your best appointment make with speed;
Tomorrow you set on.

CLAUDIO
Is there no remedy?

ISABELLA
None but such remedy as, to save a head,
To cleave a heart in twain.

CLAUDIO
But is there any?

ISABELLA
Yes, brother, you may live.
There is a devilish mercy in the judge,
If you'll implore it, that will free your life,
But fetter you till death.

CLAUDIO
Perpetual durance?

ISABELLA
Ay, just; perpetual durance, a restraint,
Though all the world's vastidity you had,
To a determin'd scope.

CLAUDIO
But in what nature?

ISABELLA
In such a one as, you consenting to 't,
Would bark your honor from that trunk you bear,
And leave you naked.

CLAUDIO
Let me know the point.

ISABELLA
O, I do fear thee, Claudio, and I quake,
Lest thou a feverous life shouldst entertain,
And six or seven winters more respect

Than a perpetual honor. Dar'st thou die?
The sense of death is most in apprehension;
And the poor beetle that we tread upon
In corporal sufferance finds a pang as great
As when a giant dies.

CLAUDIO
Why give you me this shame?
Think you I can a resolution fetch
From flow'ry tenderness? If I must die,
I will encounter darkness as a bride,
And hug it in mine arms.

ISABELLA
There spake my brother! There my father's grave
Did utter forth a voice. Yes, thou must die.
Thou art too noble to conserve a life
In base appliances. This outward-sainted deputy,
Whose settled visage and deliberate word
Nips youth i' th' head, and follies doth enew
As falcon doth the fowl, is yet a devil;
His filth within being cast, he would appear
A pond as deep as hell.

CLAUDIO
The prenzie Angelo?

ISABELLA
O, 'tis the cunning livery of hell,
The damned'st body to invest and cover
In prenzie guards! Dost thou think, Claudio,
If I would yield him my virginity,
Thou mightst be freed!

CLAUDIO
O heavens, it cannot be.

ISABELLA
Yes, he would give 't thee, from this rank offence,
So to offend him still. This night's the time
That I should do what I abhor to name,
Or else thou diest tomorrow.

CLAUDIO
Thou shalt not do 't.

ISABELLA
O, were it but my life,
I'd throw it down for your deliverance
As frankly as a pin.

CLAUDIO
Thanks, dear Isabel.

ISABELLA
Be ready, Claudio, for your death tomorrow.

CLAUDIO
Yes. Has he affections in him,
That thus can make him bite the law by th' nose,
When he would force it? Sure, it is no sin,
Or of the deadly seven, it is the least.

ISABELLA
Which is the least?

CLAUDIO
If it were damnable, he being so wise,
Why would he for the momentary trick
Be perdurably fin'd? O Isabel!

ISABELLA
What says my brother?

CLAUDIO
Death is a fearful thing.

ISABELLA
And shamed life a hateful.

CLAUDIO
Ay, but to die, and go we know not where,
To lie in cold obstruction and to rot,
This sensible warm motion to become
A kneaded clod; and the delighted spirit
To bathe in fiery floods, or to reside
In thrilling region of thick-ribbed ice;
To be imprison'd in the viewless winds
And blown with restless violence round about
The pendent world; or to be worse than worst
Of those that lawless and incertain thought
Imagine howling—'tis too horrible!
The weariest and most loathed worldly life

That age, ache, penury and imprisonment
Can lay on nature is a paradise
To what we fear of death.

ISABELLA
Alas, alas!

CLAUDIO
Sweet sister, let me live.
What sin you do to save a brother's life,
Nature dispenses with the deed so far
That it becomes a virtue.

ISABELLA
O you beast!
O faithless coward! O dishonest wretch!
Wilt thou be made a man out of my vice?
Is 't not a kind of incest, to take life
From thine own sister's shame? What should I think?
Heaven shield my mother play'd my father fair!
For such a warped slip of wilderness
Ne'er issued from his blood. Take my defiance!
Die, perish! Might but my bending down
Reprieve thee from thy fate, it should proceed.
I'll pray a thousand prayers for thy death,
No word to save thee.

CLAUDIO
Nay, hear me, Isabel.

ISABELLA
O, fie, fie, fie!
Thy sin's not accidental, but a trade.
Mercy to thee would prove itself a bawd;
'Tis best thou diest quickly.

CLAUDIO
O hear me, Isabella!

1 comfort comforting word, good news **3 affairs to** business with **4 you for** for you to be **5 leiger** resident ambassador **6 appointment** preparation **7 set on** set forth **9 twain** two parts **13 durance** imprisonment **15 vastidity** vastness **16 a determin'd scope** fixed boundaries (i.e., the perpetual regret you'll feel for the bargain you made) **18 bark** strip off (as one strips bark off a tree) **trunk** body (with a play on "tree trunk") **20 fear** fear for **21 feverous** feverish, agitated **entertain** desire, cling to **22 respect** value **24 apprehension** anticipating it

26 corporal sufferance physical suffering **29 a resolution fetch** find resolve, summon up courage **30 flow'ry tenderness** soothing figures of speech **31 as** as I would **36 In base appliances** by means of shameful remedies **37 settled visage** composed demeanor **word** speech **38 Nips . . . head** strikes youth from high above (like a falcon swoops down on its prey) **follies doth enew** drives youthful follies down into the water (i.e., "enews" them, another term from falconry) **40 cast** thrown up (?) cleared out (?) **41 prenzie** princely (?) **42 livery** uniform **43 invest** clothe **44 guards** trimmings, trappings **Dost thou think** just think of it **47–48 give . . . still** give you your freedom, in return for my foul offence, so that you might continue offending (i.e., unlawfully fornicating) **53 frankly . . . pin** freely as I would toss away a pin **55 affections** lusts **56 bite . . . nose** flout the law **57 would force** should enforce **61 trick** trifle **62 perdurably fin'd** everlastingly punished **66 cold obstruction** cessation of the body's vital functions **67 sensible** able to feel **motion** organism, body **68 kneaded clod** lump of clay **delighted spirit** spirit accustomed to experiencing delight **70 thrilling** bitterly cold **71 viewless** invisible **73 pendent** suspended in space **74 lawless . . . thought** wild and unrestrained conjecture **82 dispenses with** excuses **88 shield** forbid **fair** honorably **89 warped** perverse **slip of wilderness** (in botany) shoot of a wild stock **90 Take** accept, resign yourself to **defiance** rejection **91 Might . . . down** even if a mere bow from me could **92 it** i.e., your execution **95 fie** (an expression of disgust) **96 accidental** a chance occurance **trade** habitual practice **97 prove . . . bawd** merely procure for you further sexual indulgences

(49) HELENA AND DEMETRIUS [II.I.188]

A Midsummer Night's Dream

SCENE: A wooded area near Athens.

{Evidently, love is not only blind, but deaf as well. So infatuated is Helena with her beloved Demetrius (who, for his part, only has eyes for Hermia) that this rather heartless snub of the poor girl fails to put her off in the least.}

[*Enter Demetrius, Helena following him.*]

DEMETRIUS
I love thee not, therefore pursue me not.
Where is Lysander and fair Hermia?
The one I'll slay, the other slayeth me.
Thou told'st me they were stol'n unto this wood;

And here am I, and wode within this wood,
Because I cannot meet my Hermia.
Hence, get thee gone, and follow me no more.

HELENA
You draw me, you hard-hearted adamant;
But yet you draw not iron, for my heart
Is true as steel. Leave you your power to draw,
And I shall have no power to follow you.

DEMETRIUS
Do I entice you? Do I speak you fair?
Or, rather, do I not in plainest truth
Tell you I do not nor I cannot love you?

HELENA
And even for that do I love you the more.
I am your spaniel; and, Demetrius,
The more you beat me, I will fawn on you.
Use me but as your spaniel, spurn me, strike me,
Neglect me, lose me; only give me leave,
Unworthy as I am, to follow you.
What worser place can I beg in your love—
And yet a place of high respect with me—
Than to be used as you use your dog?

DEMETRIUS
Tempt not too much the hatred of my spirit,
For I am sick when I do look on thee.

HELENA
And I am sick when I look not on you.

DEMETRIUS
You do impeach your modesty too much
To leave the city and commit yourself
Into the hands of one that loves you not;
To trust the opportunity of night
And the ill counsel of a desert place
With the rich worth of your virginity.

HELENA
Your virtue is my privilege. For that
It is not night when I do see your face,
Therefore I think I am not in the night;
Nor doth this wood lack worlds of company,
For you in my respect are all the world.

Then how can it be said I am alone,
When all the world is here to look on me?

DEMETRIUS
I'll run from thee and hide me in the brakes,
And leave thee to the mercy of wild beasts.

HELENA
The wildest hath not such a heart as you.
Run when you will, the story shall be chang'd:
Apollo flies, and Daphne holds the chase;
The dove pursues the griffin, the mild hind
Makes speed to catch the tiger—bootless speed,
When cowardice pursues and valor flies.

DEMETRIUS
I will not stay thy questions. Let me go.
Or if thou follow me, do not believe
But I shall do thee mischief in the wood.

HELENA
Ay, in the temple, in the town, the field,
You do me mischief. Fie, Demetrius!
Your wrongs do set a scandal on my sex.
We cannot fight for love, as men may do;
We should be woo'd, and were not made to woo.

[*Exit Demetrius.*]

I'll follow thee and make a heaven of hell,
To die upon the hand I love so well.

[*Exit.*]

2 Lysander . . . Hermia (For background on the relationships between Lysander, Hermia, Helena and Demetrius, see I.i.) **5 wode** mad with anger (pronounced "wood") **8 adamant** magnet **10 Leave you** surrender, give up **12 you fair** to you courteously **27 impeach** call into question, disparage **31 desert** deserted **33 virtue . . . privilege** excellence is my license for doing so **For that** because **37 in my respect** as far as I'm concerned **40 brakes** bushes, thickets **44 Apollo . . . chase** (According to myth, Daphne ran from Apollo and was saved from rape only by being transformed into a tree. Here, Helena notes that the tables are turned, as the woman now "holds the chase.") **45 griffin** a mythical beast with an eagle's head and the body of a lion **mild** gentle **hind** female deer **46 bootless** unavailing, fruitless **48 stay thy questions** wait here to hear your talk **52 Fie** (an expression of disgust) **53 scandal . . . sex** (in that he compels her, the woman, to do the wooing) **57 upon** by

(50) BEATRICE AND BENEDICK [IV.I.254]

Much Ado About Nothing

SCENE: A church in Messina.

{Though they've long made a habit of denouncing each other, Benedick and Beatrice must finally acknowledge what has been apparent to others for some time now: they make a perfect pair. Even Beatrice's preoccupation with the plight of her cousin, Hero, cannot make a dent in the duo's new-found affection for each other.}

BENEDICK
Lady Beatrice, have you wept all this while?

BEATRICE
Yea, and I will weep a while longer.

BENEDICK
I will not desire that.

BEATRICE
You have no reason; I do it freely.

BENEDICK
Surely I do believe your fair cousin is wrong'd.

BEATRICE
Ah, how much might the man deserve of me that would right her!

BENEDICK
Is there any way to show such friendship?

BEATRICE
A very even way, but no such friend.

BENEDICK
May a man do it?

BEATRICE
It is a man's office, but not yours.

BENEDICK
I do love nothing in the world so well as you. Is not that strange?

BEATRICE
As strange as the thing I know not. It were as possible for me to say I lov'd nothing so well as you. But believe me not; and yet I lie not. I confess nothing, nor I deny nothing. I am sorry for my cousin.

BENEDICK
By my sword, Beatrice, thou lovest me.

BEATRICE
Do not swear and eat it.

BENEDICK
I will swear by it that you love me, and I will make him eat it that says I love not you.

BEATRICE
Will you not eat your word?

BENEDICK
With no sauce that can be devis'd to it. I protest I love thee.

BEATRICE
Why, then, God forgive me!

BENEDICK
What offence, sweet Beatrice?

BEATRICE
You have stay'd me in a happy hour. I was about to protest I lov'd you.

BENEDICK
And do it with all thy heart.

BEATRICE
I love you with so much of my heart that none is left to protest.

BENEDICK
Come, bid me do any thing for thee.

BEATRICE
Kill Claudio.

BENEDICK
Ha! Not for the wide world.

BEATRICE
You kill me to deny it. Farewell. [*She starts to go.*]

BENEDICK
Tarry, sweet Beatrice.

BEATRICE
I am gone, though I am here. There is no love in you. Nay, I pray you, let me go.

BENEDICK
Beatrice—

BEATRICE
In faith, I will go.

BENEDICK
We'll be friends first.

BEATRICE
You dare easier be friends with me than fight with mine enemy.

BENEDICK
Is Claudio thine enemy?

BEATRICE
Is he not approv'd in the height a villain, that hath slander'd, scorn'd, dishonor'd my kinswoman? O that I were a man! What, bear her in hand until they come to take hands, and then, with public accusation, uncover'd slander, unmitigated rancor—O God, that I were a man! I would eat his heart in the market-place.

BENEDICK
Hear me, Beatrice—

BEATRICE
Talk with a man out at a window! A proper saying!

BENEDICK
Nay, but, Beatrice—

BEATRICE
Sweet Hero! She is wrong'd, she is slander'd, she is undone.

BENEDICK
Beat—

BEATRICE
Princes and counties! Surely, a princely testimony, a goodly count, Count Comfect; a sweet gallant, surely! O that I were a man for his sake! Or that I had any friend would be a man for my sake! But manhood is melted into cur'sies, valor into compliment, and men are only turn'd into tongue, and trim ones too. He is now as valiant as Hercules that only tells a lie, and swears it. I cannot be a man with wishing, therefore I will die a woman with grieving.

BENEDICK
Tarry, good Beatrice. By this hand, I love thee.

BEATRICE
Use it for my love some other way than swearing by it.

BENEDICK
Think you in your soul the Count Claudio hath wrong'd Hero?

BEATRICE
Yea, as sure as I have a thought or a soul.

BENEDICK
Enough, I am engag'd. I will challenge him. I will kiss your hand, and so I leave you. By this hand, Claudio shall render me a dear account. As you hear of me, so think of me. Go, comfort your cousin. I must say she is dead; and so, farewell.

[*Exeunt severally.*]

5 cousin is wrong'd (See IV.i.1.) **8 even** direct, straightforward **10 office** business, affair **12 As strange** as much a stranger to me **16 eat it** go back on your oath, i.e., eat your words **20 devis'd to** bestowed upon **23 stay'd** stopped **in . . . hour** at just the right moment **protest** declare **25 protest** object **30 Tarry** wait **31 gone** (i.e., in spirit) **33 In faith** by my faith, I swear **37 approv'd . . . villain** proved a villain of the highest degree **38 kinswoman** i.e., Hero (For the events that Beatrice proceeds to refer to, see the beginning of IV.i.) **bear . . . hand** deceive her with false hopes **39 hands** i.e., in marriage **uncover'd** suddenly and openly declared **45 undone** ruined **47 counties** counts **count** (1) title of Count (2) legal indictment **48 Comfect** confection, candy **50 cur'sies** curtsies, servile bows **trim** fine (used ironically) **57 am engag'd** bound by my pledge, promise **58 render . . . account** make with me a very costly settlement **59 dead** (See IV.i.199.)

(51) DESDEMONA AND OTHELLO [III.IV.33]

Othello

SCENE: Before Othello's castle.

{By now, Othello is nearly convinced of Iago's false accusations—namely, that Othello's wife Desdemona is cheating on him, that she's doing so with his lieutenant Cassio, and that she's gone so far as to give her handkerchief to Cassio as a token of affection. In a twisted attempt to satisfy himself that the first two contentions are true, the Moor confronts a bewildered Desdemona about the third.}

DESDEMONA
How is 't with you, my lord?

OTHELLO
Well, my good lady. [*Aside*.] O, hardness to dissemble!—
How do you, Desdemona?

DESDEMONA
Well, my good lord.

OTHELLO
Give me your hand. [*She gives her hand.*] This hand is moist, my lady.

DESDEMONA
It yet hath felt no age nor known no sorrow.

OTHELLO
This argues fruitfulness and liberal heart.
Hot, hot, and moist. This hand of yours requires
A sequester from liberty, fasting and prayer,
Much castigation, exercise devout;
For here's a young and sweating devil here,
That commonly rebels. 'Tis a good hand,
A frank one.

DESDEMONA
You may, indeed, say so;
For 'twas that hand that gave away my heart.

OTHELLO
A liberal hand. The hearts of old gave hands;
But our new heraldry is hands, not hearts.

DESDEMONA
I cannot speak of this. Come now, your promise.

OTHELLO
What promise, chuck?

DESDEMONA
I have sent to bid Cassio come speak with you.

OTHELLO
I have a salt and sorry rheum offends me;
Lend me thy handkerchief.

DESDEMONA
Here, my lord. [*She gives him her handkerchief.*]

OTHELLO
That which I gave you.

DESDEMONA
I have it not about me.

OTHELLO
Not?

DESDEMONA
No, faith, my lord.

OTHELLO
That's a fault. That handkerchief
Did an Egyptian to my mother give;
She was a charmer, and could almost read
The thoughts of people. She told her, while she kept it,
'Twould make her amiable and subdue my father
Entirely to her love; but if she lost it
Or made gift of it, my father's eye
Should hold her loathed and his spirits should hunt
After new fancies. She, dying, gave it me,
And bid me, when my fate would have me wiv'd,
To give it her. I did so; and take heed on 't;
Make it a darling like your precious eye.
To lose 't or give 't away were such perdition
As nothing else could match.

DESDEMONA
Is 't possible?

OTHELLO
'Tis true; there's magic in the web of it.
A sibyl, that had numb'red in the world
The sun to course two hundred compasses,
In her prophetic fury sew'd the work;
The worms were hallowed that did breed the silk;
And it was dy'd in mummy which the skillful
Conserv'd of maidens' hearts.

DESDEMONA
I' faith! Is 't true?

OTHELLO
Most veritable. Therefore look to 't well.

DESDEMONA
Then would to God that I had never seen 't!

OTHELLO
Ha! Wherefore?

DESDEMONA
Why do you speak so startingly and rash?

OTHELLO
Is 't lost? Is 't gone? Speak, is 't out o' th' way?

DESDEMONA
Heaven bless us!

OTHELLO
Say you?

DESDEMONA
It is not lost; but what an if it were?

OTHELLO
How?

DESDEMONA
I say, it is not lost.

OTHELLO
Fetch 't, let me see 't.

DESDEMONA
Why, so I can, sir, but I will not now.
This is a trick to put me from my suit.
Pray you, let Cassio be receiv'd again.

OTHELLO
Fetch me the handkerchief! My mind misgives.

DESDEMONA
Come, come;
You'll never meet a more sufficient man.

OTHELLO
The handkerchief!

DESDEMONA
I pray, talk me of Cassio.

OTHELLO
The handkerchief!

DESDEMONA
A man that all his time
Hath founded his good fortunes on your love,
Shar'd dangers with you—

OTHELLO
The handkerchief!

DESDEMONA
I' faith, you are to blame.

OTHELLO
'Zounds!

[*Exit Othello.*]

6 liberal (Here and subsequently, Othello likely has in mind two senses of "liberal"; "generous" and "licentious.") **8 sequester** separation **9 exercise devout** religious devotion **12 frank** (1) generous (2) undisciplined, lusty (In her reply, Desdemona regards only of the first sense of the word.) **15 our . . . hearts** with the heraldry of current times, hands (given in marriage) no longer signify the giving of hearts as well **17 chuck** chick (a term of endearment) **19 salt . . . rheum** troubling watering of the eyes that **24 faith** truthfully **25 a fault** unfortunate **27 charmer** sorceress **28 while . . . it** as long as my mother kept the handkerchief **29 amiable** desirable **35 her** i.e., to my wife **37 perdition** loss **39 web** weave, material **40 sibyl** prophetess **41 course** travel **compasses** annual circlings, revolutions (the numbering of which demonstrated that the sibyl was 200 years old) **42 prophetic fury** the inspired frenzy which enabled her to prophesy **44 mummy** magic fluid extracted from embalmed bodies

45 Conserv'd of made a preserve out of, prepared out of **46 look . . . well** take good care of it **49 startingly** by fits and starts, disjointedly **53 an if** if **61 sufficient** able **63 all his time** throughout his career **67 'Zounds** by God's wounds (a mild oath)

(52) DESDEMONA AND OTHELLO [V.II.I]

Othello

SCENE: A bedchamber in Othello's castle.

{Othello has just slipped into Desdemona's room, where she lies fast asleep. Though he's come here to do away with his beloved for her supposed infidelity, it's evident that the Moor is of two minds about this whole murder thing.}

OTHELLO
It is the cause, it is the cause, my soul.
Let me not name it to you, you chaste stars!
It is the cause. Yet I'll not shed her blood,
Nor scar that whiter skin of hers than snow,
And smooth as monumental alabaster.
Yet she must die, else she'll betray more men.
Put out the light, and then put out the light.
If I quench thee, thou flaming minister,
I can again thy former light restore,
Should I repent me; but once put out thy light,
Thou cunning'st pattern of excelling nature,
I know not where is that Promethean heat
That can thy light relume. When I have pluck'd the rose,
I cannot give it vital growth again;
It must needs wither. I'll smell it on the tree. [*Kissing her.*]
O balmy breath, that dost almost persuade
Justice to break her sword! One more, one more.
Be thus when thou art dead, and I will kill thee,
And love thee after. One more, and that's the last.
So sweet was ne'er so fatal. I must weep,
But they are cruel tears. This sorrow's heavenly;
It strikes where it doth love. She wakes.

DESDEMONA
Who's there? Othello?

OTHELLO
Ay, Desdemona.

DESDEMONA
Will you come to bed, my lord?

OTHELLO
Have you pray'd tonight, Desdemon?

DESDEMONA
Ay, my lord.

OTHELLO
If you bethink yourself of any crime
Unreconcil'd as yet to heaven and grace,
Solicit for it straight.

DESDEMONA
Alack, my lord, what may you mean by that?

OTHELLO
Well, do it, and be brief; I will walk by.
I would not kill thy unprepared spirit;
No, heaven forfend! I would not kill thy soul.

DESDEMONA
Talk you of killing?

OTHELLO
Ay, I do.

DESDEMONA
Then heaven
Have mercy on me!

OTHELLO
Amen, with all my heart!

DESDEMONA
If you say so, I hope you will not kill me.

OTHELLO
Hum!

DESDEMONA
And yet I fear you; for you're fatal then
When your eyes roll so. Why I should fear I know not,
Since guiltiness I know not; but yet I feel I fear.

OTHELLO
Think on thy sins.

DESDEMONA
They are loves I bear to you.

OTHELLO
Ay, and for that thou diest.

DESDEMONA
That death's unnatural that kills for loving.
Alas, why gnaw you so your nether lip?
Some bloody passion shakes your very frame:
These are portents; but yet I hope, I hope,
They do not point on me.

OTHELLO
Peace, and be still!

DESDEMONA
I will so. What's the matter?

OTHELLO
That handkerchief which I so lov'd and gave thee
Thou gav'st to Cassio.

DESDEMONA
No, by my life and soul!
Send for the man, and ask him.

OTHELLO
Sweet soul, take heed, Take heed of perjury.
Thou art on thy deathbed.

DESDEMONA
Ay, but not yet to die.

OTHELLO
Yes, presently.
Therefore confess thee freely of thy sin;
For to deny each article with oath
Cannot remove nor choke the strong conception
That I do groan withal. Thou art to die.

DESDEMONA
Then Lord have mercy on me!

OTHELLO
I say, amen.

DESDEMONA
And have you mercy too! I never did
Offend you in my life; never lov'd Cassio
But with such general warranty of heaven
As I might love. I never gave him token.

OTHELLO
By heaven, I saw my handkerchief in 's hand.
O perjur'd woman! Thou dost stone my heart,
And makes me call what I intend to do
A murder, which I thought a sacrifice.
I saw the handkerchief.

DESDEMONA
He found it then;
I never gave it him. Send for him hither;
Let him confess a truth.

OTHELLO
He hath confess'd.

DESDEMONA
What, my lord?

OTHELLO
That he hath us'd thee.

DESDEMONA
How? Unlawfully?

OTHELLO
Ay.

DESDEMONA
He will not say so.

OTHELLO
No, his mouth is stopp'd;
Honest Iago hath ta'en order for 't.

DESDEMONA
O, my fear interprets. What, is he dead?

OTHELLO
Had all his hairs been lives, my great revenge
Had stomach for them all.

DESDEMONA
Alas! he is betray'd and I undone! [*She weeps.*]

OTHELLO
Out, strumpet! Weep'st thou for him to my face?

DESDEMONA
O, banish me, my lord, but kill me not!

OTHELLO
Down, strumpet!

DESDEMONA
Kill me tomorrow; let me live tonight!

OTHELLO
Nay, if you strive—

DESDEMONA
But half an hour!

OTHELLO
Being done, there is no pause.

DESDEMONA
But while I say one prayer!

OTHELLO
It is too late.

[*He smothers her.*]

1 cause i.e., the cause of justice (Othello believes that the infidelity he ascribes to Desdemona is tantamount to a crime; a transgression which, even if he were to set aside the matter of his personal honor, he would still feel duty-bound to punish.) **7 the light . . . light** the candle, and then end her life **11 cunning'st** most marvelous **12 Promethean heat** life-giving fire (alludes to the fire that Prometheus stole from heaven) **13 relume** rekindle **16 balmy** delightfully fragrant **21–22 This . . . love** (an allusion to the biblical passage found at Hebrews 12:6) **28 bethink yourself** can think **crime** sin **30 straight** at once, straightaway **34 forfend** forbid **39 fatal** menacing **44 unnatural** cruel, without normal human feeling **48 point on** point to, aim at **50 handkerchief** (See III.iv.) **55 presently** immediately, at once **58 conception** belief (of your guilt) **59 withal** with **63 warranty**

permission, approval **64 token** i.e., a token of my affection (such as her handkerchief) **66 stone** harden, turn to stone **68 thought** had (up till now) thought was **75 ta'en . . . 't** taken steps to see to it **80 Out** (An exclamation of reproach or indignation.) **85 Being done** (1) since I've already made up my mind (2) since everything has been said and done

(53) LADY ANNE AND RICHARD, DUKE OF GLOUCESTER [I.II.33]

Richard III

SCENE: A street in London.

{In the midst of escorting the remains of her father-in-law, Henry VI, to its final resting place, Lady Anne is confronted by the last person she wants to see—King Henry's assassin, the Duke of Gloucester.}

GLOUCESTER
Stay, you that bear the corse, and set it down.

LADY ANNE
What black magician conjures up this fiend,
To stop devoted charitable deeds?

GLOUCESTER
Villains, set down the corse, or, by Saint Paul,
I'll make a corse of him that disobeys.

LADY ANNE
What do you tremble? Are you all afraid?
Alas, I blame you not, for you are mortal,
And mortal eyes cannot endure the devil.
Avaunt, thou dreadful minister of hell!
Thou hadst but power over his mortal body,
His soul thou canst not have. Therefore be gone.

GLOUCESTER
Sweet saint, for charity, be not so curst.

LADY ANNE
Foul devil, for God's sake hence, and trouble us not;
For thou hast made the happy earth thy hell,
Fill'd it with cursing cries and deep exclaims.
If thou delight to view thy heinous deeds,

Behold this pattern of thy butcheries.
[*She uncovers the corpse.*]
O, gentlemen, see, see dead Henry's wounds
Open their congeal'd mouths and bleed afresh!
Blush, Blush, thou lump of foul deformity;
For 'tis thy presence that exhales this blood
From cold and empty veins where no blood dwells.
Thy deeds inhuman and unnatural
Provoke this deluge most unnatural.
O God, which this blood mad'st, revenge his death!
O earth, which this blood drink'st revenge his death!
Either heav'n with lightning strike the murd'rer dead,
Or earth gape open wide and eat him quick,
As thou dost swallow up this good king's blood,
Which his hell-govern'd arm hath butchered!

GLOUCESTER
Lady, you know no rules of charity,
Which renders good for bad, blessings for curses.

LADY ANNE
Villain, thou know'st nor law of God nor man.
No beast so fierce but knows some touch of pity.

GLOUCESTER
But I know none, and therefore am no beast.

LADY ANNE
O wonderful, when devils tell the truth!

GLOUCESTER
More wonderful, when angels are so angry.
Vouchsafe, divine perfection of a woman,
Of these supposed crimes to give me leave
By circumstance but to acquit myself.

LADY ANNE
Vouchsafe, defus'd infection of a man,
For these known evils, but to give me leave,
By circumstance, to curse thy cursed self.

GLOUCESTER
Fairer than tongue can name thee, let me have
Some patient leisure to excuse myself.

LADY ANNE
Fouler than heart can think thee, thou canst make
No excuse current but to hang thyself.

GLOUCESTER
By such despair I should accuse myself.

LADY ANNE
And by despairing shalt thou stand excused
For doing worthy vengeance on thyself,
That didst unworthy slaughter upon others.

GLOUCESTER
Say that I slew them not?

LADY ANNE
Then say they were not slain.
But dead they are, and, devilish slave, by thee.

GLOUCESTER
I did not kill your husband.

LADY ANNE
Why, then he is alive.

GLOUCESTER
Nay, he is dead; and slain by Edward's hand.

LADY ANNE
In thy foul throat thou li'st! Queen Margaret saw
Thy murd'rous falchion smoking in his blood;
The which thou once didst bend against her breast,
But that thy brothers beat aside the point.

GLOUCESTER
I was provoked by her sland'rous tongue,
That laid their guilt upon my guiltless shoulders.

LADY ANNE
Thou wast provoked by thy bloody mind,
That never dream'st on aught but butcheries.
Didst thou not kill this king?

GLOUCESTER
I grant ye.

LADY ANNE
Dost grant me, hedgehog? Then God grant me too

Thou mayst be damned for that wicked deed!
O, he was gentle, mild, and virtuous!

GLOUCESTER
The better for the King of Heaven that hath him.

LADY ANNE
He is in heaven, where thou shalt never come.

GLOUCESTER
Let him thank me that holp to send him thither;
For he was fitter for that place than earth.

LADY ANNE
And thou unfit for any place but hell.

GLOUCESTER
Yes, one place else, if you will hear me name it.

LADY ANNE
Some dungeon.

GLOUCESTER
Your bedchamber.

LADY ANNE
Ill rest betide the chamber where thou liest!

GLOUCESTER
So will it, madam, till I lie with you.

LADY ANNE
I hope so.

GLOUCESTER
I know so. But, gentle Lady Anne,
To leave this keen encounter of our wits
And fall something into a slower method,
Is not the causer of the timeless deaths
Of these Plantagenets, Henry and Edward,
As blameful as the executioner?

LADY ANNE
Thou wast the cause, and most accurs'd effect.

GLOUCESTER
Your beauty was the cause of that effect—
Your beauty, that did haunt me in my sleep

To undertake the death of all the world,
So I might live one hour in your sweet bosom.

LADY ANNE
If I thought that, I tell thee, homicide,
These nails should rend that beauty from my cheeks.

GLOUCESTER
These eyes could not endure that beauty's wrack;
You should not blemish it, if I stood by.
As all the world is cheered by the sun,
So I by that. It is my day, my life.

LADY ANNE
Black night o'ershade thy day, and death thy life!

GLOUCESTER
Curse not thyself, fair creature—thou art both.

LADY ANNE
I would I were, to be reveng'd on thee.

GLOUCESTER
It is a quarrel most unnatural
To be reveng'd on him that loveth thee.

LADY ANNE
It is a quarrel just and reasonable
To be reveng'd on him that kill'd my husband.

GLOUCESTER
He that bereft thee, lady, of thy husband,
Did it to help thee to a better husband.

LADY ANNE
His better doth not breathe upon the earth.

GLOUCESTER
He lives that loves thee better than he could.

LADY ANNE
Name him.

GLOUCESTER
Plantagenet.

LADY ANNE
Why, that was he.

GLOUCESTER
The selfsame name, but one of better nature.

LADY ANNE
Where is he?

GLOUCESTER
Here.

[*She spits at him.*]

Why dost thou spit at me?

LADY ANNE
Would it were mortal poison, for thy sake!

GLOUCESTER
Never came poison from so sweet a place.

LADY ANNE
Never hung poison on a fouler toad.
Out of my sight! Thou dost infect my eyes.

GLOUCESTER
Thine eyes, sweet lady, have infected mine.

LADY ANNE
Would they were basilisks, to strike thee dead!

1 corse corpse **3 devoted** holy **6 What** why **9 Avaunt** away, be gone **12 curst** disagreeable, shrewish **13 hence** away from here **15 deep exclaims** heartfelt exclamations **17 pattern** example **19 bleed afresh** (It was commonly believed that a murder victim's wounds would bleed anew in the presence of the murderer.) **21 exhales** draws forth, induces the flow of **23 unnatural** cruel, wicked **24 unnatural** supernatural **28 quick** alive **33 nor . . . nor man** neither . . . nor law of man **34 No** (there is) no **38–40 Vouchsafe . . . myself** allow me, you divine and perfect woman, to, by detailed argument, acquit myself of these supposed crimes **41 defus'd infection** misshapen corruption **47 current** acceptable **48 I should accuse** I would incriminate **57 falchion** curved sword **58 bend** aim **63 aught** anything **65 hedgehog** (Alludes to Richard's badge, which featured a wild hog.) **70 holp** helped **75 betide** befall **79 something into a** into a somewhat **80 timeless** untimely **83 effect** agent **84 effect** result **88 homicide** murderer **90 wrack** destruction **97 unnatural** cruel **101 bereft** deprived **104 He lives that** i.e., there is a man who **he** i.e., Prince Edward **105 Plantagenet** (Both Richard and Edward were members of the Plantagenet family.) **110 toad** (Toads were commonly thought to be poisonous.) **112 infected** i.e., with love (There was some thought back then that love entered through one's eyes.) **113 basilisks** legendary reptiles that could kill by staring

(54) QUEEN ELIZABETH AND KING RICHARD III [IV.IV.199]

Richard III

SCENE: Before the royal palace in London.

{No sooner does Elizabeth, widow of King Edward IV, finish denouncing Richard for his litany of heinous deeds (among which is responsibility for the murder of her two sons) than Richard himself appears on the scene to present his unseemly side of things.}

KING RICHARD
Stay, madam; I must talk a word with you.

QUEEN ELIZABETH
I have no more sons of the royal blood
For thee to slaughter. For my daughters, Richard,
They shall be praying nuns, not weeping queens;
And therefore level not to hit their lives.

KING RICHARD
You have a daughter call'd Elizabeth,
Virtuous and fair, royal and gracious.

QUEEN ELIZABETH
And must she die for this? O, let her live,
And I'll corrupt her manners, stain her beauty,
Slander myself as false to Edward's bed;
Throw over her the veil of infamy;
So she may live unscarr'd of bleeding slaughter,
I will confess she was not Edward's daughter.

KING RICHARD
Wrong not her birth, she is a royal princess.

QUEEN ELIZABETH
To save her life, I'll say she is not so.

KING RICHARD
Her life is safest only in her birth.

QUEEN ELIZABETH
And only in that safety died her brothers.

KING RICHARD
Lo, at their births good stars were opposite.

QUEEN ELIZABETH
No, to their lives ill friends were contrary.

KING RICHARD
All unavoided is the doom of destiny.

QUEEN ELIZABETH
True, when avoided grace makes destiny.
My babes were destin'd to a fairer death,
If grace had bless'd thee with a fairer life.

KING RICHARD
You speak as if that I had slain my cousins.

QUEEN ELIZABETH
Cousins, indeed, and by their uncle cozen'd
Of comfort, kingdom, kindred, freedom, life.
Whose hand soever lanch'd their tender hearts,
Thy head, all indirectly, gave direction.
No doubt the murd'rous knife was dull and blunt
Till it was whetted on thy stone-hard heart,
To revel in the entrails of my lambs.
But that still use of grief makes wild grief tame,
My tongue should to thy ears not name my boys
Till that my nails were anchor'd in thine eyes;
And I, in such a desp'rate bay of death,
Like a poor bark, of sails and tackling reft,
Rush all to pieces on thy rocky bosom.

KING RICHARD
Madam, so thrive I in my enterprise
And dangerous success of bloody wars,
As I intend more good to you and yours
Than ever you or yours were by me harm'd!

QUEEN ELIZABETH
What good is cover'd with the face of heaven,
To be discover'd, that can do me good?

KING RICHARD
Th' advancement of your children, gentle lady.

QUEEN ELIZABETH
Up to some scaffold, there to lose their heads?

KING RICHARD
Unto the dignity and height of fortune,
The high imperial type of this earth's glory.

QUEEN ELIZABETH
Flatter my sorrow with report of it;
Tell me what state, what dignity, what honor,
Canst thou demise to any child of mine?

KING RICHARD
Even all I have—ay, and myself and all—
Will I withal endow a child of thine,
So in the Lethe of thy angry soul
Thou drown the sad remembrance of those wrongs
Which thou supposest I have done to thee.

QUEEN ELIZABETH
Be brief, lest that the process of thy kindness
Last longer telling than thy kindness' date.

KING RICHARD
Then know that from my soul I love thy daughter.

QUEEN ELIZABETH
My daughter's mother thinks it with her soul.

KING RICHARD
What do you think?

QUEEN ELIZABETH
That thou dost love my daughter from thy soul;
So from thy soul's love didst thou love her brothers,
And from my heart's love I do thank thee for it.

KING RICHARD
Be not so hasty to confound my meaning.
I mean that with my soul I love thy daughter,
And do intend to make her Queen of England.

QUEEN ELIZABETH
Well then, who dost thou mean shall be her king?

KING RICHARD
Even he that makes her queen. Who else should be?

QUEEN ELIZABETH
What, thou?

KING RICHARD
Even so. How think you of it, madam?

QUEEN ELIZABETH
How canst thou woo her?

KING RICHARD
That would I learn of you,
As one being best acquainted with her humor.

QUEEN ELIZABETH
And wilt thou learn of me?

KING RICHARD
Madam, with all my heart.

QUEEN ELIZABETH
Send to her, by the man that slew her brothers,
A pair of bleeding hearts; thereon engrave
"Edward" and "York"; then haply she will weep.
Therefore present to her—as sometime Margaret
Did to thy father, steep'd in Rutland's blood—
A handkerchief, which, say to her, did drain
The purple sap from her sweet brother's body;
And bid her wipe her weeping eyes withal.
If this inducement move her not to love,
Send her a letter of thy noble deeds.
Tell her thou mad'st away her uncle Clarence,
Her uncle Rivers, ay, and, for her sake,
Mad'st quick conveyance with her good aunt Anne.

KING RICHARD
Come, come, you mock me; this is not the way
To win your daughter.

QUEEN ELIZABETH
There is no other way
Unless thou couldst put on some other shape,
And not be Richard that hath done all this.

KING RICHARD
Say that I did all this for love of her.

QUEEN ELIZABETH
Nay, then indeed she cannot choose but hate thee,
Having bought love with such a bloody spoil.

1 Stay wait **5 level** aim **9 manners** morals **12 bleeding** bloody **16 birth** noble lineage **18 opposite** adverse, antagonistic **19 contrary** opposed **20 unavoided** unavoidable **21 avoided grace** i.e., Richard, who is void of grace **23 grace** divine grace **25 cozen'd** cheated **27 Whose hand soever** whatever hand it was that **lanch'd** pierced **28 all** although, even if **32 But** except **still** continual **33 should** would **35 desp'rate . . . death** treacherously dangerous inlet **36 bark** small sailing vessel **reft** robbed, bereft **38–40 so . . . intend** i.e., as certainly as I succeed in my dangerous and bloody endeavors, so do I intend to do **42 cover'd with** masked by **47 type** sign, symbol (i.e., the crown) **50 demise** convey **53 Lethe** forgetfulness (Lethe was the river of Hades that produced forgetfulness.) **56 process** tale **57 telling** in the telling of it **thy kindness' date** the duration of your kindness **58 from** with (But in her ensuing lines, the Queen uses the word in its "apart from" sense.) **64 confound** confuse **71 humor** nature, temperament **76 sometime** once **76–77 Margaret Did** (See *Henry VI, Part 3*, I.iv.) **79 purple** blood-red **80 withal** with that **83 mad'st away** did away with, killed **85 conveyance with** rid of **93 spoil** slaughter (A term from hunting.)

(55) QUEEN ELIZABETH AND KING RICHARD III [IV.IV.291]

Richard III

SCENE: Before the royal palace in London.

{Devil incarnate he may well be, but you can't deny that Richard sure has chutzpah. Take for example this continuation of the preceding scene, in which the evil King doggedly and unashamedly pursues the favor of a woman who is anything but amenable to his cause.}

KING RICHARD
Look what is done cannot be now amended.
Men shall deal unadvisedly sometimes,
Which after hours give leisure to repent.
If I did take the kingdom from your sons,
To make amends, I'll give it to your daughter.
And when this arm of mine hath chastised
The petty rebel, dull-brain'd Buckingham,

Bound with triumphant garlands will I come
And lead thy daughter to a conqueror's bed;
To whom I will retail my conquest won,
And she shall be sole victress, Caesar's Caesar.

QUEEN ELIZABETH
What were I best to say? Her father's brother
Would be her lord? Or shall I say her uncle?
Or, he that slew her brothers and her uncles?
Under what title shall I woo for thee,
That God, the law, my honor and her love
Can make seem pleasing to her tender years?

KING RICHARD
Infer fair England's peace by this alliance.

QUEEN ELIZABETH
Which she shall purchase with still lasting war.

KING RICHARD
Say that the King, that may command, entreats.

QUEEN ELIZABETH
That at her hands which the King's King forbids.

KING RICHARD
Say she shall be a high and mighty queen.

QUEEN ELIZABETH
To vail the title, as her mother doth.

KING RICHARD
Say I will love her everlastingly.

QUEEN ELIZABETH
But how long shall that title "ever" last?

KING RICHARD
Sweetly in force unto her fair life's end.

QUEEN ELIZABETH
But how long fairly shall her sweet life last?

KING RICHARD
As long as heaven and nature lengthens it.

QUEEN ELIZABETH
As long as hell and Richard likes of it.

KING RICHARD
Say I, her sovereign, am her subject low.

QUEEN ELIZABETH
But she, your subject, loathes such sovereignty.

KING RICHARD
Be eloquent in my behalf to her.

QUEEN ELIZABETH
An honest tale speeds best being plainly told.

KING RICHARD
Then plainly to tell her my loving tale.

QUEEN ELIZABETH
Plain and not honest is too harsh a style.

KING RICHARD
Your reasons are too shallow and too quick.

QUEEN ELIZABETH
O no, my reasons are too deep and dead—
Too deep and dead, poor infants, in their grave.

KING RICHARD
Harp not on that string, madam; that is past.

QUEEN ELIZABETH
Harp on it still shall I till heartstrings break.

KING RICHARD
Now, by my George, my garter, and my crown—

QUEEN ELIZABETH
Profan'd, dishonor'd, and the third usurp'd.

KING RICHARD
I swear—

QUEEN ELIZABETH
By nothing; for this is no oath.
Thy George, profan'd, hath lost his lordly honor;
Thy garter, blemish'd, pawn'd his knightly virtue;
Thy crown, usurp'd, disgrac'd his kingly glory.
If something thou wouldst swear to be believ'd,
Swear then by something that thou hast not wrong'd.

KING RICHARD
Then, by myself—

QUEEN ELIZABETH
Thyself is self-misus'd.

KING RICHARD
Now, by the world—

QUEEN ELIZABETH
'Tis full of thy foul wrongs.

KING RICHARD
My father's death—

QUEEN ELIZABETH
Thy life hath it dishonor'd.

KING RICHARD
Why then, by God—

QUEEN ELIZABETH
God's wrong is most of all.
If thou didst fear to break an oath with Him,
The unity the King thy brother made
Thou hadst not broken, nor my brothers died.
If thou hadst fear'd to break an oath by Him,
Th' imperial metal, circling now thy head,
Had grac'd the tender temples of my child,
And both the princes had been breathing here,
Which now, two tender bedfellows for dust,
Thy broken faith hath made the prey for worms.
What canst thou swear by now?

1 Look what whatever **10 retail** relate **15 what title** which of your titles **17 tender** youthful **18 Infer** allege, imply **19 still** ever **21 King's King** i.e., God **23 vail** devalue, lower (as a sign of submission) **29 likes of** is fond of, approves of **33 speeds** succeeds **34 plainly** straightforwardly, frankly **35 harsh a style** discordant a combination **36 quick** hasty, rushed (Though in the following line, the Queen plays on the word's "alive" sense.) **41 George** a badge that pictured St. George slaying a dragon **garter** a blue velvet ribbon symbolizing the Order of the Garter **47 to** is to **52 God's wrong is** (swearing by) God is wrong **54 unity** i.e., the peace King Edward brokered between Queen Elizabeth and her enemies. See II.i.)
57 Th' imperial metal the royal crown

(56) JULIET AND ROMEO [II.II.2]

Romeo and Juliet

SCENE: Capulet's orchard.

{Wandering alone among the trees of Capulet's garden, Romeo suddenly finds himself a stone's throw away from his beloved Juliet's balcony. As for the maid herself, she can't seem to stop thinking about that handsome young man she encountered back at the party.}

ROMEO

But, soft! What light through yonder window breaks?
It is the east, and Juliet is the sun.
Arise, fair sun, and kill the envious moon,
Who is already sick and pale with grief,
That thou, her maid, art far more fair than she.
[*Juliet appears at her window.*]
It is my lady, O, it is my love!
O, that she knew she were!

JULIET

Ay me!

ROMEO

She speaks!
O, speak again, bright angel, for thou art
As glorious to this night, being o'er my head,
As is a winged messenger of heaven
Unto the white-upturned wond'ring eyes
Of mortals that fall back to gaze on him
When he bestrides the lazy puffing clouds
And sails upon the bosom of the air.

JULIET

O Romeo, Romeo, wherefore art thou Romeo?
Deny thy father and refuse thy name.
Or, if thou wilt not, be but sworn my love,
And I'll no longer be a Capulet.

ROMEO

[*Aside.*] Shall I hear more, or shall I speak at this?

JULIET

'Tis but thy name that is my enemy;
Thou art thyself, though not a Montague.

What's Montague? It is nor hand, nor foot,
Nor arm, nor face, nor any other part
Belonging to a man. O, be some other name!
What's in a name? That which we call a rose
By any other name would smell as sweet;
So Romeo would, were he not Romeo call'd,
Retain that dear perfection which he owes
Without that title. Romeo, doff thy name,
And for thy name, which is no part of thee,
Take all myself.

ROMEO
[*Reveals himself.*] I take thee at thy word!
Call me but love, and I'll be new baptized;
Henceforth I never will be Romeo.

JULIET
What man art thou that thus bescreen'd in night
So stumblest on my counsel?

ROMEO
By a name
I know not how to tell thee who I am.
My name, dear saint, is hateful to myself,
Because it is an enemy to thee;
Had I it written, I would tear the word.

JULIET
My ears have not yet drunk a hundred words
Of thy tongue's uttering, yet I know the sound.
Art thou not Romeo and a Montague?

ROMEO
Neither, fair maid, if either thee dislike.

JULIET
How camest thou hither, tell me, and wherefore?
The orchard walls are high and hard to climb,
And the place death, considering who thou art,
If any of my kinsmen find thee here.

ROMEO
With love's light wings did I o'erperch these walls,
For stony limits cannot hold love out.
And what love can do, that dares love attempt;
Therefore thy kinsmen are no stop to me.

JULIET
If they do see thee, they will murder thee.

ROMEO
Alack, there lies more peril in thine eye
Than twenty of their swords. Look thou but sweet,
And I am proof against their enmity.

JULIET
I would not for the world they saw thee here.

ROMEO
I have night's cloak to hide me from their eyes;
And but thou love me, let them find me here.
My life were better ended by their hate,
Than death prorogued, wanting of thy love.

JULIET
By whose direction found'st thou out this place?

ROMEO
By love, that first did prompt me to inquire.
He lent me counsel, and I lent him eyes.
I am no pilot; yet, wert thou as far
As that vast shore wash'd with the farthest sea,
I should adventure for such merchandise.

JULIET
Thou knowest the mask of night is on my face,
Else would a maiden blush bepaint my cheek
For that which thou hast heard me speak tonight.
Fain would I dwell on form, fain, fain deny
What I have spoke; but farewell compliment!
Dost thou love me? I know thou wilt say "Ay,"
And I will take thy word. Yet, if thou swear'st,
Thou mayst prove false. At lovers' perjuries
They say, Jove laughs. O gentle Romeo,
If thou dost love, pronounce it faithfully.
Or if thou thinkest I am too quickly won,
I'll frown and be perverse and say thee nay,
So thou wilt woo; but else, not for the world.
In truth, fair Montague, I am too fond,
And therefore thou mayst think my behavior light.
But trust me, gentleman, I'll prove more true
Than those that have more coying to be strange.

I should have been more strange, I must confess,
But that thou overheard'st, ere I was ware,
My true-love passion. Therefore pardon me,
And not impute this yielding to light love,
Which the dark night hath so discovered.

ROMEO
Lady, by yonder blessed moon I vow,
That tips with silver all these fruit-tree tops—

JULIET
O, swear not by the moon, th' inconstant moon,
That monthly changes in her circled orb,
Lest that thy love prove likewise variable.

ROMEO
What shall I swear by?

JULIET
Do not swear at all;
Or, if thou wilt, swear by thy gracious self,
Which is the god of my idolatry,
And I'll believe thee.

ROMEO
If my heart's dear love—

JULIET
Well, do not swear. Although I joy in thee,
I have no joy of this contract tonight.
It is too rash, too unadvis'd, too sudden,
Too like the lightning, which doth cease to be
Ere one can say "It lightens." Sweet, good night!
This bud of love, by summer's ripening breath,
May prove a beauteous flow'r when next we meet.
Good night, good night! As sweet repose and rest
Come to thy heart as that within my breast!

ROMEO
O, wilt thou leave me so unsatisfied?

JULIET
What satisfaction canst thou have tonight?

ROMEO
Th' exchange of thy love's faithful vow for mine.

JULIET
I gave thee mine before thou didst request it;
And yet I would it were to give again.

ROMEO
Wouldst thou withdraw it? For what purpose, love?

JULIET
But to be frank, and give it thee again.
And yet I wish but for the thing I have.
My bounty is as boundless as the sea,
My love as deep; the more I give to thee,
The more I have, for both are infinite.
[*Nurse calls within.*]
I hear some noise within; dear love, adieu!—
Anon, good nurse!-Sweet Montague, be true.
Good night, good night! Parting is such sweet sorrow,
That I shall say good night till it be morrow. [*Exit.*]

ROMEO
Sleep dwell upon thine eyes, peace in thy breast!
Would I were sleep and peace, so sweet to rest!
Hence will I to my ghostly father's cell,
His help to crave, and my dear hap to tell

1 soft wait **5 maid** follower, devotee (of Diana, mood-goddess and patroness of virgins) **11 white-upturned** rolled upward such that the whites of the eyes are prominent **15 wherefore** why **21 Thou . . . Montague** i.e., you would still be your same self, even if you changed your name **28 owes** possesses **30 for** in exchange for **35 bescreen'd in** hidden by **36 counsel** private thoughts **44 thee dislike** displeases you **45 hither** to this place **49 o'erperch** fly over **50 stony limits** i.e., stone walls **52 stop** obstacle, impediment **56 proof** protected, armored **59 but** unless **61 prorogued** prolonged **wanting of** lacking **66 vast** desolate **67 should adventure** would dare journey there **71 Fain** gladly **72 compliment** modest behavior, social conventions **79 perverse** intentionally unreasonable **80 So thou wilt** so that you will **82 light** frivolous **84 coying** coyness **strange** aloof, reserved **86 ware** aware (you were nearby) **89 discovered** uncovered, revealed **93 orb** sphere (Astronomers of the day believed that heavenly bodies like the moon revolved around the earth while fixed inside transparent spheres.) **100 contract** exchanging of vows **101 rash** hasty **unadvis'd** impetuous, ill-advised **114 frank** generous **120 Anon** in a moment **125 ghostly father's** spiritual mentor's, i.e., Friar Laurence **cell** room **126 dear hap** good fortune

(57) Katharina and Petruchio [II.i.182]

The Taming of the Shrew

SCENE: Baptista's house.

{Petruchio has come a courtin', lured in large part by the generous dowry that goes to any man sturdy enough to win Katharina's hand. But tried and true shrew that she is, Kate's not inclined to cooperate.}

[*Enter Katharina.*]

PETRUCHIO
Good morrow, Kate; for that's your name, I hear.

KATHARINA
Well have you heard, but something hard of hearing.
They call me Katharine that do talk of me.

PETRUCHIO
You lie, in faith; for you are call'd plain Kate,
And bonny Kate, and sometimes Kate the curst;
But Kate, the prettiest Kate in Christendom,
Kate of Kate Hall, my super-dainty Kate,
For dainties are all Kates, and therefore, Kate,
Take this of me, Kate of my consolation:
Hearing thy mildness prais'd in every town,
Thy virtues spoke of, and thy beauty sounded,
Yet not so deeply as to thee belongs,
Myself am mov'd to woo thee for my wife.

KATHARINA
Mov'd? In good time! Let him that mov'd you hither
Remove you hence. I knew you at the first
You were a moveable.

PETRUCHIO
Why, what's a moveable?

KATHARINA
A join'd-stool.

PETRUCHIO
Thou hast hit it. Come, sit on me.

KATHARINA
Asses are made to bear, and so are you.

PETRUCHIO
Women are made to bear, and so are you.

KATHARINA
No such jade as you, if me you mean.

PETRUCHIO
Alas, good Kate, I will not burden thee,
For knowing thee to be but young and light.

KATHARINA
Too light for such a swain as you to catch,
And yet as heavy as my weight should be.

PETRUCHIO
Should be! Should—buzz!

KATHARINA
Well ta'en, and like a buzzard.

PETRUCHIO
O slow-wing'd turtle, shall a buzzard take thee?

KATHARINA
Ay, for a turtle, as he takes a buzzard.

PETRUCHIO
Come, come, you wasp; i' faith, you are too angry.

KATHARINA
If I be waspish, best beware my sting.

PETRUCHIO
My remedy is then to pluck it out.

KATHARINA
Ay, if the fool could find it where it lies.

PETRUCHIO
Who knows not where a wasp does wear his sting?
In his tail.

KATHARINA
In his tongue.

PETRUCHIO
Whose tongue?

KATHARINA
Yours, if you talk of tails; and so farewell.

PETRUCHIO
What, with my tongue in your tail? Nay, come again,
Good Kate; I am a gentleman.

KATHARINA
That I'll try. [*She strikes him.*]

PETRUCHIO
I swear I'll cuff you, if you strike again.

KATHARINA
So may you lose your arms.
If you strike me, you are no gentleman;
And if no gentleman, why then no arms.

PETRUCHIO
A herald, Kate? O, put me in thy books!

KATHARINA
What is your crest, a coxcomb?

PETRUCHIO
A combless cock, so Kate will be my hen.

KATHARINA
No cock of mine; you crow too like a craven.

PETRUCHIO
Nay, come, Kate, come; you must not look so sour.

KATHARINA
It is my fashion, when I see a crab.

PETRUCHIO
Why, here's no crab; and therefore look not sour.

KATHARINA
There is, there is.

PETRUCHIO
Then show it me.

KATHARINA
Had I a glass, I would.

PETRUCHIO
What, you mean my face?

KATHARINA
Well aim'd of such a young one.

PETRUCHIO
Now, by Saint George, I am too young for you.

KATHARINA
Yet you are wither'd.

PETRUCHIO
'Tis with cares.

KATHARINA
I care not.

PETRUCHIO
Nay, hear you, Kate. In sooth you scape not so.

KATHARINA
I chafe you if I tarry. Let me go.

PETRUCHIO
No, not a whit. I find you passing gentle.
'Twas told me you were rough and coy and sullen,
And now I find report a very liar;
For thou are pleasant, gamesome, passing courteous,
But slow in speech, yet sweet as spring-time flowers.
Thou canst not frown, thou canst not look askance,
Nor bite the lip, as angry wenches will,
Nor hast thou pleasure to be cross in talk;
But thou with mildness entertain'st thy wooers,
With gentle conference, soft and affable.
Why does the world report that Kate doth limp?
O sland'rous world! Kate like the hazel-twig
Is straight and slender, and as brown in hue
As hazel nuts, and sweeter than the kernels.
O, let me see thee walk. Thou dost not halt.

KATHARINA
Go, fool, and whom thou keep'st command.

PETRUCHIO
Did ever Dian so become a grove
As Kate this chamber with her princely gait?

O, be thou Dian, and let her be Kate;
And then let Kate be chaste and Dian sportful!

KATHARINA
Where did you study all this goodly speech?

PETRUCHIO
It is extempore, from my mother-wit.

KATHARINA
A witty mother! Witless else her son.

PETRUCHIO
Am I not wise?

KATHARINA
Yes, keep you warm.

PETRUCHIO
Marry, so I mean, sweet Katharine, in thy bed.
And therefore, setting all this chat aside,
Thus in plain terms: your father hath consented
That you shall be my wife; your dowry 'greed on;
And, will you, nill you, I will marry you.
Now, Kate, I am a husband for your turn;
For, by this light, whereby I see thy beauty—
Thy beauty that doth make me like thee well—
Thou must be married to no man but me.
For I am he am born to tame you Kate,
And bring you from a wild Kate to a Kate
Conformable as other household Kates.
Never make denial; I must and will
Have Katharine to my wife.

2 something are somewhat **4 faith** truth **7 Kate Hall** (The idea being that Kate is so well regarded, her residence takes its name from her rather from than her father or family, as was customary.) **8 dainties** delicacies, confections **Kates** (with a play on "cates," another word for "delicacies") **9 of me** from me **11 sounded** proclaimed **12 deeply** loudly, resonantly **14 In good time** indeed **16 moveable** something easily portable (e.g., small furniture like a "joined-stool") **17 join'd-stool** a finely crafted stool with parts carefully joined together **18 bear** carry weight **19 bear** i.e., (1) bear children (2) support the weight of men during intercourse **20 jade** unruly or poorly-conditioned horse **22 For knowing** because I know **light** (1) of delicate build (2) wanton **23 light** elusive **swain** bumpkin, clod **25 buzz** (Petruchio plays on the sound a "bee" makes.) **buzzard** (Here, Katharina means the word in its figurative "fool" sense; next, Petruchio refers to the inferior kind of hawk fit only to capture a slow-flying turtledove; lastly, Katharina concludes by meaning the sort of buzzing insect easily snapped up by a turtle.) **28 wasp** i.e., peevish, waspy woman (but also with a play on Katharina's buzzing insect) **29 sting** stinger **36 talk of tails** idly tell "tales" **38 try** put to the test **42 arms** coat of arms **43 herald** authority on heraldry **books** (1) heraldric registers (2) good books, i.e., favor **44 crest** (1) family crest (2) tuft on a cock's head **coxcomb** cap worn by a professional fool **45 combless** tame, humble **46 too** too much **craven** a cock unwilling to fight **48 crab** crab apple **51 glass** looking glass **53 aim'd of** guessed for **young** inexperienced **54 young** (Petruchio opts for the word's "vigorous" sense.) **56 sooth** truth **scape** escape **57 chafe** (1) irritate (2) excite, arouse **59 coy** disdainful **61 gamesome** playful **passing** exceedingly **62 But slow** never anything but deliberate **63 askance** scornfully **67 conference** conversation **72 halt** limp **73 whom . . . command** i.e., command your servants, not me **74 Dian** Diana, the moon goddess and goddess of chastity **77 sportful** wanton **79 mother-wit** natural intelligence **80 Witless . . . son** otherwise her son would be completely witless **82 keep you warm** (Alludes to the saying, "wit enough to keep oneself warm," which she implies is the sum total of his wit.) **83 Marry** indeed **85 Thus** here it is **87 will you, nill you** whether you will or will not (consent to this marriage) **88 husband . . . turn** suitable husband for a woman of your character and inclination **94 Conformable** obedient, submissive **household** domesticated

(58) MIRANDA AND FERDINAND [III.i.i]

The Tempest

SCENE: The island, before Prospero's cell.

{Prospero has commanded Ferdinand—son to the King of Naples—to pile up some logs, apparently believing that this is a suitable way to test the young man's love for Prospero's daughter, Miranda. Miranda, on the other hand, seems to disagree with her father's methodology, and she's not afraid to say so when she spots her beloved Ferdinand performing his labor of love.}

[*Enter Ferdinand, bearing a log.*]

FERDINAND

There be some sports are painful, and their labor
Delight in them sets off; some kinds of baseness
Are nobly undergone; and most poor matters

Point to rich ends. This my mean task
Would be as heavy to me as odious, but
The mistress which I serve quickens what's dead
And makes my labors pleasures. O, she is
Ten times more gentle than her father's crabbed,
And he's compos'd of harshness. I must remove
Some thousands of these logs and pile them up,
Upon a sore injunction. My sweet mistress
Weeps when she sees me work, and says such baseness
Had never like executor. I forget;
But these sweet thoughts do even refresh my labors,
Most busy lest, when I do it.

[*Enter Miranda.*]

MIRANDA

Alas, now, pray you,
Work not so hard. I would the lightning had
Burnt up those logs that you are enjoin'd to pile!
Pray, set it down and rest you. When this burns,
'Twill weep for having wearied you. My father
Is hard at study; pray now, rest yourself.
He's safe for these three hours.

FERDINAND

O most dear mistress,
The sun will set before I shall discharge
What I must strive to do.

MIRANDA

If you'll sit down,
I'll bear your logs the while. Pray give me that.
I'll carry it to the pile.

FERDINAND

No, precious creature,
I had rather crack my sinews, break my back,
Than you should such dishonor undergo,
While I sit lazy by.

MIRANDA

It would become me
As well as it does you; and I should do it
With much more ease, for my good will is to it,
And yours it is against. You look wearily.

FERDINAND

No, noble mistress, 'tis fresh morning with me
When you are by at night. I do beseech you—
Chiefly that I might set it in my prayers—
What is your name?

MIRANDA

Miranda.—O my father,
I have broke your hest to say so!

FERDINAND

Admir'd Miranda!
Indeed the top of admiration! Worth
What's dearest to the world! Full many a lady
I have ey'd with best regard, and many a time
Th' harmony of their tongues hath into bondage
Brought my too diligent ear. For several virtues
Have I lik'd several women, never any
With so full soul but some defect in her
Did quarrel with the noblest grace she ow'd
And put it to the foil. But you, O you,
So perfect and so peerless, are created
Of every creature's best!

MIRANDA

I do not know
One of my sex; no woman's face remember,
Save, from my glass, mine own. Nor have I seen
More that I may call men than you, good friend,
And my dear father. How features are abroad,
I am skilless of; but, by my modesty,
The jewel in my dower, I would not wish
Any companion in the world but you,
Nor can imagination form a shape,
Besides yourself, to like of. But I prattle
Something too wildly, and my father's precepts
I therein do forget.

FERDINAND

I am in my condition
A prince, Miranda; I do think, a king—
I would, not so!—and would no more endure
This wooden slavery than to suffer
The flesh-fly blow my mouth. Hear my soul speak:
The very instant that I saw you, did
My heart fly to your service; there resides,

To make me slave to it; and for your sake
Am I this patient log-man.

MIRANDA
Do you love me?

FERDINAND
O heaven, O earth, bear witness to this sound,
And crown what I profess with kind event
If I speak true! If hollowly, invert
What best is boded me to mischief! I,
Beyond all limit of what else i' th' world
Do love, prize, honor you.

MIRANDA
[*Weeping*.] I am a fool
To weep at what I am glad of.

FERDINAND
Wherefore weep you?

MIRANDA
At mine unworthiness, that dare not offer
What I desire to give, and much less take
What I shall die to want. But this is trifling,
And all the more it seeks to hide itself,
The bigger bulk it shows. Hence, bashful cunning,
And prompt me, plain and holy innocence!
I am your wife, it you will marry me;
If not, I'll die your maid. To be your fellow
You may deny me, but I'll be your servant,
Whether you will or no.

FERDINAND
My mistress, dearest,
And I thus humble ever.

MIRANDA
My husband, then?

FERDINAND
Ay, with a heart as willing
As bondage e'er of freedom. Here's my hand.

MIRANDA
And mine, with my heart in 't, And now farewell
Till half an hour hence.

FERDINAND

A thousand thousand!

[*Exeunt Ferdinand and Miranda severally.*]

2 sets off offsets **baseness** menial work **6 quickens** gives life to **8 crabbed** peevish, petulant **11 sore injunction** harsh command (of Prospero's) **13 Had . . . executor** never had someone so noble doing it **15 Most . . . it** i.e., the hardest work made easier when I think of her **19 weep** i.e., secrete resin **21 He's safe** i.e., you are safe from him **26 sinews** strength **36 hest to say** command by saying **41 several** particular **44 ow'd** owned **45 put . . . foil** attempt to vanquish it (i.e., the grace) in combat **49 glass** looking glass **51 abroad** elsewhere **52 skilless** ignorant, unaware **58 condition** rank, status **61 wooden slavery** drudgery of carrying wood **62 flesh-fly** insect that feeds and deposits its eggs on flesh **blow** befoul (by depositing eggs) **68 kind event** favorable outcome **69 hollowly** insincerely **70 boded** destined for **77 want** lack, be without **79 Hence** away **bashful cunning** coyness **82 maid** handmaid, attendant **fellow** mate **89 a thousand** i.e., a thousand farewells

(59) VIOLA AND FESTE [III.i.1]

Twelfth Night

SCENE: Olivia's garden.

{Viola, still in disguise as a boy named "Cesario," has arrived here once more to press Duke Orsino's suit for Olivia's hand. But before she can proceed with her appointed task, she must first deal with the barbed tongue and biting wit of Feste the Clown.}

[*Enter Viola and clown, Feste, with a tabor.*]

VIOLA
Save thee, friend, and thy music. Dost thou live by thy tabor?

FESTE
No, sir, I live by the church.

VIOLA
Art thou a churchman?

FESTE

No such matter, sir. I do live by the church; for I do live at my house, and my house doth stand by the church.

VIOLA

So thou mayst say, the king lies by a beggar, if a beggar dwell near him; or, the church stands by thy tabor, if thy tabor stand by the church.

FESTE

You have said, sir. To see this age! A sentence is but a chev'ril glove to a good wit. How quickly the wrong side may be turn'd outward!

VIOLA

Nay, that's certain. They that dally nicely with words may quickly make them wanton.

FESTE

I would therefore my sister had had no name, sir.

VIOLA

Why, man?

FESTE

Why, sir, her name's a word, and to dally with that word might make my sister wanton. But indeed, words are very rascals since bonds disgrac'd them.

VIOLA

Thy reason, man?

FESTE

Troth, sir, I can yield you none without words, and words are grown so false I am loath to prove reason with them.

VIOLA

I warrant thou art a merry fellow and car'st for nothing.

FESTE

Not so, sir, I do care for something; but in my conscience, sir, I do not care for you. If that be to care for nothing, sir, I would it would make you invisible.

VIOLA

Art not thou the Lady Olivia's fool?

FESTE

No, indeed, sir. The Lady Olivia has no folly. She will keep no fool, sir, till she be married; and fools are as like husbands as pilchers are to herrings, the husband's the bigger. I am indeed not her fool, but her corrupter of words.

VIOLA
I saw thee late at the Count Orsino's.

FESTE
Foolery, sir, does walk about the orb like the sun, it shines everywhere. I would be sorry, sir, but the fool should be as oft with your master as with my mistress. I think I saw your wisdom there.

VIOLA
Nay, an thou pass upon me, I'll no more with thee. Hold, there's expenses for thee. [*Gives him a coin.*]

FESTE
Now Jove, in his next commodity of hair, send thee a beard!

VIOLA
By my troth, I'll tell thee, I am almost sick for one—[*Aside.*] though I would not have it grow on my chin.—Is thy lady within?

FESTE
Would not a pair of these have bred, sir?

VIOLA
Yes, being kept together and put to use.

FESTE
I would play Lord Pandarus of Phrygia, sir, to bring a Cressida to this Troilus.

VIOLA
I understand you, sir; 'tis well begged. [*Gives another coin.*]

FESTE
The matter, I hope, is not great, sir, begging but a beggar; Cressida was a beggar. My lady is within, sir. I will conster to them whence you come. Who you are and what you would are out of my welkin—I might say "element," but the word is overworn. [*Exit.*]

VIOLA
This fellow is wise enough to play the fool,
And to do that well craves a kind of wit.
He must observe their mood on whom he jests,
The quality of persons, and the time,
And, like the haggard, check at every feather
That comes before his eye. This is a practice
As full of labor as a wise man's art;
For folly that he wisely shows is fit,
But wise men, folly-fall'n, quite taint their wit.

1 Save God save **live by** make your living by playing **tabor** small drum **3 churchman** clergyman **6 by a beggar** i.e., with a beggar **7 stands by** i.e., is supported by **8 sentence** statement, utterance **chev'ril** fine leather **11 wanton** unruly **15 wanton** lustful, unchaste **bonds** sworn statements **17 Troth** short for "by my troth," a mild oath affirming one's truthfulness **19 car'st for nothing** do not worry about a thing **20–21 care for you** (Ignoring Viola's meaning, Feste opts for care's "have affection" sense.) **21 invisible** i.e., nothing **22 fool** (Both "clown" and "fool" are alternate titles given to those in Feste's line of work, that of a professional jester.) **24 pilchers** small fish that closely resemble herring **26 late** of late, recently **27 orb** earth (The sun was then thought to revolve ("walk") around the earth.) **28 but** unless **29 your wisdom** i.e., you (This is Feste's playful take on "your honor" or "your worship.") **30 an . . . me** if you fence (verbally) with me **32 commodity** consignment, allotment **33 one** i.e., a man—Orsino **35 these** i.e., coins **36 put to use** loaned out at interest **37 Pandarus** (Pandarus was the go-between in the love story of Troilus and Cressida.) **39–40 Cressida . . . beggar** (One version of the Cressida tale has her becoming a beggar.) **40 conster** explain **41 would** wish **welkin** sky **element** i.e., sphere of influence ("element" is a synonym for "sky") **44 craves** requires **46 quality** character **time** occasion **47 haggard** wild hawk **47–48 check . . . eye** strike at every bird it sees, i.e., maneuver deftly from one subject to the next **48 practice** exercise of skill **49 art** skill, method **50 folly . . . fit** the cleverness he exhibits is a proper skill **51 folly-fall'n** having lapsed into folly **taint their wit** call into question their intelligence

(60) HERMIONE AND LEONTES [II.i.36]

The Winter's Tale

SCENE: A room in Leontes' palace.

{Hermione, her ladies in waiting and her young son Maxmillius are all enjoying a bit of playtime fun when in strides an obviously agitated Leontes. It seems that, for no apparent reason, Leontes is convinced that Hermione has been stepping out on him with his friend and fellow monarch, Polixenes. Now the time's come, evidently, for Leontes to confront his queen.}

LEONTES
How blest am I
In my just censure, in my true opinion!
Alack, for lesser knowledge! How accurs'd
In being so blest! There may be in the cup

A spider steep'd, and one may drink, depart,
And yet partake no venom, for his knowledge
Is not infected; but if one present
Th' abhorr'd ingredient to his eye, make known
How he hath drunk, he cracks his gorge, his sides,
With violent hefts. I have drunk, and seen the spider.
Give me the boy. I am glad you did not nurse him.
Though he does bear some signs of me, yet you
Have too much blood in him.

HERMIONE

What is this? Sport?

LEONTES

Bear the boy hence; he shall not come about her.
Away with him! And let her sport herself
With that she's big with, for 'tis Polixenes
Has made thee swell thus. [*Maxmillius is led away.*]

HERMIONE

But I'd say he had not,
And I'll be sworn you would believe my saying,
Howe'er you lean to th' nayward.

LEONTES

You, my lords,
Look on her, mark her well; be but about
To say "She is a goodly lady," and
The justice of your hearts will thereto add
"'Tis pity she's not honest, honorable."
Praise her but for this her without-door form,
Which on my faith deserves high speech, and straight
The shrug, the hum or ha, these petty brands
That calumny doth use—O, I am out,
That mercy does, for calumny will sear
Virtue itself-these shrugs, these hums and ha's,
When you have said she's goodly, come between
Ere you can say she's honest. But be 't known,
From him that has most cause to grieve it should be,
She's an adulteress.

HERMIONE

Should a villain say so,
The most replenish'd villain in the world,
He were as much more villain. You, my lord,
Do but mistake.

LEONTES

You have mistook, my lady,
Polixenes for Leontes. O thou thing!
Which I'll not call a creature of thy place,
Lest barbarism, making me the precedent,
Should a like language use to all degrees,
And mannerly distinguishment leave out
Betwixt the prince and beggar. I have said
She's an adulteress; I have said with whom.
More, she's a traitor, and Camillo is
A federary with her, and one that knows
What she should shame to know herself
But with her most vile principal—that she's
A bed-swerver, even as bad as those
That vulgars give bold'st titles; ay, and privy
To this their late escape.

HERMIONE

No, by my life.
Privy to none of this. How will this grieve you,
When you shall come to clearer knowledge, that
You thus have publish'd me! Gentle my lord,
You scarce can right me throughly then to say
You did mistake.

LEONTES

No; if I mistake
In those foundations which I build upon,
The center is not big enough to bear
A school-boy's top. Away with her, to prison!
He who shall speak for her is afar off guilty
But that he speaks.

HERMIONE

There's some ill planet reigns.
I must be patient till the heavens look
With an aspect more favorable. Good my lords,
I am not prone to weeping, as our sex
Commonly are, the want of which vain dew
Perchance shall dry your pities; but I have
That honorable grief lodg'd here which burns
Worse than tears drown. Beseech you all, my lords,
With thoughts so qualified as your charities
Shall best instruct you, measure me; and so
The King's will be perform'd!

LEONTES

Shall I be heard?

HERMIONE

Who is 't that goes with me? Beseech your Highness,
My women may be with me, for you see
My plight requires it. Do not weep, good fools;
There is no cause. When you shall know your mistress
Has deserv'd prison, then abound in tears
As I come out. This action I now go on
Is for my better grace. Adieu, my lord.
I never wish'd to see you sorry; now
I trust I shall. My women, come; you have leave.

LEONTES

Go, do our bidding; hence!

[*Exit Hermione, guarded, with Ladies.*]

2 censure judgment **3 Alack** (an exclamation of despair) **for lesser knowledge** i.e., if only I knew less **7 one** i.e., one should happen to **9 cracks** bursts **gorge** throat **10 hefts** heavings, retchings **13 Sport** a joke **14 hence** away from here **about** near, around **15 sport** amuse **16 that . . . with** i.e., the child she's pregnant with **17 I'd** I have only to **19 to th' nayward** in the opposite direction **21 goodly** beautiful, fine **23 honest** virtuous **24 without-door** outward, external **25 on my faith** i.e., by my faith (a mild oath) **speech** praise **straight** straightaway, at once **26 hum** utterance of the interjection "hum" (indicating contempt or displeasure) **27 out** in error, wrong **28 does** uses (Leontes is pointing out that no one will be defaming Hermione by suggesting with a shrug or a "hum" that she is not virtuous; calumny, he notes, harms "virtue itself," not Hermione's mere pretense of virtue.) **30 come between** interrupt (you) **34 replenish'd** complete **35 as** again as **38 Which . . . place** on whom ("which") I will not bestow a name appropriate to your stature and rank **39 making me** using me as **40 a like** the same **use . . . degrees** apply to people of all ranks **41 mannerly distinguishment** a proper distinction **45 federary** confederate, accomplice **47 principal** partner **48 bed-swerver** adulteress (literally, one who strays from her marriage bed) **49 vulgars . . . titles** common people call by the rudest names **50 their late** Polixenes' and Camillo's recent **53 publish'd** publicly proclaimed **Gentle my** my noble **54 throughly** thoroughly **57 center** earth **59–60 afar . . . speaks** indirectly guilty merely because he speaks **64 want** lack **68 qualified** tempered **charities** senses of compassion **69 measure** judge **70 heard** i.e., obeyed **72 women** ladies-in-waiting **73 fools** (used here as a term of endearment toward her ladies) **74 cause** reason **76 action** legal action **77 for . . . grace** to my greater honor (when I am ultimately vindicated) **79 leave** permission to depart **80 our** (Leontes is employing the royal plural.)

A GUIDE TO PRONUNCIATION

If your aim is to proclaim to one and all, "I'm in over my head with this Shakespeare stuff and I don't know what I'm doing," letting loose a mispronunciation might well be the quickest way to do just that. Botching the name of a person or place is guaranteed to distract every audience member in the know. It will hustle them away from the world you've been working so diligently to create, and direct their focus on your lack of preparation rather than on your compelling characterization.

Fortunately, this all-too-common misstep is a simple one to prevent. All you need is the resolve to get things right, and a resource to help you do so. The first part of the equation is your responsibility. The second is taken care of with the following guide to pronunciation.

Listed below are the most widely accepted pronunciations of character and location names appearing in *Shakespeare For Two*. Commonly recognized terms like "Henry" and "Verona" have been omitted since most everyone knows them already, and those who don't can turn for help to any standard dictionary.

The essentials of the guide are as follows:

- Syllables are separated by a hyphen.
- Accented syllables are CAPITALIZED.
- Syllables or parts of syllables that are *italicized* indicate vowel sounds that are lightly articulated. For example, the sound of <*uh*> is identical to that of <uh>, but it's uttered for a shorter length of time. An eighth note versus a quarter, if you will.

In an attempt to strike a happy medium between ease of use and precision, a phonetic-based key to pronunciation has been adopted. Its basic elements are provided below.

Vowel Sounds

A

A, a . . . as in MAN, ASK, FLAP

AH, ah . . . as in DOT, ODD, JOG

AHR, ahr . . . as in CAR, FAR, MARK

AIR, air . . . as in CARE, WEAR, FAIR

AY, ay . . . as in DAY, WEIGHT, THEY

AW, aw . . . as in RAW, BALL, TALK

E

E, e . . . as in PET, LESS, WRECK

EE, ee . . . as in EAT, WE, DEED

EER, eer . . . as in JEER, NEAR, PIER

I

I, i . . . as in TRIP, SIT, PIN

Y, y . . . as in ICE, TRY, NIGHT

O

OH, oh . . . as in TOE, DOUGH, OLD

OO, oo . . . as in OOZE, TWO, SOUP

OR, or . . . as in FOR, WAR, MORE

OOR, oor . . . as in TOUR, LURE

OW, ow . . . as in HOW, POUT, DOWN

OY, oy . . . as in TOY, OIL, COIN

U

UH, uh . . . as in DUMB, SON, UP

UR, ur . . . as in SPUR, STIR, EARN

UU, uu . . . as in HOOD, PULL, TOOK

Consonant Sounds

B, b . . . as in BOB, CRAB
CH, ch . . . as in CHOP, DUTCH
D, d . . . as in DID, POD
F, f . . . as in FLUFF, LAUGH
G, g . . . as in GAG, RUG
H, h . . . as in HOT, HIP
J, j . . . as in JUICE, CAGE
K, k . . . as in CAKE, COOK
L, l . . . as in LULL, ALE
M, m . . . as in MOM, SOME
N, n . . . as in NUN, SOON
NG, ng . . . as in RING, BANG
P, p . . . as in POP, MAP
R, r . . . as in RIP, MORE
S, s . . . as in SASS, SIP
T, t . . . as in TOT, CAST
TH, th . . . as in PATH, THOUGHT

V, v . . . as in VERY, HIVE
W, w . . . as in WOW, QUIT
Y, y . . . as in YES, YAWN
Z, z . . . as in HAZE, ZOO
ZH, zh . . . as in BEIGE

ADRIANA	(ay-dree-AH-n*uh*)
ALCIBIADES	(al-si-BY-*uh*-deez)
ANGIERS	(AN-jeerz)
ANJOU	(AN-joo)
ANTIGONUS	(an-TIG-*oh*-nuhs)
ANTIPHOLUS	(an-TIF-oh-luhs)
ANTONY	(AN-t*oh*-nee)
AUTOLYCUS	(aw-TAHL-i-kuhs)
BAPTISTA	(bap-TEES-t*ah*)
BEATRICE	(BEE-*uh*-tris)
BERTRAM	(BUR-t*ruhm*)
BOHEMIA	(boh-HEE-mee-*uh*)
CAESAR, JULIUS	(JOOL-yuhs SEE-zur)
CAIUS MARCIUS	(KAY-uhs or KAY-yuhs MAHR-shuhs)
CAPULET	(KAP-yoo-let)
CASSIO	(KAS-ee-oh)
CASSIUS	(KAS-ee-uhs)
CAWDOR	(KAW-dur)
CERIMON	(SER-i-mahn)
CESARIO	(se-ZAH-ree-oh)
CLOTEN	(KLOH-t*uhn*)
COLOSSUS	(k*o*-LAHS-*uh*s)
COMINIUS	(kah-MIN-ee-uhs)
CORDELIA	(kor-DEE-lyuh)
CORIOLANUS	(kor-ee-oh-LAY-nuhs)
CRESSIDA	(KRES-i-d*uh*)
CYMBELINE	(SIM-be-leen)
DE LA POLE	(DE LAH POOL)
DEMETRIUS	(d*ee*-MEE-tri-uhs)
DESDEMONA	(dez-de-MOH-n*uh*)
DIAN	(DY-an)
DROMIO	(DROH-mee-oh)

ELSINORE	(EL-si-nohr)
EPHESUS	(EF-e-suhs)
FALSTAFF	(FAWL-staf)
FORTINBRAS	(FOR-tin-brahs)
FULVIA	(FUHL-vee-*uh*)
GLAMIS	(GLAHM-is)
GLOUCESTER	(GLAHS-tur)
HARFLEUR	(HAHR-flur)
HERMIA	(HUR-mee-*uh*)
HERMIONE	(hur-MY-*oh*-n*ee*)
HERO	(HE-roh)
HORATIO	(hoh-RAY-shoh)
IACHIMO	(EEAH-k*i*-moh or EEAH-kee-moh)
IAGO	(EEAH-goh)
IMOGEN	(IM-oh-jen)
ISABELLA	(iz-*uh*-BEL-*uh*)
JAQUES	(JAY-kweez)
JULIA	(JYOOL-i-*uh*)
JULIET	(JYOOL-yet or JYOO-lee-et)
KATHARINA	(kat-*uh*-REE-n*uh*)
LAPUCELLE	(LAHpuu-SEL)
LAERTES	(lay-UR-teez)
LAUNCE	(LAHNS or LAWNS)
LEONATO	(lee-oh-NAH-toh or lay-oh-NAH-toh)
LEONTES	(lee-AHN-teez)
LUCENTIO	(loo-CHEN-seeoh)
LUCIANA	(loo-shee-AH-n*uh*)
LUCIUS	(LOO-shuhs)
MACBETH	(mak-BETH)
MENENIUS AGRIPPA	(me-NEE-nee-uhs *uh*-GRIP-*uh*)
MILAN	(mi-LAN)
MONTAGUE	(MAHN-t*uh*-gyoo)
NERISSA	(ne-RIS-*uh*)
NYM	(NIM)

OCTAVIUS	(ahk-TAY-vee-uhs)
OPHELIA	(oh-FEEL-y*uh*)
OTHELLO	(oh-THEL-oh)
PALATINE	(PAL-*uh*-tyn or PAL-*uh*-tin)
PAROLLES	(pah-RAHL-es or pay-rohl-es)
PETRUCHIO	(pe-TROOCH-eeoh or pe-TROO-keeoh)
PISANIO	(pee-ZAH-neeoh)
PLANTAGENET	(plan-TAJ-*uh*-net)
POLIXENES	(poh-LIKS-*uh*-neez)
POLONIUS	(p*oh*-LOH-nee-uhs)
PORTIA	(POR-sh*uh*)
POSTHUMUS	(PAHS-tyoo-muhs)
PROSPERO	(PRAHS-pe-roh)
PROTEUS	(PROH-tee-uhs)
RODERIGO	(rahd-*uh*-REE-goh)
ROMEO	(ROH-meeoh)
ROSALIND	(RAHZ-*uh*-lind)
ROSSILLION	(roo-SIL-y*uh*n)
SEBASTIAN	(se-BAS-ti*uh*n)
SILVIA	(SIL-vee-*uh*)
SUFFOLK	(SUHF-*uh*k)
THESEUS	(THEE-see-uhs)
TIMON	(TY-m*uh*n)
TROILUS	(TROY-luhs)
TULLUS AUFIDIUS	(TUHL-uhs aw-FID-ee-uhs)
TYBALT	(TIB-*uh*lt)
URSULA	(UR-syoo-l*uh*)
VALENTINE	(VAL-*uh*n-tyn)
VINCENTIO	(veen-CHEN-seeoh)
VIOLA	(VEE-oh-lah or VY-oh-lah)
YORICK	(YOR-ik)

JUST THE FACTS, MA'AM

Keeping straight the twists and turns of Shakespeare's 37 plots is a Herculean task all by itself. To make your labor a little easier, you may wish to call from time to time on the synopses provided below.

As duly noted in the introduction to this volume, these thumbnail sketches are in no way intended as substitutes for reading the plays themselves. They are here merely to help you recall the who, what and where of each story as they relate to the scenes of *Shakespeare For Two*.

All's Well that Ends Well

When Bertram ventures off to Paris with his companion Parolles, Helena is devastated. Though she's long adored the young Count, the lowborn Helena has always believed him to be unattainable. But things start looking up when, shortly after her own arrival in Paris, Helena cures the King of France of a serious ailment, and by way of reward is granted her one true wish—to have Bertram for her husband.

Though Bertram is duty-bound to do his king's bidding, he clearly resents having to wed Helena. Not long after the wedding ceremony, he spurns his bride and marches off to the wars.

Some time later, Helena learns that her wayward husband is in Florence courting a young woman named Diana. Before long Helena, along with Diana and her mother the Widow Capilet, have concocted an intricate scheme to insure that Bertram is Helena's once and for all. After a few unexpected twists and turns, their plan eventually succeeds: Bertram at last sees the error of his ways, he professes to Helena his undying love, and just as promised . . . all's well that ends well.

Antony and Cleopatra

Even the considerable charms of Cleopatra cannot detain Antony when word of his wife's death and the threat of an impending civil war compels his return to Rome. Once he's back home, Antony smoothes over a little trouble with his fellow triumvir, Octavius Caesar, by marrying Octavius's sister, Octavia. The peace proves short-lived, however, when Antony abandons Rome and his new wife in favor of a return to Egypt and its beguiling Queen of the Nile. War between Antony and Caesar soon follows.

After an initial triumph, Antony's military fortunes soon turn sour when his navy deserts him. Disheartened by defeat, and under the false impression that Cleopatra has died, Antony mortally wounds himself. A short time later he expires in his beloved's arms. For her part, Cleopatra decides to end things on her own terms rather than succumb to a fate as Octavius's war prize. With loyal attendants by her side, Egypt's queen applies a poisonous snake to her breast and dies.

As You Like It

Orlando, fearing for his life and fed up with his brother Oliver's neglectful guardianship, decides to seek his fortune elsewhere. Accompanied by his old friend and servant Adam, he arrives in the Forest of Arden and joins the company of Duke Senior, who's been living in banishment since his evil brother Frederick usurped his title.

When Orlando's beloved Rosalind is likewise banished by Frederick, she disguises herself as a boy and, accompanied her cousin Celia and Touchstone the fool, she strikes out in search of her father, Duke Senior. When she and Orlando happen to meet in the forest, Rosalind decides to exploit the fact that he cannot see through her disguise by offering to school him on the finer points of romance.

Elsewhere in the forest, Silvius the shepherd is having no luck at all in wooing the affections of a local maiden named Phebe. After Rosalind overhears Phebe's heartless rebuff of poor Silvius, she steps in to severely upbraid the maid for her cruelty—and, by doing so, induces Phebe to fall in love with her.

Eventually, everything turns out swell: Rosalind drops her disguise and reunites with Orlando, Phebe makes up with Silvius, a repentant Oliver shows up just in time to pair off with Celia, a similarly reformed Frederick restores to Duke Senior his rightful position, and even Touchstone finds love as marriage and merriment abound.

Comedy of Errors

Twenty-three years ago, there was a ship that foundered in a storm. Among the ship's passengers tossed into the raging sea were a merchant, his wife, their twin baby boys (both named Antipholus), and another set of infant twins (both named Dromio) being raised by them.

Fortunately, everyone was rescued; unfortunately, not by the same rescue parties. As things turned out, the merchant, one Antipholus and one Dromio were taken to Syracuse, while the merchant's wife, the other Antipholus and the other Dromio ended up in the city of Ephesus.

After turning eighteen, the pair of twins from Syracuse set out in search of their long-lost brothers, and five years into their quest finally arrive in Ephesus. Because no one realizes that there are now two Antipholuses and two Dromios in town, a series of mistaken identifications and general mayhem ensue. Eventually, of course, everything is set right and the long-separated families are reunited.

Coriolanus

Though roundly criticized for his arrogance and lack of compassion in a time of famine, Coriolanus is nonetheless the man the people turn to when Rome comes under the threat of attack by the Volscian army. His courageous leadership brings victory to the Romans, for which he is duly praised. But his contemptuous ways soon incite the masses (and some jealous tribunes) against him, and before long he is banished.

Looking to exact some revenge, Coriolanus offers to join his former enemy, the Volscian general Aufidius, in his assault upon Rome. Only a last-minute plea by Coriolanus's mother, Volumnia, persuades Coriolanus to preempt the attack and instead arrange a truce between the two armies.

But when Aufidius too grows jealous of Coriolanus's rising popularity, he decries the Roman's efforts for peace as a betrayal of the Volscian people. Aufidius's propaganda soon bears fruit: Coriolanus is ultimately murdered at the behest of a mob and at the hands of Aufidius's assassins.

Cymbeline

Cymbeline simply would not stand for his daughter Imogen's secret marriage to Posthumus, and so he had the poor lad banished. Landing on his feet in Rome, Posthumus wagers with a local scoundrel named Iachimo that his beloved Imogen cannot be corrupted. Though Iachimo fails miserably in his attempt to seduce Imogen, he returns from Britain with enough misleading evidence to convince Posthumus otherwise.

Incensed by his wife's apparent betrayal, Posthumus dashes off a letter to Pisanio (his manservant back in Britain) that instructs him to murder Imogen. Pisanio, however, is unable to do his master's bidding. Instead, he persuades Imogen to make her way to Rome—for safety's sake, disguised as a boy—and set matters straight with her husband.

Pursuing Imogen into the countryside is Cymbeline's stepson, Cloten, who intends to forcibly return her to the fold. Along the way, however, he tangles with banished lord Belarius and his two sons, and is forthwith beheaded for his trouble.

Meanwhile, the war between Rome and Britain has escalated. Posthumus returns to Britain just in time to assist both Belarius and his boys (who are actually Cymbeline's sons, kidnapped by Belarius when they were babies) in rallying the British forces. Before all is said and done, the Roman invaders are routed, Posthumus and Imogen are reunited, and there is peace once more in the British Isles.

Hamlet

Only two months after the untimely death of his father, Hamlet's mother Gertrude has already remarried—and to her late husband's brother, at that. Though Hamlet soon discovers that it was this selfsame uncle of his, Claudius, who murdered King Hamlet in the first place, vengeance is inexplicably slow in coming.

Even as he feigns madness and abuses poor Ophelia, Hamlet continuously agonizes over how best to proceed in the matter before him. When Claudius tumbles to the fact that Hamlet is onto him, he devises an elaborate plot designed to do away with his rival. The plan involves goading Hamlet into a friendly little fencing match with Ophelia's brother Laertes, during which the Prince is slated to be mortally wounded by a poison-tipped rapier.

All does not go quite as planned, however. Before the final thrusts and parries are made, Hamlet has indeed met his demise . . . but so too have Gertrude, Laertes, and even Claudius himself.

Henry VI, Part I

Mother England's present situation is not a pretty one: Good King Henry V has recently died, his young son is not yet of sufficient age to assume his royal duties as Henry VI, and England's war with France has reached full speed. To make matters worse, a young Frenchwoman by the name of Joan La Pucelle (also known as Joan of Arc) takes the battlefield by storm, inspiring France's forces to one victory after another.

As if that weren't enough, young Henry's game attempt to smooth over an smoldering feud between the Duke of Somerset and the Duke of York has but a transient effect. A tenuous truce between the two houses soon disintegrates into a barrage of mutual recriminations on the French battlefield. Yet, just when England appears on the brink of defeat, Joan of Arc's spiritual mentors suddenly desert her, and France's troops are routed. La Pucelle is subsequently taken prisoner by the Duke of York and burned at the stake.

Meanwhile, the Earl of Suffolk has taken a prisoner of his own: Margaret, daughter to the King of Naples. Suffolk sees Margaret as his personal spoil of war, and by engineering a marriage between her and King Henry, he intends to control both the next queen and the crown.

Henry VI, Part II

When the Duke of Gloucester dares to criticize certain provisions of England's recent treaty with France—a peace that resulted in, among other things, the marriage of Margaret to King Henry—the new (and seditious) Queen does not take it well. Ably assisted by her fellow conspirators, the Earl of Suffolk and Cardinal Beaufort, Margaret immediately sets about eliminating Gloucester and his influence on the King. Before long Margaret has seen to it that the Duchess of Gloucester is banished, and that Gloucester himself is accused of treason, and ultimately murdered.

Direct from Ireland, enter Jack Cade. Somehow, this oddest of ducks manages to lead a motley crew of insurgents all the way to the streets of London. But the ad hoc rebellion quickly fizzles out when Cade's men desert him, leaving Cade to meet his end at the hands of Alexander Iden.

Elsewhere, the Wars of The Roses have begun in earnest. Claiming that he is the rightful King of England, the Duke of York leads his armies to an initial victory over the King's forces at the Battle of St. Alban's, at which point the action moves on to London and *Henry VI, Part 3.*

Henry VI, Part III

When his forces suffer defeat at the first Battle of St. Alban's (see *Henry VI, Part 2*) King Henry has little choice but to strike a bargain with his adversary, the Duke of York. Their agreement calls for Henry to continue ruling England as long as he lives, with York winning official recognition as the royal heir. But since this also amounts to the disinheritance of her son, Queen Margaret declares the arrangement unacceptable.

Joining forces with Lord Clifford, Margaret resolves to wage war against York and his followers. Round one of the ensuing struggle goes to the Queen's faction as York's army is routed at Wakefield, and York himself is stabbed to death by Margaret and Clifford.

York's sons, Edward and Richard, mount an impressive comeback, however. Clifford is slain and the royal forces are defeated at Towton, after which Edward assumes the title of King Edward IV and ascends England's throne.

As for Margaret, her alliance with King Lewis of France proves insufficient to avert a resounding defeat at Tewkesbury. Margaret is taken captive and eventually returned to France in exchange for a healthy ransom. Meanwhile, Margaret's husband suffers a somewhat more dreadful fate: while a prisoner in the Tower of London, Henry is mercilessly butchered by the Duke of Gloucester—a slaying designed to shove Gloucester one step closer to his reign as King Richard III.

Julius Caesar

Fearing that Caesar's immense popularity will one day translate into the end of Roman democracy, Cassius and a few other prominent Roman citizens have decided the time has come for action. The budding conspiracy's final piece falls into place when Brutus's devotion to the republic outweighs even his love for Caesar, and he reluctantly agrees to sign on to the plan.

Shortly after entering the Capitol building, Caesar is surrounded by the group of conspirators, and stabbed to death. Though Brutus manages to tranquilize an irate Roman citizenry with his considerable oratory prowess, the pacifying effect proves short-lived. Mark Antony soon arrives on the scene and, with an impassioned elocutionary display of his own, moves the masses so profoundly that Brutus and the other conspirators are forced to flee.

A triumvirate of Antony, Octavius and Lepidus is formed to lead Rome and its armies in battle against the forces of Brutus and Cassius. After a series of confrontations, the rebel forces are finally defeated on the plains of Philippi. Rather than face being captured, both Cassius and Brutus elect to die by their own swords.

King John

Full-scale war between their two countries is apparently averted when England's King John and France's King Philip agree to a royal marriage between John's niece and Philip's son. The truce soon falls by the wayside, however. Under threat of excommunication by the Catholic church, Philip reneges on his agreement with John (whom the Church has declared a heretic), and the war is back on.

England's armies emerge victorious on the battlefield near Angiers, where young Arthur—living in France with his mother, Constance, and arguably the rightful heir to the English throne—is taken captive and returned to England.

Viewing Arthur as a threat to his grip on the crown, John intimates to Hubert De Burgh that it would be better if the boy were dead. Though good Hubert proves unable to commit the foul deed, Arthur dies while attempting to escape.

When word spreads of Arthur's death, a number of English noblemen smell a rat and defect to France, which in turn renews its fight with England. The French invasion founders, though, when Philip the Bastard assumes England's helm and the renegade nobles return to the fold.

King John, meanwhile, has retired to Swinstead Abbey. His death there by poison clears the way for the reign of his son, Henry III.

King Lear

Lear's plan to divide his kingdom among his three daughters hits a snag when his youngest child, Cordelia, refuses to join her two older sisters in showering their father with disingenuous praise. Goneril and Regan thus split the spoils in half, while Cordelia rebounds from her disinheritance by marrying the King of France.

The madness of Lear's method soon becomes evident, however, when both Goneril and Regan humiliate the King by refusing to accommodate his retinue of boisterous knights. Enraged by his daughters' ingratitude, Lear storms off into the tempestuous night.

Elsewhere, the Earl of Gloucester has his own problems. Through a series of sinister machinations, the Earl has been convinced by his bastard son Edmund that his other (and legitimate) son, Edgar, covets his wealth and wishes him dead. Edgar, fearing for his life, takes on the guise of a madman and escapes into the countryside. It is there that, some time later, Edgar encounters his father, who has been blinded by Regan's husband

Cornwall for providing assistance to Lear. Both the blind Gloucester, led by his son Edgar, and the mad Lear, aided by his true friend Kent, end up near Dover, where Cordelia has landed with French troops in order to rescue her father. Cordelia is reunited with her father, but her soldiers suffer defeat at the hands of Edmund and his forces, and both Cordelia and Lear are taken captive.

Before all the shouting is over, Cordelia is hanged by order of Edmund, Goneril poisons Regan before dying by her own hand, Edmund is slain by Edgar, and poor old Lear dies of grief.

Macbeth

On his way home from a successful military campaign, Macbeth encounters three witches who hail him as Thane of Cawdor and "king hereafter." When word soon arrives that King Duncan has in fact named Macbeth as the new Thane of Cawdor, Macbeth starts to thinking. Before long, his lust for the crown and Lady Macbeth's prodding have turned those thoughts to murder. After weathering a few fleeting pangs of conscience, Macbeth slays Duncan in his sleep, and is crowned king.

Though Duncan's sons, Malcolm and Donalbain, are initially suspected of the King's murder, it isn't long before Macbeth is identified as the true culprit. When Macbeth's former comrade, Macduff, convinces Malcolm to fight for his rightful place on the Scottish throne, Macbeth's fate seems all but sealed.

Left twisting in the wind by his friends and Lady Macbeth (who descends into madness and kills herself), Macbeth is eventually set upon by Macduff in the fields of Dunsinane, and is slain. Soon thereafter, Malcolm is hailed as the new King of Scotland.

Measure for Measure

Duke Vincentio has made known his intention to leave Vienna and turn control of the city over to his deputy, Angelo. But in fact, it's all a ruse. After merely pretending to leave town, the Duke adopts the guise of a friar so that he might clandestinely observe local events as they unfold.

Suddenly flush with power, Deputy Angelo sets about addressing what he views as the city's declining morality. First up is the sentencing of young Claudio to death for impregnating his girlfriend, Juliet, before the two could be legally married. When Claudio's sister, Isabella, appears before Angelo to beg that he spare her brother's life, Angelo agrees to do just that—if she agrees to be his mistress. Unable to compromise her honor, Isabella spurns the deputy's vile offer and informs Claudio that she cannot save him.

Just in the nick of time, reenter Duke Vincentio. After orchestrating a bit of intrigue that involved Angelo's former betrothed, Mariana, the Duke dispenses with his friar disguise, spares Claudio's life, condemns Angelo's hypocrisy (even as he compels him to wed Mariana), and to top things off, requests of Isabella her hand in marriage.

The Merchant of Venice

Bassanio wants in the worst way to travel to Belmont and court the heiress Portia, but he needs money to do so. Upon looking to his merchant friend Antonio for financial assistance, Bassanio learns that he too is cash-poor at the moment. Even so, Antonio manages to secure a loan from the moneylender Shylock—but only by agreeing to a most severe condition: if Antonio defaults, he must forfeit to Shylock a pound of his own flesh.

In Belmont, Portia is bound by her late father's will to marry the first suitor who can choose correctly from among three chests made of gold, silver and lead, respectively. When Bassanio arrives on the scene, he quickly manages to succeed where all others before him have failed—the lead chest it is. Portia is elated by Bassanio's winning guess, and the two lovers are soon married.

Joy is short-lived, however, as word arrives that Antonio's ships have wrecked at sea. Unable to repay the loan, the merchant is now faced with meeting Shylock's demand for a pound of his flesh. Bassanio rushes off to his friend's aid, followed shortly thereafter by Portia, who, disguised as a male lawyer, proves to be instrumental in saving Antonio's hide. In court it is determined that the conditions of Shylock's loan are not only pernicious, but virtually impossible to enforce. Antonio is thus spared (and so, it turns out, were his ships), while Shylock is sent off to a life of Christianity.

The Merry Wives of Windsor

In dire need of some cash, Falstaff decides to court Mistresses Ford and Page, hoping he can thereby gain access to their husbands' purses. The ladies are understandably revolted by Falstaff's amorous overtures, but decide to lead him on anyway just for the fun of it. Employing Mistress Quickly as their go-between, the two wives begin their intrigue by arranging separate assignations with the clueless Sir John.

Elsewhere, a disgruntled pair of Falstaff's followers have alerted Masters Ford and Page to Falstaff's designs on their wives. Unlike Page, Ford takes the warning to heart, but is frustrated in his two attempts to catch his wife and Sir John in the act.

After Mistresses Ford and Page finally inform one and all of their shenanigans with Falstaff. everyone agrees it would be swell to stage one last, elaborate humiliation of the fat knight. The plan comes off swimmingly, of course, and afterwards the conspirators all saunter over to the Page's house for a bit of country cheer.

A Midsummer Night's Dream

Helena loves Demetrius, but Demetrius only has eyes for Hermia. Hermia, on the other hand, has just run off with Lysander. Before long, all four lovers end up in a forest outside Athens.

In the very same woods reside the King and Queen of the Fairies, Oberon and Titania, who have recently locked horns over the services of a young boy. Determined that he shall be the one who employs the lad, Oberon manages to anoint Titania's eyes with a potion which will induce her to fall in love with the first creature she sees. If Oberon's plot unfolds as intended, Titania will be so humiliated she will be forced to relinquish the boy to him.

For good measure, Oberon instructs his servant, Puck, to similarly enchant Demetrius, whose heartless rejection of Helena the fairy King has just witnessed. Puck botches the job, however, and ends up sprinkling both Demetrius and Lysander with the potion, thereby inducing them to passionately pursue a bewildered Helena.

Meanwhile, a bewitched Titania is in hot pursuit herself. The object of her lust is a local simpleton named Bottom—this despite the fact that Bottom's head has of late been changed into that of an ass, courtesy of the impish Puck. Mayhem ensues, of course, until Oberon finally sets things right by releasing Lysander, Bottom and Titania from their spells.

By story's end, marriages and merriment are everywhere, as one and all gather to enjoy an unforgettable performance of "Pyramus And Thisby," courtesy of Bottom and his fellow players.

Much Ado About Nothing

Benedick is no fan of Beatrice, while Beatrice has little but scorn for Benedick. It's a bit surprising then that friends of each are soon conspiring to convince both Benedick and Beatrice that one is madly in love with the other.

Elsewhere in Messina, another plot unfolds. Because Don John resents the close friendship forged between his brother Don Pedro and young Claudio, he has decided to undermine Claudio's plans to marry Hero, daughter to Leonato.

Don John's scheme plays out precisely as planned when Claudio and Don Pedro happen to glimpse a servant disguised as Hero dallying with another man in Hero's bedroom window. Thus convinced that he's been betrayed by his betrothed, Claudio publicly humiliates Hero at the altar by refusing her hand in marriage.

Everything appears to have completely unraveled when, thanks in part to some dubious police work by Constable Dogberry, Don John's villainy is revealed and Claudio and Hero are reunited. As for Beatrice and Benedick, they eventually tumble to the fact that their would-be romance was founded on their friends' machinations, but even so resign themselves to the bonds of matrimony.

Othello

Othello and Desdemona fell in love and were secretly married, much to the chagrin of the bride's father, Brabantio. Othello's subsequent appearance before the Duke of Venice to defend his conduct is interrupted by news of an impending attack on Cyprus by the Turks. The Moor is sent to defend the island, and Desdemona is permitted to accompany him.

Enter Iago. Recently passed over for promotion to lieutenant in favor of the dashing Cassio, Iago vowed revenge on all concerned. Through a series of intricate machinations, he manages to make good on his word. First he secures Cassio's professional disgrace by getting the lieutenant drunk while on duty. Next, Iago contrives a plot to convince Othello that his wife and Cassio are having an affair.

While Cassio manages to survive an attempt on his life by Roderigo (a dupe of Iago's who's infatuated with Desdemona), Othello's beloved wife is not so lucky. Consumed by jealousy, the Moor slinks into Desdemona's bedchamber and smothers her in her sleep.

When Iago's villainy is finally revealed, an enraged Othello attempts to slay him, but failing that, slays himself instead. Iago is then arrested and led off to his just rewards.

Richard III

Though a bevy of would-be royal heirs stand between Richard and the throne of England, he is bound and determined to be the man who succeeds his ailing brother, King Edward IV. Even as Richard somehow manages to woo and wed the fair Lady Anne—this despite the fact that he killed her betrothed, the Prince of Wales—he embarks in earnest upon his plan to usurp the crown.

First of the potential successors to be eliminated from contention is Richard's brother the Duke of Clarence, who, at Richard's behest, is slain while imprisoned in the Tower of London. With Clarence out of the way, the death of King Edward enables Richard to finagle his way to the throne, which he quickly does through a series of subtle and not-so-subtle machinations.

To make sure he stays on top, Richard proceeds to tie up a few loose ends. For one thing, he sees to it that Edward's two young sons (and rightful heirs to the crown) are murdered. Next up: Richard's wife, Lady Anne, is neatly disposed of so that Richard can woo the late King Edward's daughter—a match that would further tighten his grip on the crown.

But when forces led by the Earl of Richmond arrive to do battle with the royal army at Bosworth Field, King Richard's day of reckoning comes at last. Richard's army goes down to defeat, while the King himself (sans horse) is slain by Richmond in hand-to-hand combat. The Wars of the Roses are finally over, and Richmond is hailed as King Henry VII.

Romeo and Juliet

It's love at first sight when Romeo and Juliet meet during a masked ball being held in the house of Capulet—this despite the fact that their families are embroiled in a protracted blood feud. By the next afternoon, the two are secretly wed by Friar Laurence.

It's not long after that when a street fight ends tragically with Romeo's friend, Mercutio, dead at the hands of Juliet's cousin, Tybalt—who in turn is slain by Romeo. For his part in the brawl, Romeo is banished, and after spending the night with his new bride, he retreats to the nearby city of Mantua.

Meanwhile, unaware of his daughter's recent elopement, Capulet has arranged for Juliet to marry a young nobleman named Paris. When Juliet's resistance to the idea is overruled by her insistent parents, the desperate newlywed turns to Friar Laurence for help. The Friar's solution is to provide Juliet with a potion that will make her appear dead for forty-two hours. If all goes as planned, Romeo will arrive at the Capulet burial vault shortly after Juliet is laid to rest, and spirit her away from Verona.

But alas, all does not go as planned. Because a messenger fails to reach Romeo with word of the Friar's scheme, Romeo arrives at Juliet's tomb believing that she has actually died. No sooner does Romeo imbibe a lethal potion he had earlier procured, than Juliet awakens. Discovering her dead husband beside her, Juliet stabs herself, and dies.

The Taming of the Shrew

Baptista has declared that, despite her many suitors, his younger daughter Bianca can be courted only after his older, shrewish one, Katharina, is first married off.

Attracted by the prospect of her sizable dowry, Petruchio gamely embraces the challenge of wooing Kate. A series of fiery confrontations between the two ensue, until Petruchio at last manages to both wed and tame the recalcitrant Kate.

The Tempest

Twelve years ago, Prospero was ousted as the Duke of Milan by his brother Antonio, and set adrift at sea along with his baby daughter Miranda. The two castaways eventually washed up on a remote island inhabited only by a cantankerous creature named Caliban. It is there that Prospero, as possessor of strange and supernatural powers, now prepares to exact his revenge.

A storm worked up by Prospero has shipwrecked the King of Naples and his company (including Prospero's brother Antonio) on the island. With the assistance of Ariel, his indentured spirit, Prospero proceeds to conjure a series of wondrous spectacles, all of which serve to thoroughly confound Antonio and the others. Once he's made his point, Prospero takes pity on his bewildered guests, provides them with safe passage to Naples, renounces his magic and grants Ariel his freedom.

Timon of Athens

Through years of misguided largess and lavish living, Timon has managed to squander his entire personal fortune. When creditors come calling, Timon turns for help to his friends—and promptly discovers that the same folk who for so long wallowed in his generosity now offer him nothing but empty sympathy and the bum's rush.

So it is that an embittered and vengeful Timon decides to regale his fair-weather pals with one final mock-banquet in their dishonor, and then turns his back on Athens for the life of a cave-dwelling recluse.

Some time later, two senators come crawling before Timon's cave to enlist his help in defending Athens against an impending attack by the banished Athenian captain, Alcibiades. Timon's reply is to offer them a tree upon which to hang themselves.

As Alcibiades stands before Athens' walls negotiating a peace with the city's leaders, word arrives that Timon, "who, alive, all living men did hate," is dead.

Twelfth Night

After being shipwrecked on the coast of Illyria, Viola adopts the guise of a young man named Cesario, and finds employment as a page to Duke Orsino. Since the Duke has made no headway of late in his attempts to woo the rich widow Olivia, he instructs Cesario to act as emissary between himself and the lady. Unfortunately, because Cesario does such a bang-up job of arguing Orsino's cause, Olivia falls for the messenger instead of the message. What's more, Olivia's beloved Cesario finds he/she has fallen in love with the Duke.

Further complicating matters is the sudden appearance in town of Viola's twin brother Sebastian, who was assumed to have been lost at sea.

Predictably enough, mistaken identities and misplaced affections soon become the order of the day. Though confusion reigns for a time, things eventually sort themselves out: Sebastian marries Olivia, while Viola drops her disguise and professes her love for her husband-to-be, the Duke.

The Two Gentlemen of Verona

Valentine and Proteus arrive at the court of the Duke of Milan intending to acquire a bit of worldly experience. In almost no time both gentlemen of Verona fall in love with the Duke's daughter, Silvia. Since Silvia quickly takes a shine to Valentine as well, she and he make plans to run away together. But their plans fall apart when the Duke hears from Proteus of his daughter's intentions, and promptly banishes Valentine.

Proteus's subsequent attempt to win Silvia for himself is a dismal failure. Silvia rebuffs his advances and sets off for the woods in search of her beloved Valentine.

Meanwhile Julia, Proteus's girlfriend back in Verona, has decided to adopt the guise of a page and pursue Proteus to Milan. Once there, Julia discovers her beau's infatuation with Silvia. Undeterred (and still in disguise), Julia then joins Proteus as he seeks out Silvia—a mission that culminates in Proteus rescuing the Silvia from a band of outlaws.

Things begin to settle a bit when Valentine appears on the scene and Julia reveals her true identity. Eventually, Proteus realizes that it is Julia he truly loves, and Valentine is granted Silvia's hand in marriage.

The Winter's Tale

For no good reason whatsoever, Leontes, the King of Sicilia, accuses his wife Hermione of cheating on him with his friend, Polixenes. Though Polixenes manages to escape the wrath of Leontes by returning to his home in Bohemia, Hermione is not so fortunate.

Shortly after being thrown in prison by her husband, Hermione gives birth to a daughter, who Leontes declares is "a bastard by Polixenes," and so orders it abandoned in some remote place. Although Hermione is cleared at her trial of any wrongdoing, it's only when word arrives that she has suddenly taken ill and died that a repentant Leontes finally sees the error of his ways.

Hermione's babe, meanwhile, is abandoned on the coast of Bohemia. But fortunately, the tot is soon discovered by a kindly shepherd, who proceeds to raise her as his own daughter, Perdita.

At the age of sixteen, Perdita falls in love with Florizel, the son of Polixenes. Since Polixenes deems a poor shepherd's daughter unworthy of his son, he thwarts their plans for marriage. The two lovers thus sail off to Sicilia, where Leontes soon figures out that Perdita is his long lost daughter. Eventually, Polixenes and Leontes are reconciled, and arrangements are made for the marriage of Florizel and Perdita. Adding to the happy proceedings is a surprise appearance by Hermione; evidently, news of the Queen's death was greatly exaggerated.

THE BARD IN BRIEF

It's no secret that Shakespeare could be a tad long-winded from time to time. But that didn't stop him from frequently employing terse, two-person scenes to develop his characters and advance his plots.

Unfortunately, many of these exchanges are too brief for any sort of traditional scene work, so they weren't included in the main body of *Shakespeare For Two.* Still, as opportunities to explore William's work with a minimum of time and fuss, they seemed way too much fun to pass up entirely.

Below you'll find the best of these sketches, twenty scenes that run no more than thirty lines and can easily be played in a minute or two. Run to your nearest collected Shakespeare and give them a look-see. You'll find they offer most everything the big boys do, just not quite as much of it.

Scenes for Two Actresses

ADRIANA *AND* LUCIANA *The Comedy of Errors* **[IV.ii.1]**
"Ah, Luciana . . . though my tongue do curse."

QUEEN *AND* LADY *Richard II* **[III.iv.1]**
"What sport shall we devise . . . woe is forerun with woe."

BIANCA *AND* KATHARINA *The Taming of the Shrew* **[II.i.1]**
"Good sister, wrong me not . . . then all the rest was so."

Scenes for Two Actors

MARCIUS *AND* AUFIDIUS *Coriolanus* **[II.viii.1]**
"I'll fight with none but thee . . . Thou shouldst not scape me here."

SICINIUS *AND* BRUTUS *Coriolanus* **[I.i.250]**
"Was ever man so proud . . . Let's along."

CLOTEN *AND* GUIDERIUS *Cymbeline* [IV.II.73]
"Soft, what are you . . . Yield, rustic mountaineer!."

PISTOL *AND* KING HENRY *Henry V* [IV.I.33]
"Che vous lá . . . It sorts well with your fierceness."

WINCHESTER *AND* GLOUCESTER *Henry VI, Part 2* [I.III.29]
"How now, ambitious Humphrey . . . Out, scarlet hypocrite!."

CORNWALL *AND* EDMUND *King Lear* [III.V.I]
"I will have my revenge . . . a dearer father in my love."

GRATIANO *AND* BASSANIO *The Merchant of Venice* [II.II.166]
"Signior Bassanio! . . . But we will visit you at supper-time."

PISTOL *AND* NYM *The Merry Wives of Windsor* [I.III.84]
"Let vultures gripe thy guts . . . I second thee; troop on."

KING RICHARD *AND* BUCKINGHAM *Richard III* [IV.II.I]
"Stand all apart . . . High-reaching Buckingham grows circumspect."

FRIAR JOHN *AND* FRIAR LAURENCE *Romeo and Juliet* [V.II.I]
"Holy Franciscan friar! . . . clos'd in a dead man's tomb!."

Scenes for One Actress and One Actor

PORTIA *AND* SOOTHSAYER *Julius Caesar* [II.IV.20]
"Come hither, fellow . . . what he doth say to thee."

LADY MACDUFF *AND* ROSS *Macbeth* [IV.II.I]
"What had he done . . . I take my leave at once."

LORENZO *AND* JESSICA *The Merchant of Venice* [V.I.I]
"The moon shines bright . . . I hear the footing of a man."

FENTON *AND* QUICKLY *The Merry Wives of Windsor* [I.IV.125]
"How now, good woman . . . What have I forgot?."

LYSANDER *AND* HERMIA *A Midsummer Night's Dream* [II.II.35]
"Fair love, you faint . . . the wisher's eyes be press'd!."

PARIS *AND* JULIET *Romeo and Juliet* [IV.I.19]
"Happily met, my lady . . . and keep this holy kiss."

TROILUS *AND* CRESSIDA *Troilus and Cressida* [IV.II.I]
"Dear, trouble not yourself . . . I shall have such a life!."

OUTTAKES

As mentioned in the introduction, Shakespeare's dramatic works comprise more than 400 two-person scenes, each running anywhere from just under 20 to just over 200 lines. With its sixty selections, *Shakespeare For Two* highlights the best of these dialogues, every one a crowd pleaser. For most of us, that's plenty.

But for those who seek more, you've come to the right page. Listed below are the best of the rest—scenes that, though they might require you to clear a hurdle or two, still have a lot to offer. A few are awfully short, and a couple are frighteningly long; some favor one character over the other, while others lag a bit in the way of dramatic flair. Even so, one of them might be just the sort of thing you're looking for. (And when looking, keep in mind that line numbers indicating location will vary a bit from one edition of the play to another.)

Scenes for Two Actresses

HELENA *AND* **WIDOW CAPILET** *All's Well That Ends Well* [III.vii.1-48]
ROSALIND *AND* **CELIA** *As You Like It* [I.ii.1-54]
ROSALIND *AND* **CELIA** *As You Like It* [I.iii.1-38]
ROSALIND *AND* **CELIA** *As You Like It* [III.iv.1-44]
ADRIANA *AND* **LUCIANA** *The Comedy of Errors* [II.i.1-43]
KATHARINE *AND* **ALICE** *Henry V* [III.iv.1-60]
ANNE BULLEN *AND* **OLD LADY** *Henry VIII* [II.iii.1-49]
MISTRESS FORD *AND* **MISTRESS PAGE** *The Merry Wives of Windsor* [III.iii.82-123]
MARINA *AND* **DIONYZA** *Pericles* [IV.i.14-52]
JULIET *AND* **NURSE** *Romeo and Juliet* [III.ii.1-143]
JULIET *AND* **NURSE** *Romeo and Juliet* [III.v.205-243]
VIOLA *AND* **OLIVIA** *Twelfth Night* [III.i.84-164]
JULIA *AND* **LUCETTA** *The Two Gentlemen of Verona* [II.vii.1-90]

Scenes for Two Actors

MENAS *AND* **LORD TALBOT** *Antony and Cleopatra* [II.vi.83-136]
ORLANDO *AND* **ADAM** *As You Like It* [II.iii.1-76]
ROMAN *AND* **VOLSCE** *Coriolanus* [IV.iii.1-50]
HAMLET *AND* **POLONIUS** *Hamlet* [II.ii.169-219]
HAMLET *AND* **ROSENCRANTZ** *Hamlet* [III.ii.1-32]
FIRST CLOWN *AND* **SECOND CLOWN** *Hamlet* [V.i.1-64]
FALSTAFF *AND* **PRINCE HENRY** *Henry IV, Part 1* [I.ii.1-103]
FALSTAFF *AND* **CHIEF JUSTICE** *Henry IV, Part 2* [I.ii.91-231]
PRINCE HENRY *AND* **POINS** *Henry IV, Part 2* [II.ii.1-65]
LORD TALBOT *AND* **JOHN TALBOT** *Henry VI, Part 1* [IV.v.1-55]
CARDINAL WOLSEY *AND* **KING HENRY** *Henry VIII* [III.ii.136-227]
GARDINER *AND* **LOVELL** *Henry VIII* [V.i.2-55]
CASSIUS *AND* **BRUTUS** *Julius Caesar* [I.ii.25-189]
EDMUND *AND* **GLOUCESTER** *King Lear* [I.ii.1-136]
MALCOLM *AND* **MACDUFF** *Macbeth* [IV.iii.1-140]
DUKE VINCENTIO *AND* **PROVOST** *Measure For Measure* [IV.ii.72-209]
OLD GOBBO *AND* **LAUNCELOT GOBBO** *The Merchant of Venice* [II.ii.30-107]
PERICLES *AND* **ANTIOCHUS** *Pericles* [I.i.1-143]
PERICLES *AND* **SIMONIDES** *Pericles* [II.v.14-66]
ROMEO *AND* **FRIAR LAURENCE** *Romeo and Juliet* [II.iii.31-94]
ROMEO *AND* **FRIAR LAURENCE** *Romeo and Juliet* [III.iii.1-78]
ARIEL *AND* **PROSPERO** *The Tempest* [I.ii.189-306]
SEBASTIAN *AND* **ANTONIO** *The Tempest* [II.i.200-298]
LUCULLUS *AND* **FLAMINIUS** *Timon of Athens* [III.i.5-64]
TIMON *AND* **APEMANTUS** *Timon of Athens* [IV.iii.178-402]
TIMON *AND* **FLAVIUS** *Timon of Athens* [IV.iii.463-541]
SIR TOBY *AND* **SIR ANDREW** *Twelfth Night* [I.iii.79-138]
VALENTINE *AND* **PROTEUS** *The Two Gentlemen of Verona* [II.iv.119-211]
CAMILLO *AND* **LEONTES** *The Winter's Tale* [I.ii.209-363]
CAMILLO *AND* **POLIXENES** *The Winter's Tale* [I.ii.363-464]

Scenes for One Actress and One Actor

HELENA *AND* **PAROLES** *All's Well That Ends Well* [I.I.81-228]
HELENA *AND* **KING OF FRANCE** *All's Well That Ends Well* [II.I.99-210]
COUNTESS OF ROSSILLION *AND* **LAVATCH** *All's Well That Ends Well* [II.II.1-68]
CLEOPATRA *AND* **MESSENGER** *Antony and Cleopatra* [II.V.23-106]
ROSALIND *AND* **ORLANDO** *As You Like It* [III.II.293-423]
ROSALIND *AND* **ORLANDO** *As You Like It* [IV.I.30-192]
LUCIANA *AND* **ANTIPHOLUS OF SYRACUSE** *The Comedy of Errors* [III.II.1-70]
IMOGEN *AND* **CLOTEN** *Cymbeline* [II.III.88-138]
LADY PERCY *AND* **HOTSPUR** *Henry IV, Part 1* [II.III.73-116]
COUNTESS OF AUVERGNE *AND* **LORD TALBOT** *Henry VI, Part 1* [II.III.14-82]
QUEEN MARGARET *AND* **SUFFOLK** *Henry VI, Part 2* [III.II.300-366]
LADY MACBETH *AND* **MACBETH** *Macbeth* [I.VII.1-83]
LADY MACBETH *AND* **MACBETH** *Macbeth* [III.II.6-59]
ISABELLA *AND* **ANGELO** *Measure For Measure* [II.IV.19-187]
DESDEMONA *AND* **OTHELLO** *Othello* [III.III.41-94]
EMILIA *AND* **OTHELLO** *Othello* [V.II.92-174]
DIONYZA *AND* **CLEON** *Pericles* [IV.III.1-51]
MARINA *AND* **LYSIMACHUS** *Pericles* [IV.VI.66-118]
MARINA *AND* **PERICLES** *Pericles* [V.I.85-222]
QUEEN ISABELLA *AND* **KING RICHARD** *Richard II* [V.I.1-50]
DUCHESS OF YORK *AND* **KING RICHARD** *Richard III* [IV.IV.136-196]
JULIET *AND* **ROMEO** *Romeo and Juliet* [III.V.1-36]
JULIET *AND* **PARIS** *Romeo and Juliet* [IV.I.44-126]
TAMORA *AND* **TITUS** *Titus Andronicus* [V.II.1-80]
CRESSIDA *AND* **TROILUS** *Troilus and Cressida* [III.II.60-204]
PERDITA *AND* **FLORIZEL** *The Winter's Tale* [IV.IV.1-54]